SAVING
GRACE

[redacted]

SAVING GRACE

GRACE WILSON

JONATHAN CAPE
LONDON

1 3 5 7 9 10 8 6 4 2

JONATHAN CAPE, AN IMPRINT OF VINTAGE
20 VAUXHALL BRIDGE ROAD, LONDON, SW1V 2SA

JONATHAN CAPE IS PART OF THE PENGUIN RANDOM HOUSE GROUP OF COMPANIES WHOSE ADDRESSES CAN BE FOUND AT
GLOBAL.PENGUINRANDOMHOUSE.COM

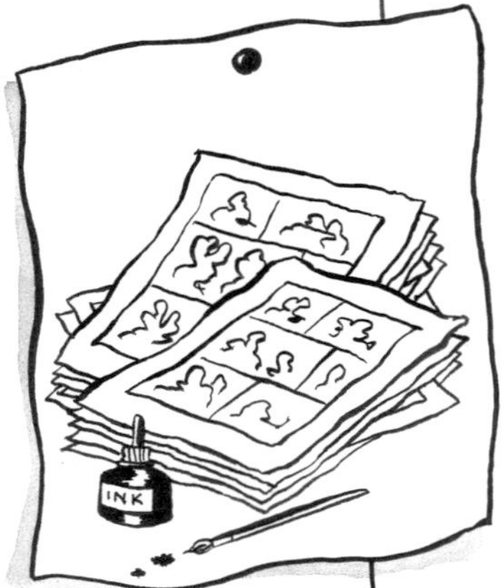
INK

FIRST PUBLISHED BY JONATHAN CAPE IN 2016

PENGUIN.CO.UK/VINTAGE

A CIP CATALOGUE RECORD FOR THIS BOOK IS AVAILABLE FROM THE BRITISH LIBRARY
ISBN 9780224102544

PRINTED AND BOUND IN ITALY BY L.E.G.O. S.p.A, VICENZA

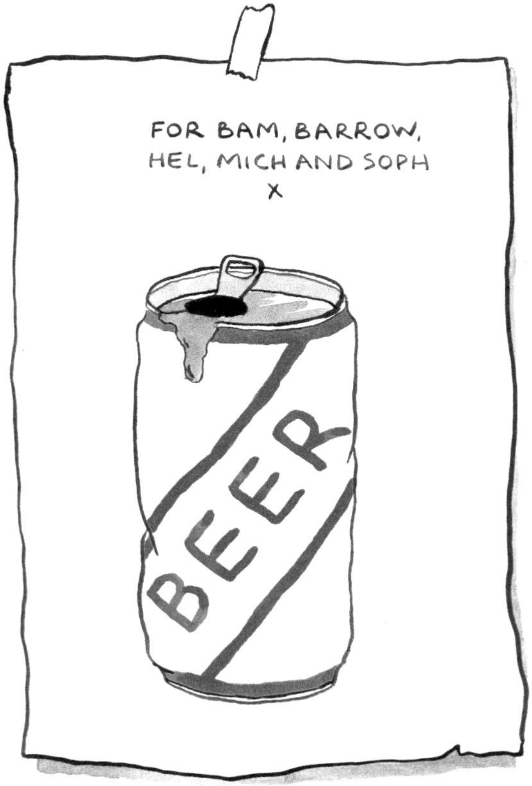
FOR BAM, BARROW,
HEL, MICH AND SOPH
X
BEER

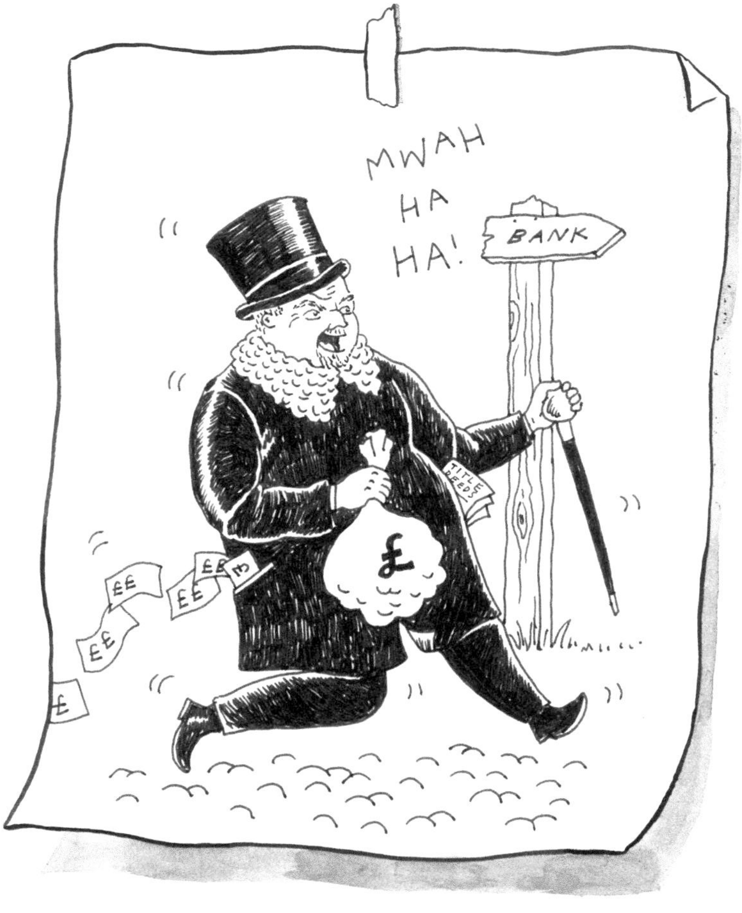
MWAH
HA
HA!
BANK
TITLE DEEDS
£

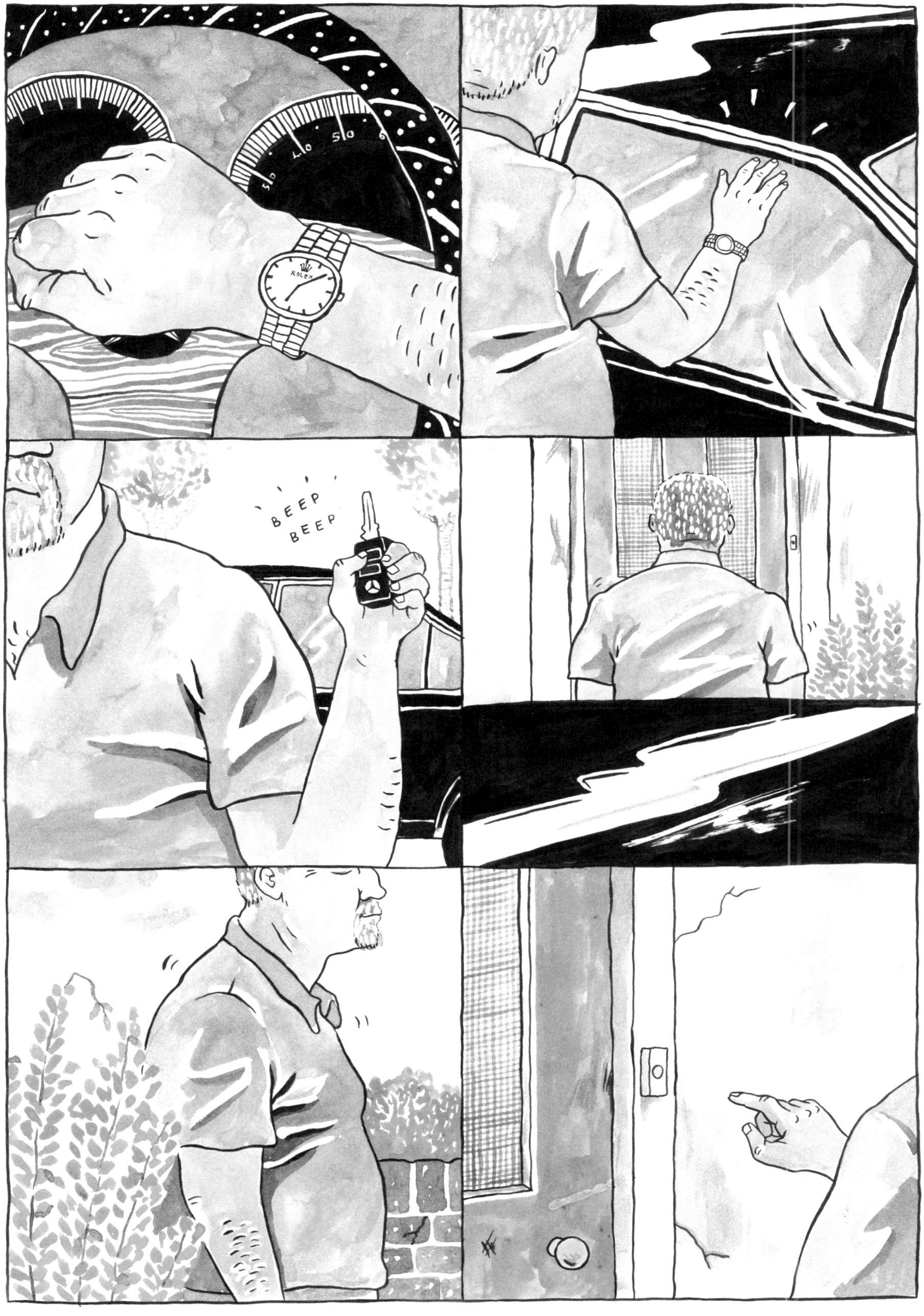
ROLEX
BEEP
BEEP

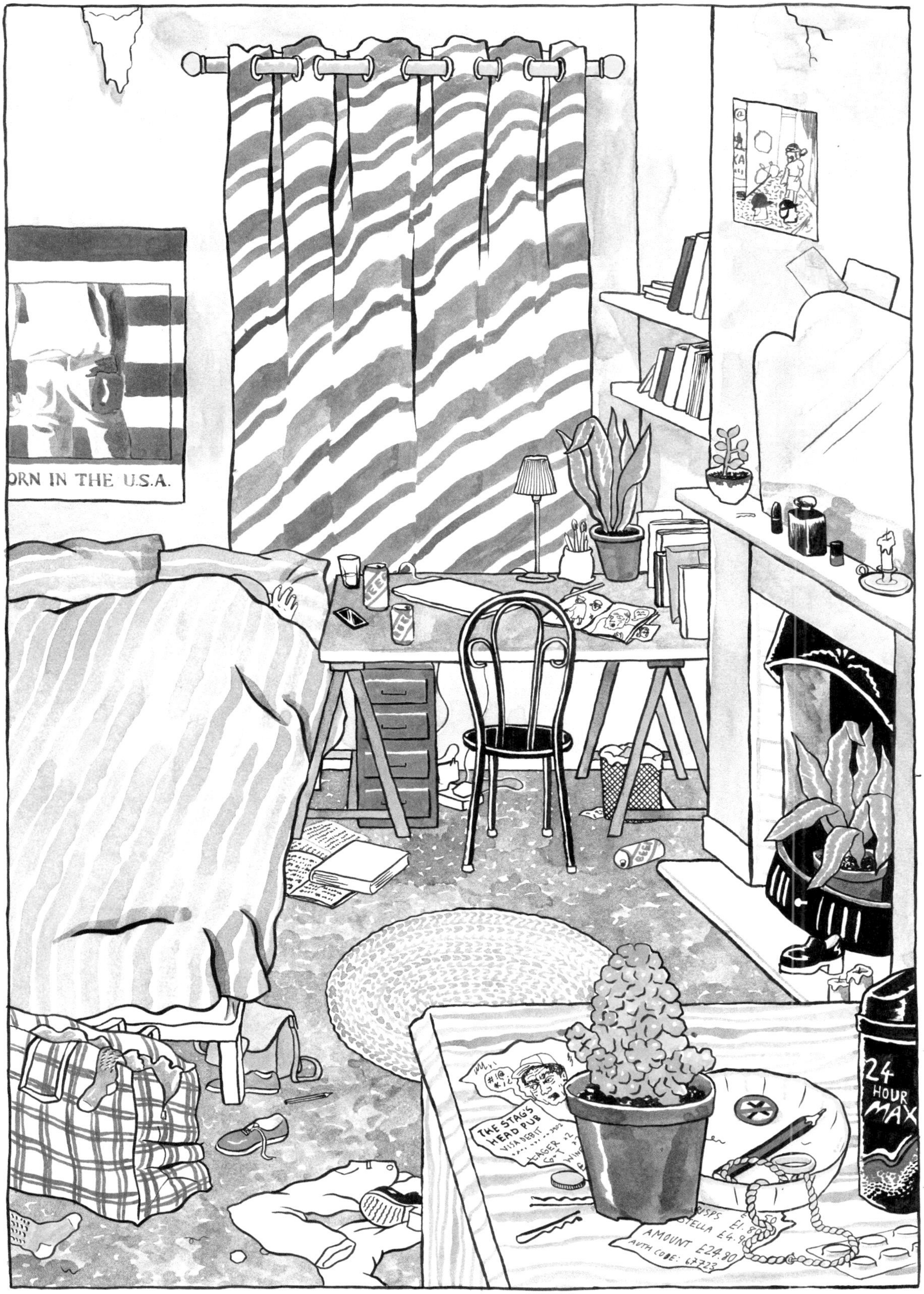
ORN IN THE U.S.A.
THE STAG'S HEAD PUB
VISA DEBIT
AMOUNT £24.80
AUTH CODE: 67723
24 HOUR MAX

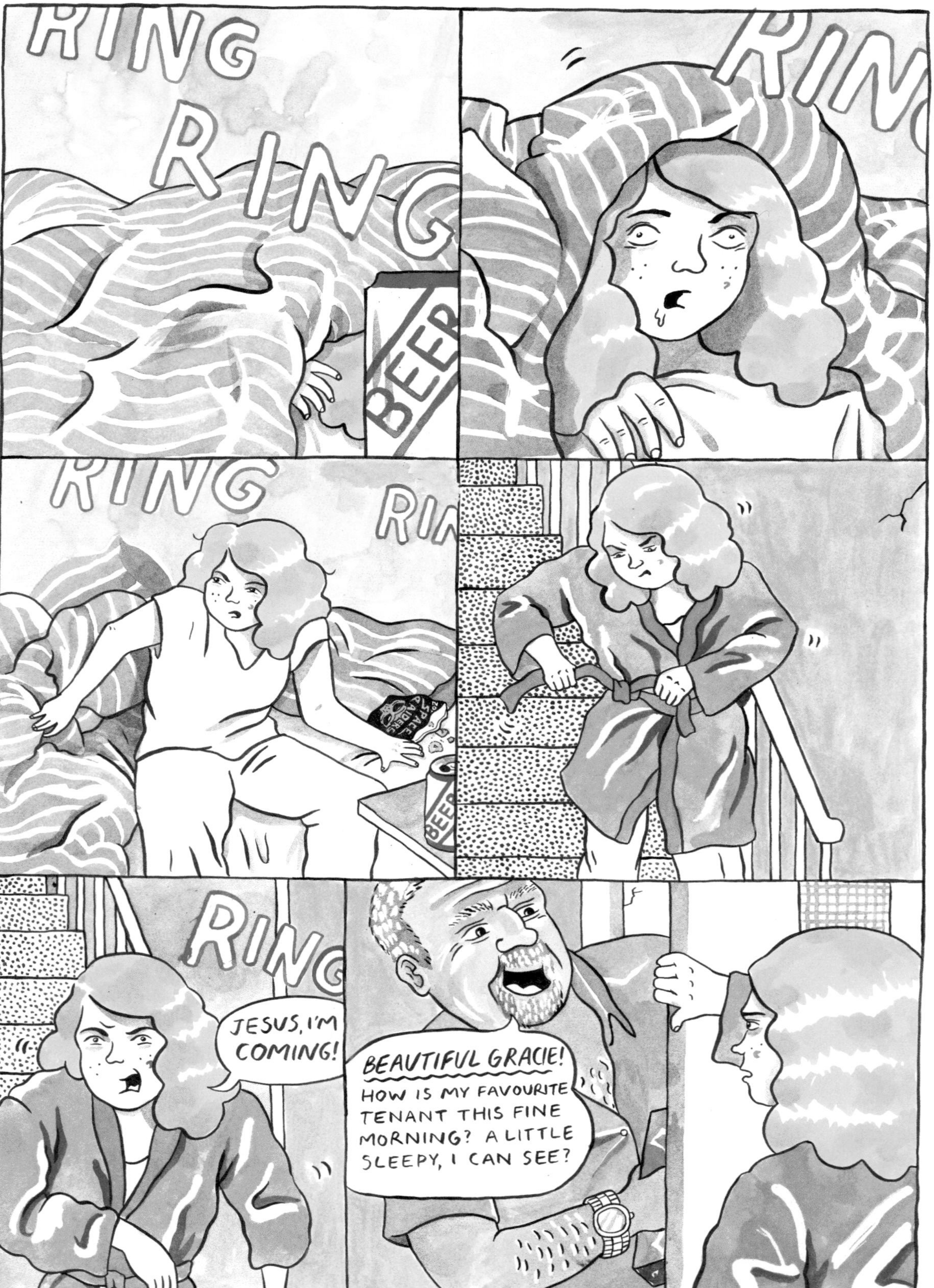
RING
RING
RING
BEER
RIN
RING
RIN
SPACE RAIDERS
BEER
RING
JESUS, I'M COMING!
BEAUTIFUL GRACIE!
HOW IS MY FAVOURITE TENANT THIS FINE MORNING? A LITTLE SLEEPY, I CAN SEE?

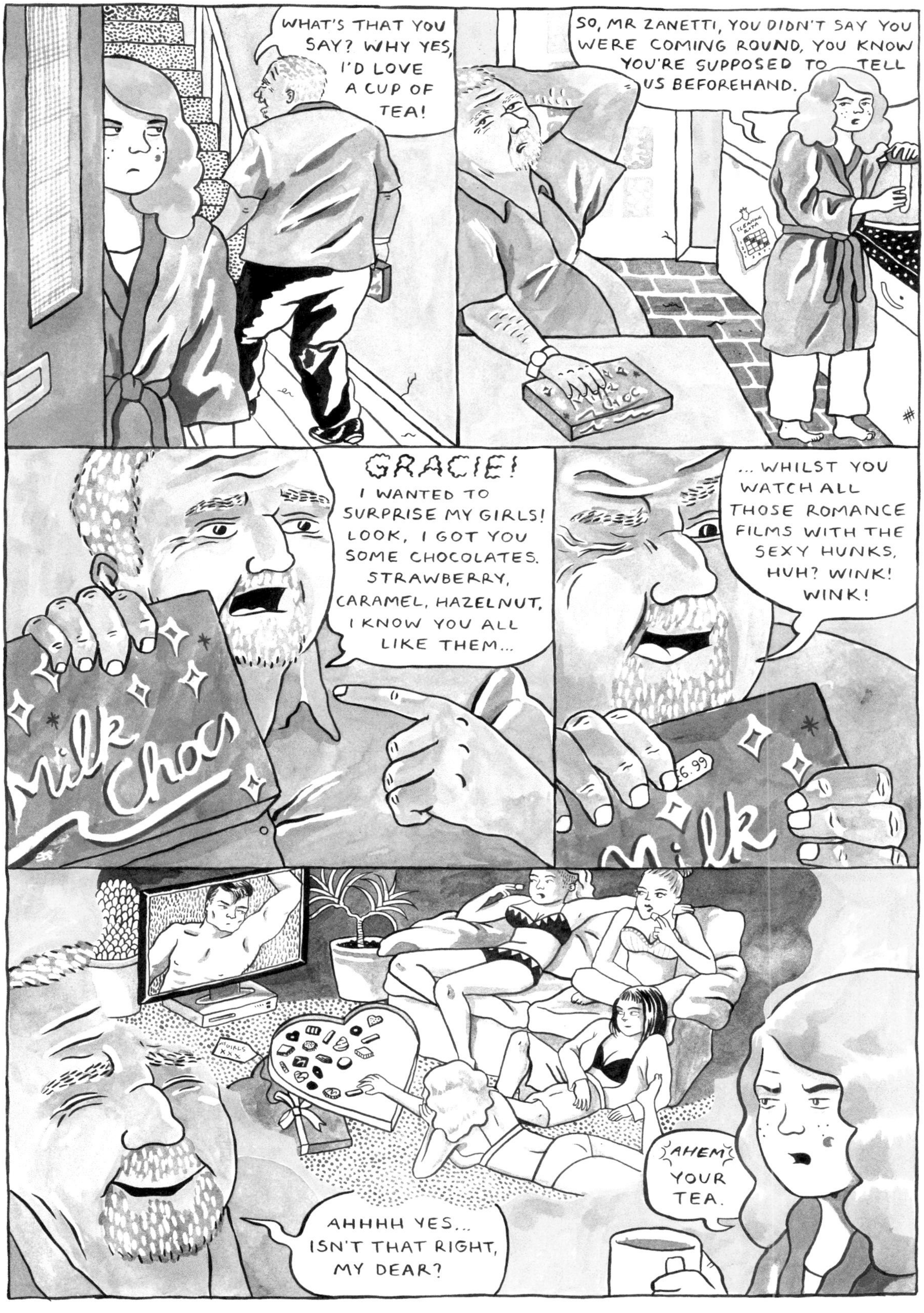
WHAT'S THAT YOU SAY? WHY YES, I'D LOVE A CUP OF TEA!
SO, MR ZANETTI, YOU DIDN'T SAY YOU WERE COMING ROUND, YOU KNOW YOU'RE SUPPOSED TO TELL US BEFOREHAND.
GRACIE!
I WANTED TO SURPRISE MY GIRLS! LOOK, I GOT YOU SOME CHOCOLATES. STRAWBERRY, CARAMEL, HAZELNUT, I KNOW YOU ALL LIKE THEM...
Milk Chocs
... WHILST YOU WATCH ALL THOSE ROMANCE FILMS WITH THE SEXY HUNKS, HUH? WINK! WINK!
Milk
AHEM
YOUR TEA.
AHHHH YES... ISN'T THAT RIGHT, MY DEAR?

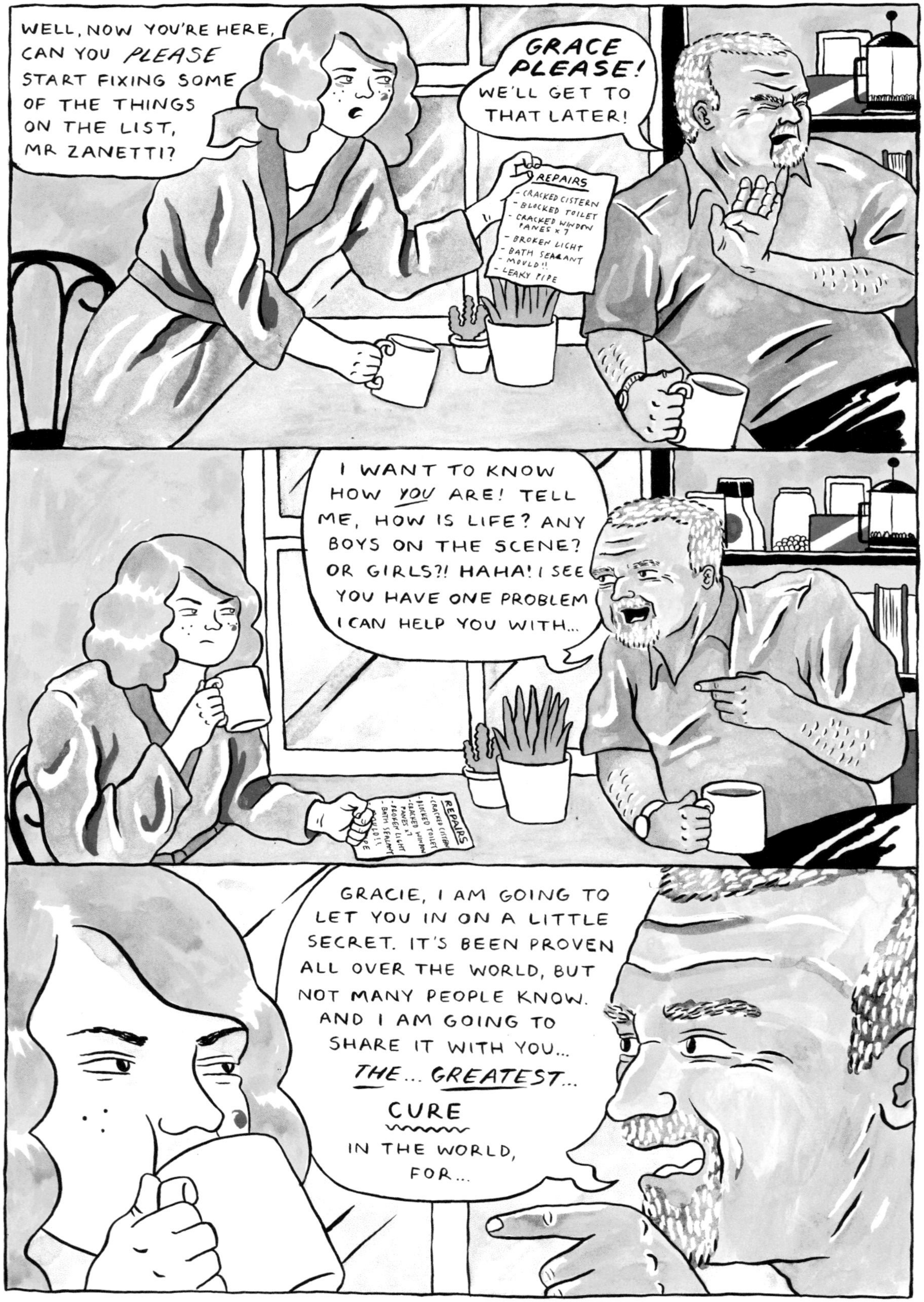
WELL, NOW YOU'RE HERE, CAN YOU PLEASE START FIXING SOME OF THE THINGS ON THE LIST, MR ZANETTI?
GRACE PLEASE! WE'LL GET TO THAT LATER!
REPAIRS
- CRACKED CISTERN
- BLOCKED TOILET
- CRACKED WINDOW PANES x 7
- BROKEN LIGHT
- BATH SEALANT
- MOULD!!
- LEAKY PIPE
I WANT TO KNOW HOW YOU ARE! TELL ME, HOW IS LIFE? ANY BOYS ON THE SCENE? OR GIRLS?! HAHA! I SEE YOU HAVE ONE PROBLEM I CAN HELP YOU WITH...
GRACIE, I AM GOING TO LET YOU IN ON A LITTLE SECRET. IT'S BEEN PROVEN ALL OVER THE WORLD, BUT NOT MANY PEOPLE KNOW. AND I AM GOING TO SHARE IT WITH YOU... THE... GREATEST... CURE IN THE WORLD, FOR...

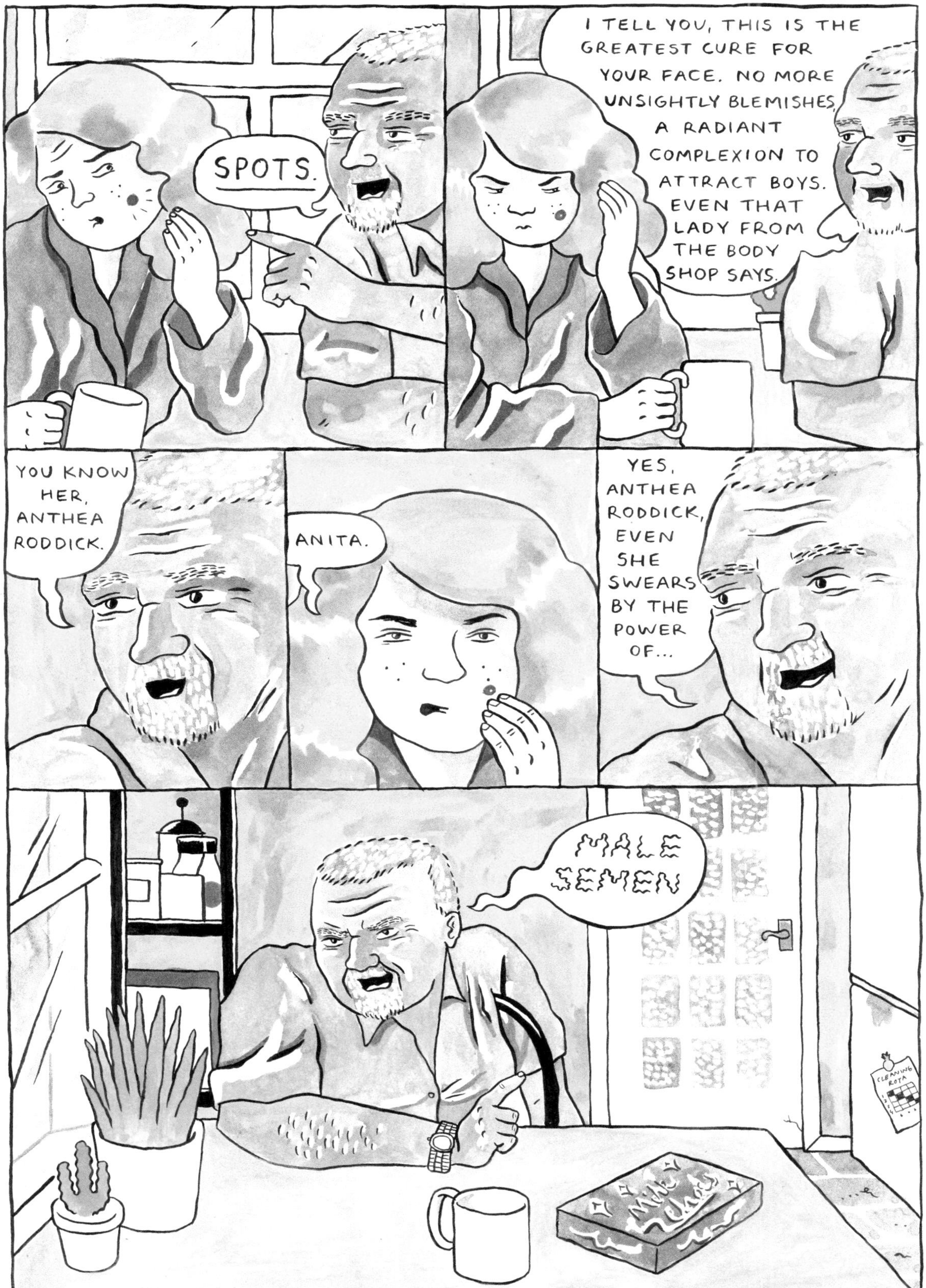
SPOTS.
I TELL YOU, THIS IS THE GREATEST CURE FOR YOUR FACE. NO MORE UNSIGHTLY BLEMISHES, A RADIANT COMPLEXION TO ATTRACT BOYS. EVEN THAT LADY FROM THE BODY SHOP SAYS.
YOU KNOW HER, ANTHEA RODDICK.
ANITA.
YES, ANTHEA RODDICK, EVEN SHE SWEARS BY THE POWER OF...
MALE SEVEN
CLEANING ROTA

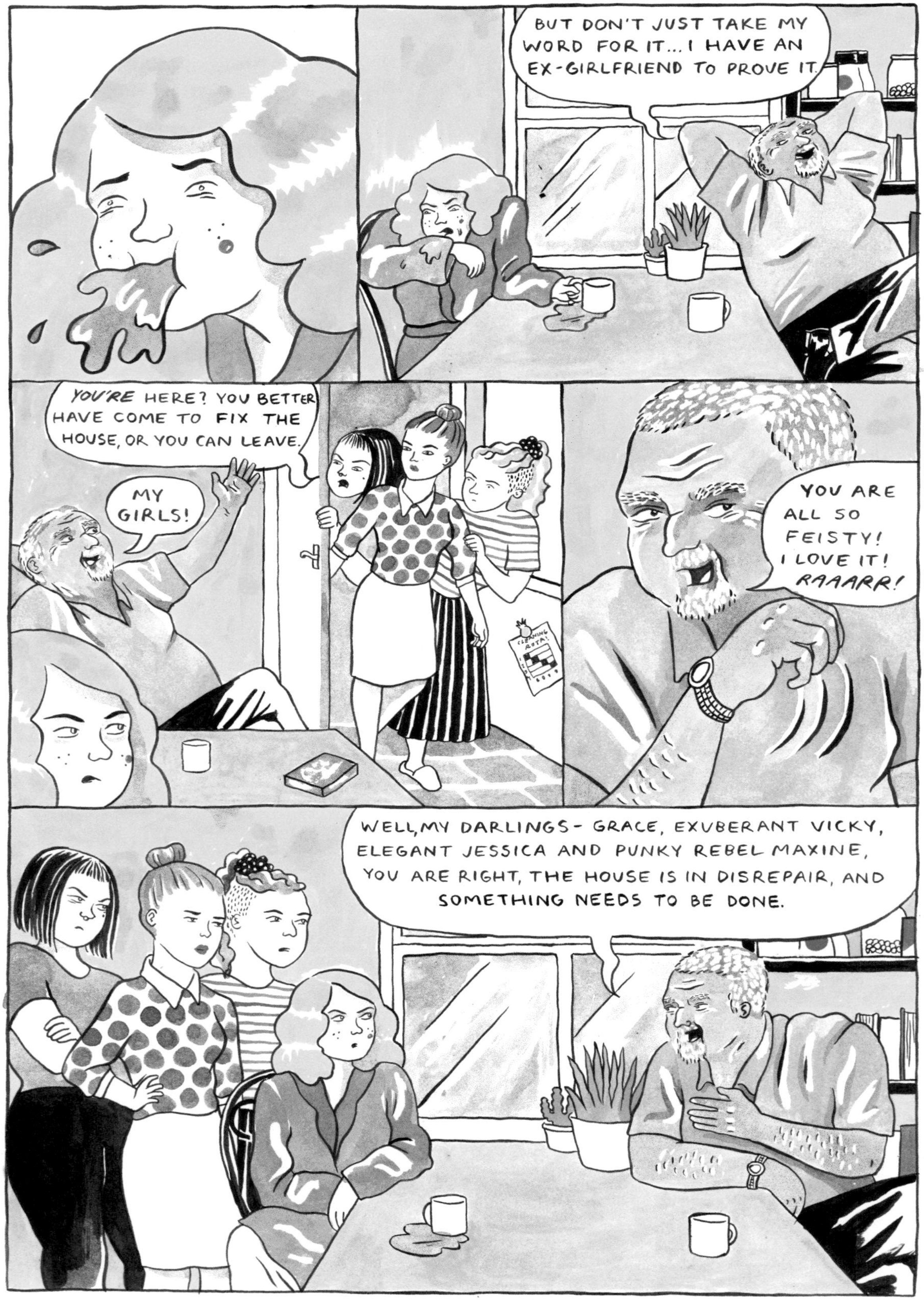
BUT DON'T JUST TAKE MY WORD FOR IT... I HAVE AN EX-GIRLFRIEND TO PROVE IT.
YOU'RE HERE? YOU BETTER HAVE COME TO FIX THE HOUSE, OR YOU CAN LEAVE.
MY GIRLS!
CLEANING ROTA!
YOU ARE ALL SO FEISTY! I LOVE IT! RAAARR!
WELL, MY DARLINGS - GRACE, EXUBERANT VICKY, ELEGANT JESSICA AND PUNKY REBEL MAXINE, YOU ARE RIGHT, THE HOUSE IS IN DISREPAIR, AND SOMETHING NEEDS TO BE DONE.

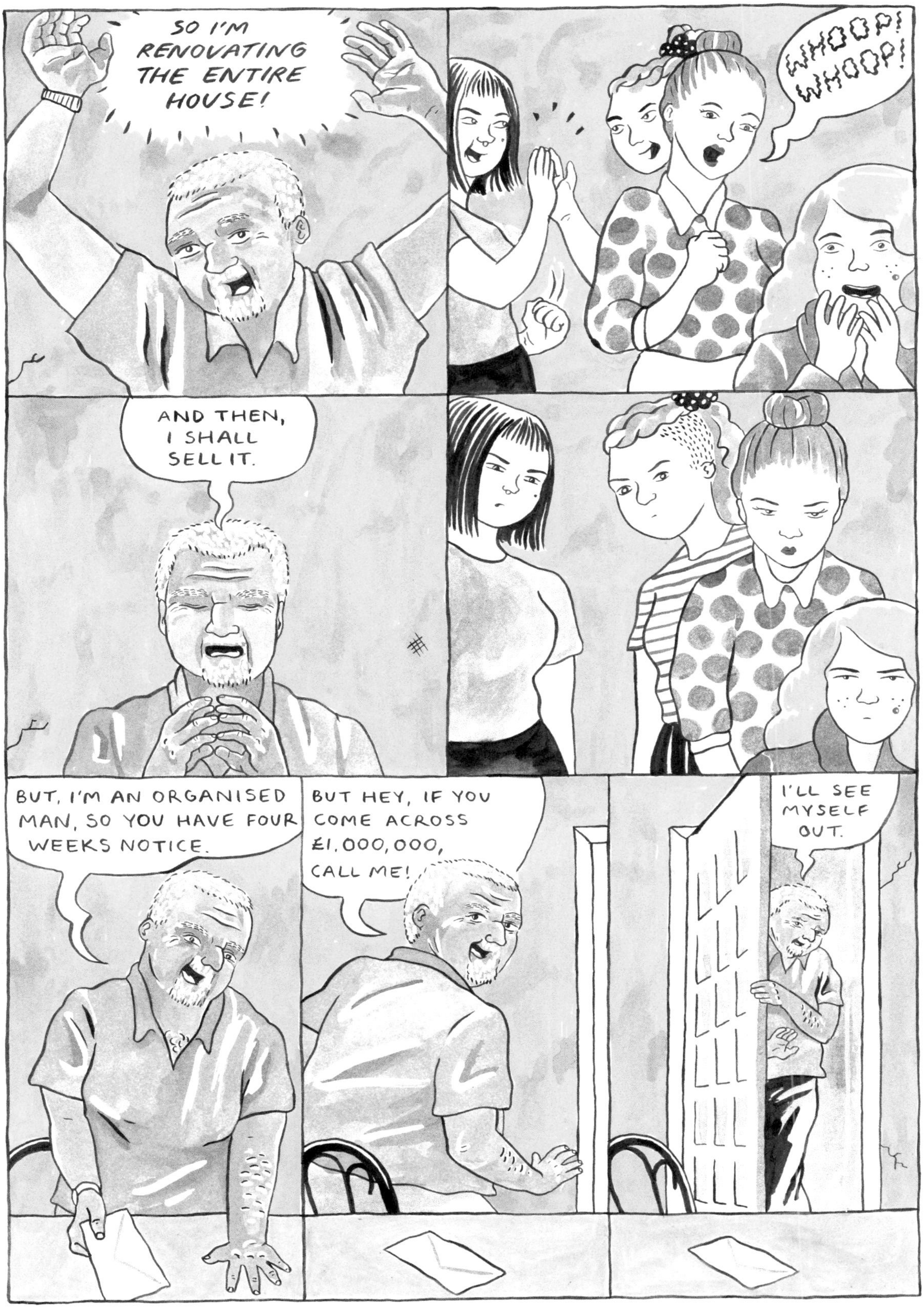
SO I'M RENOVATING THE ENTIRE HOUSE!
WHOOP! WHOOP!
AND THEN, I SHALL SELL IT.
BUT, I'M AN ORGANISED MAN, SO YOU HAVE FOUR WEEKS NOTICE.
BUT HEY, IF YOU COME ACROSS £1,000,000, CALL ME!
I'LL SEE MYSELF OUT.

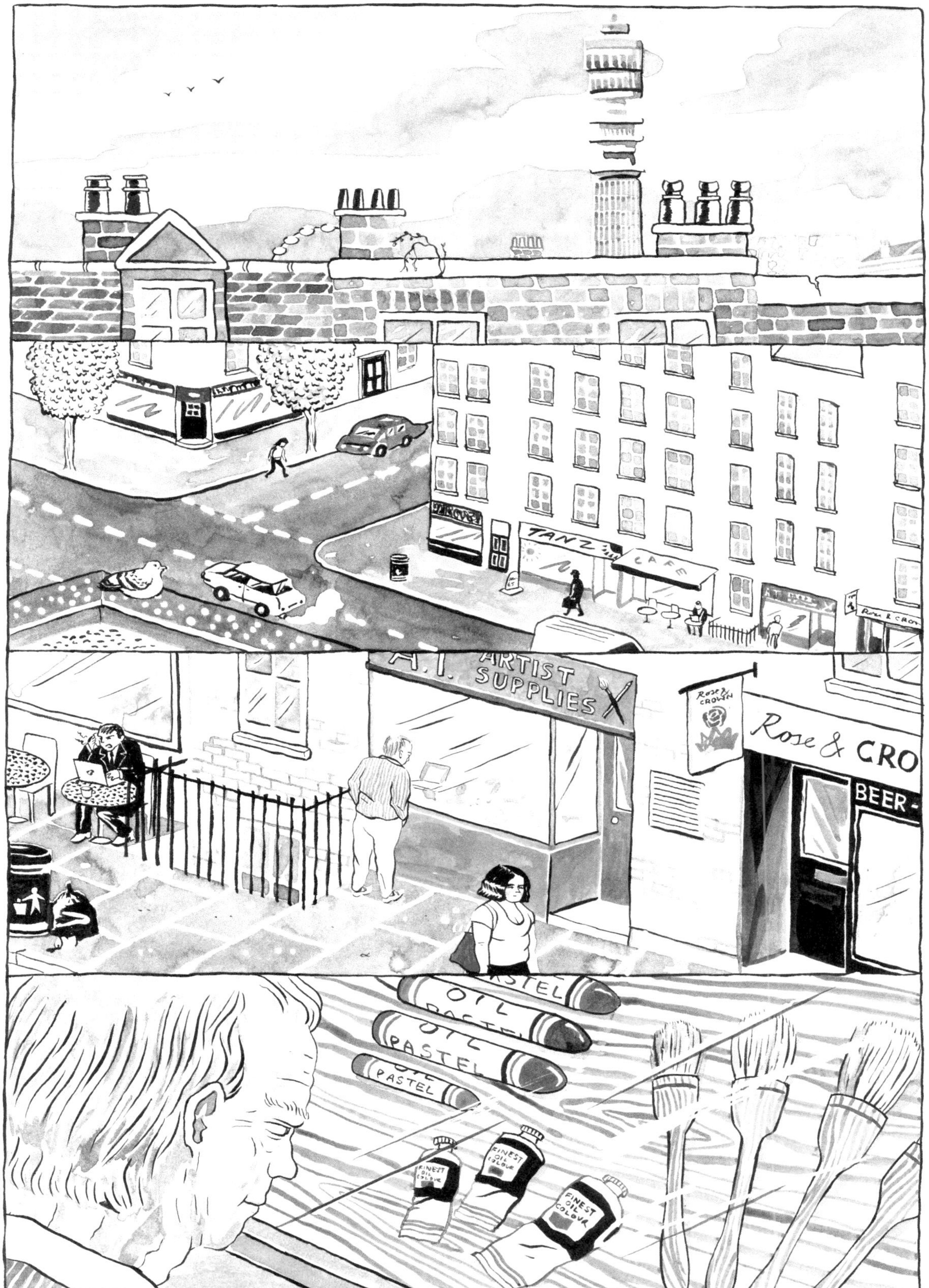
TANZ
CAFE
ARTIST SUPPLIES
Rose & CRO
BEER
PASTEL
OIL PASTEL
OIL PASTEL
PASTEL
FINEST OIL COLOUR
FINEST OIL COLOUR
FINEST OIL COLOUR

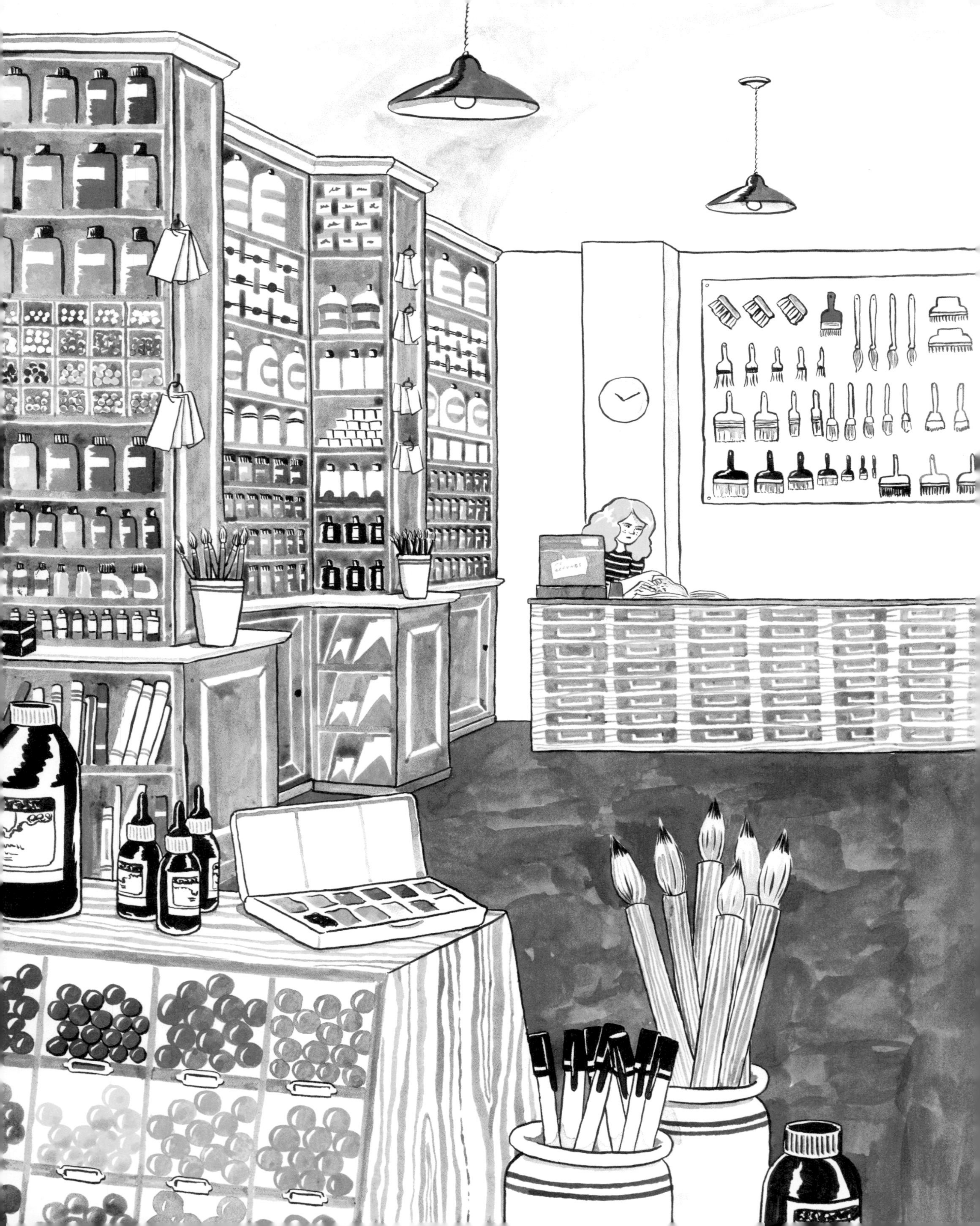

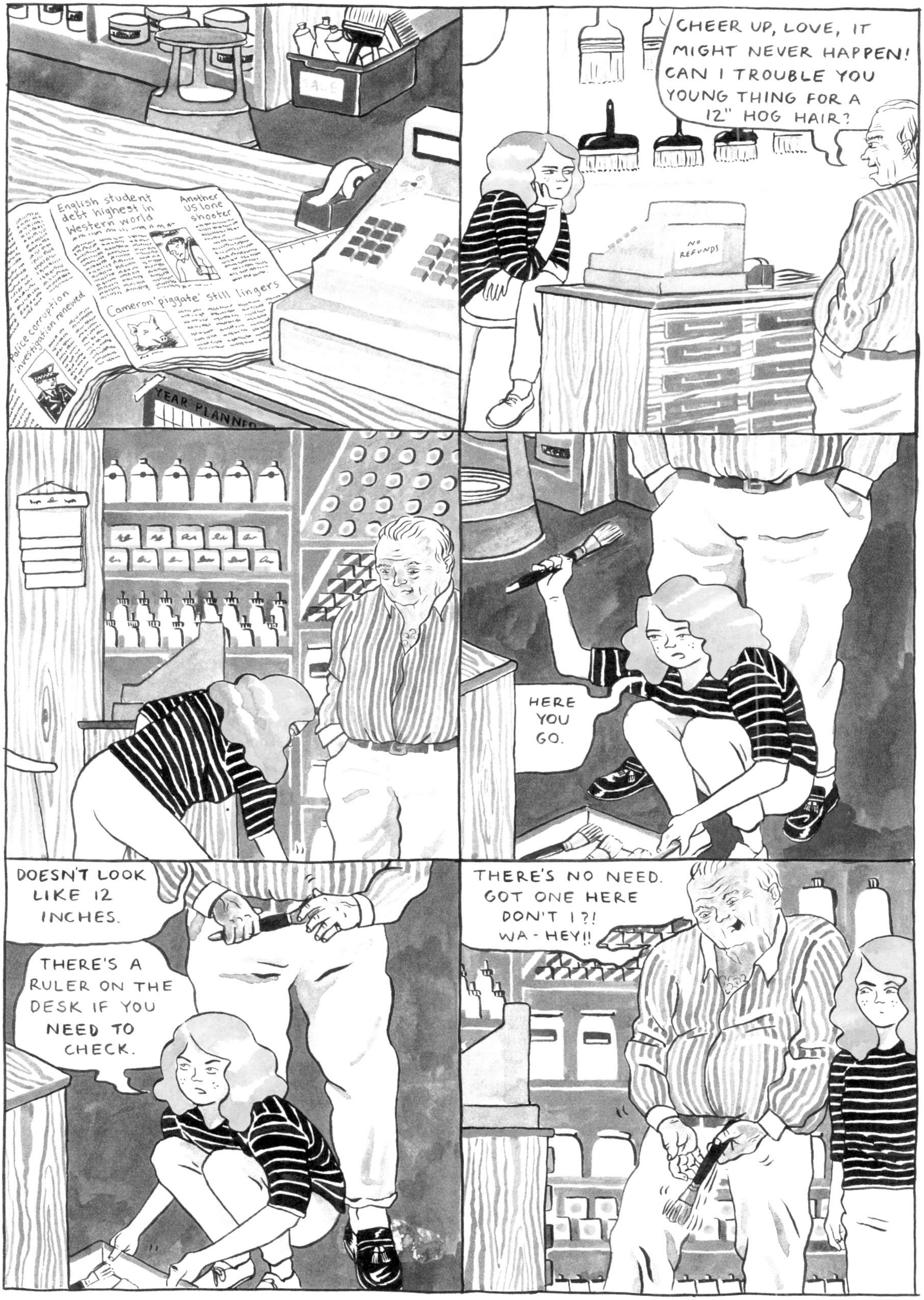
English student debt highest in Western world
Another US lone shooter
Cameron 'piggate' still lingers
Police corruption investigation renewed
CHEER UP, LOVE, IT MIGHT NEVER HAPPEN! CAN I TROUBLE YOU YOUNG THING FOR A 12" HOG HAIR?
NO REFUNDS
HERE YOU GO.
DOESN'T LOOK LIKE 12 INCHES.
THERE'S A RULER ON THE DESK IF YOU NEED TO CHECK.
THERE'S NO NEED. GOT ONE HERE DON'T I?! WA-HEY!!

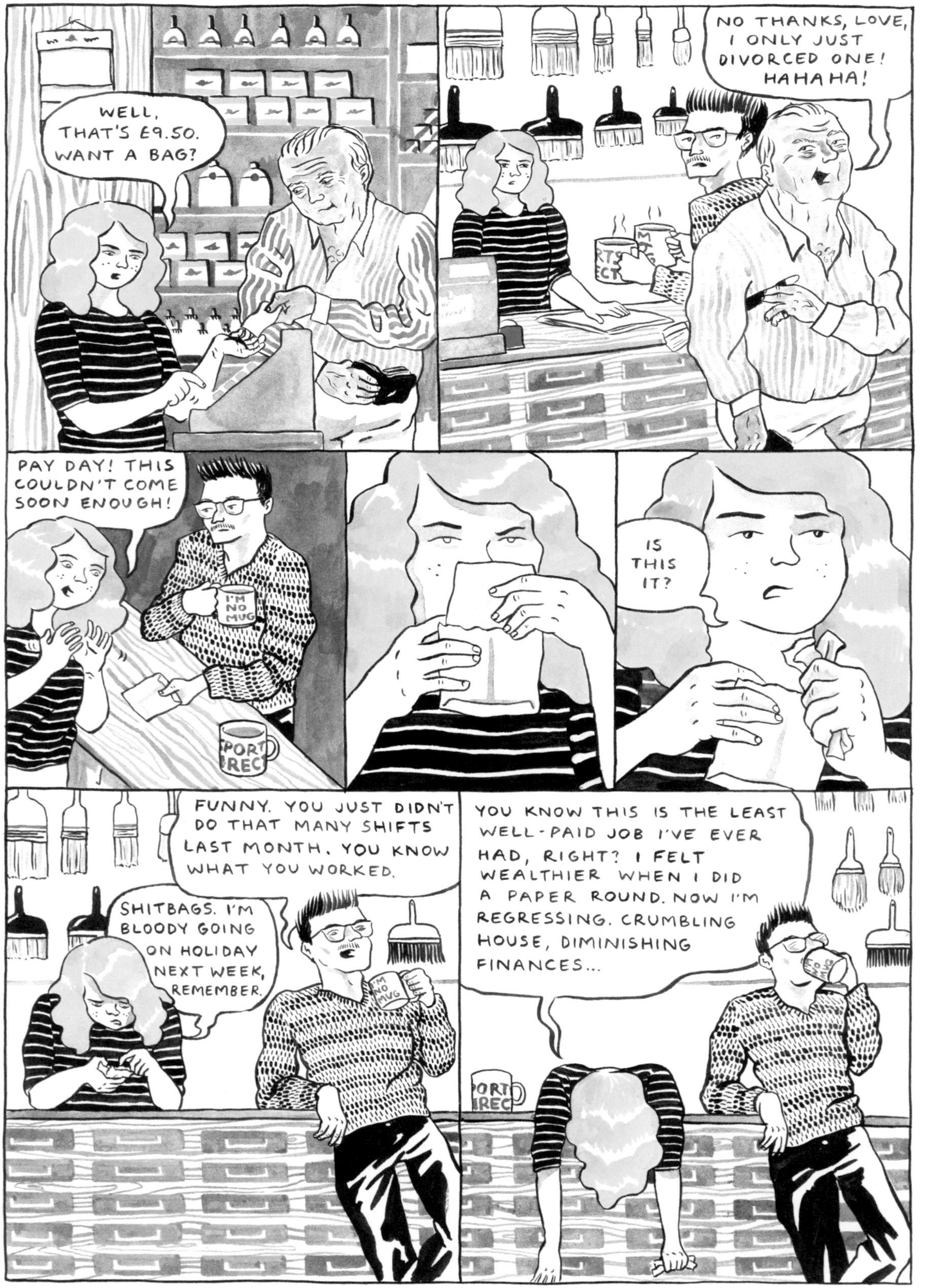
WELL, THAT'S £9.50. WANT A BAG?
NO THANKS, LOVE, I ONLY JUST DIVORCED ONE! HAHAHA!
PAY DAY! THIS COULDN'T COME SOON ENOUGH!
I'M NO MUG
IS THIS IT?
FUNNY. YOU JUST DIDN'T DO THAT MANY SHIFTS LAST MONTH. YOU KNOW WHAT YOU WORKED.
SHITBAGS. I'M BLOODY GOING ON HOLIDAY NEXT WEEK, REMEMBER.
I'M NO MUG
YOU KNOW THIS IS THE LEAST WELL-PAID JOB I'VE EVER HAD, RIGHT? I FELT WEALTHIER WHEN I DID A PAPER ROUND. NOW I'M REGRESSING. CRUMBLING HOUSE, DIMINISHING FINANCES...

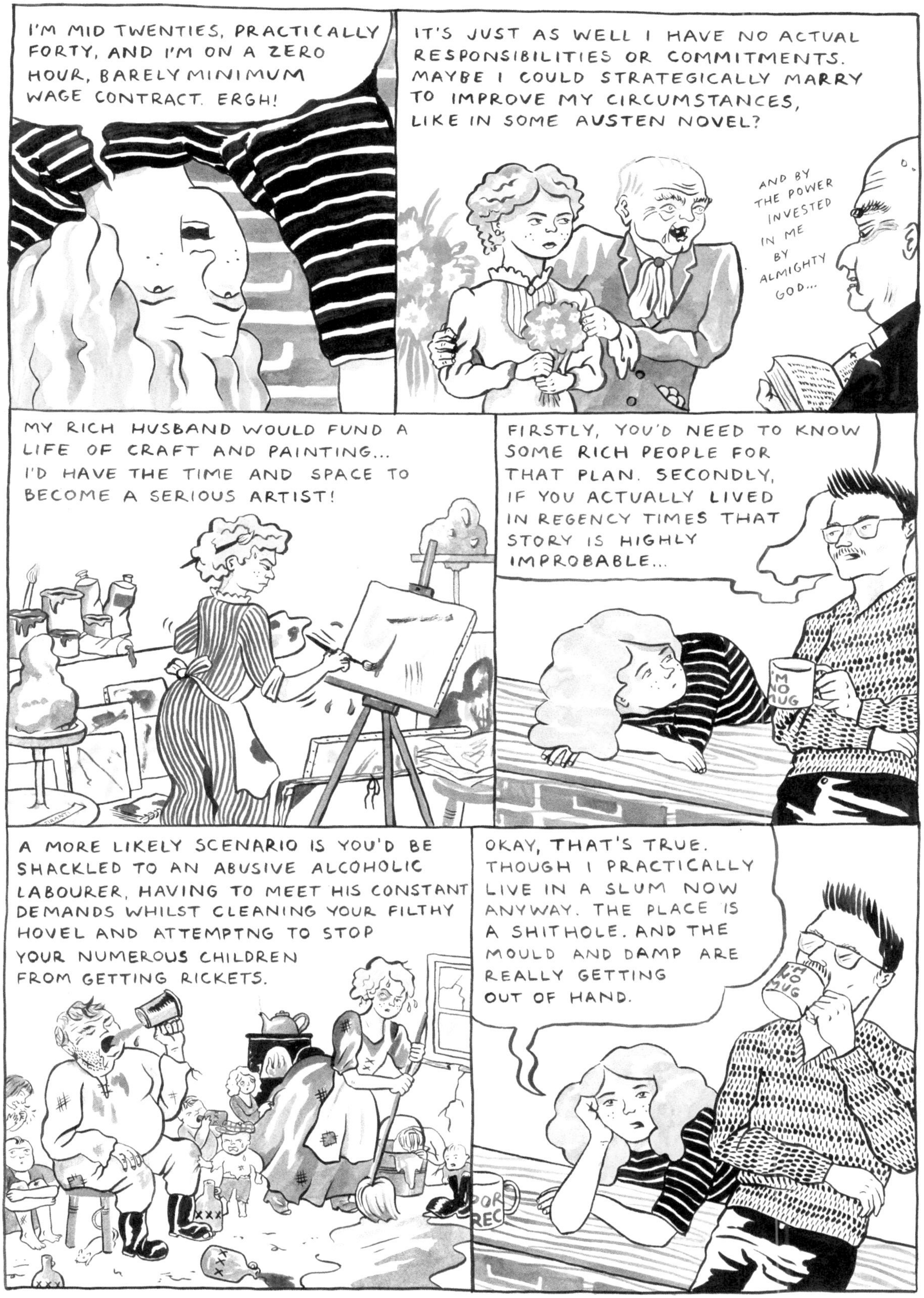

I'M MID TWENTIES, PRACTICALLY FORTY, AND I'M ON A ZERO HOUR, BARELY MINIMUM WAGE CONTRACT. ERGH!
IT'S JUST AS WELL I HAVE NO ACTUAL RESPONSIBILITIES OR COMMITMENTS. MAYBE I COULD STRATEGICALLY MARRY TO IMPROVE MY CIRCUMSTANCES, LIKE IN SOME AUSTEN NOVEL?
AND BY THE POWER INVESTED IN ME BY ALMIGHTY GOD...
MY RICH HUSBAND WOULD FUND A LIFE OF CRAFT AND PAINTING... I'D HAVE THE TIME AND SPACE TO BECOME A SERIOUS ARTIST!
FIRSTLY, YOU'D NEED TO KNOW SOME RICH PEOPLE FOR THAT PLAN. SECONDLY, IF YOU ACTUALLY LIVED IN REGENCY TIMES THAT STORY IS HIGHLY IMPROBABLE...
I'M NO MUG
A MORE LIKELY SCENARIO IS YOU'D BE SHACKLED TO AN ABUSIVE ALCOHOLIC LABOURER, HAVING TO MEET HIS CONSTANT DEMANDS WHILST CLEANING YOUR FILTHY HOVEL AND ATTEMPTNG TO STOP YOUR NUMEROUS CHILDREN FROM GETTING RICKETS.
OKAY, THAT'S TRUE. THOUGH I PRACTICALLY LIVE IN A SLUM NOW ANYWAY. THE PLACE IS A SHITHOLE. AND THE MOULD AND DAMP ARE REALLY GETTING OUT OF HAND.

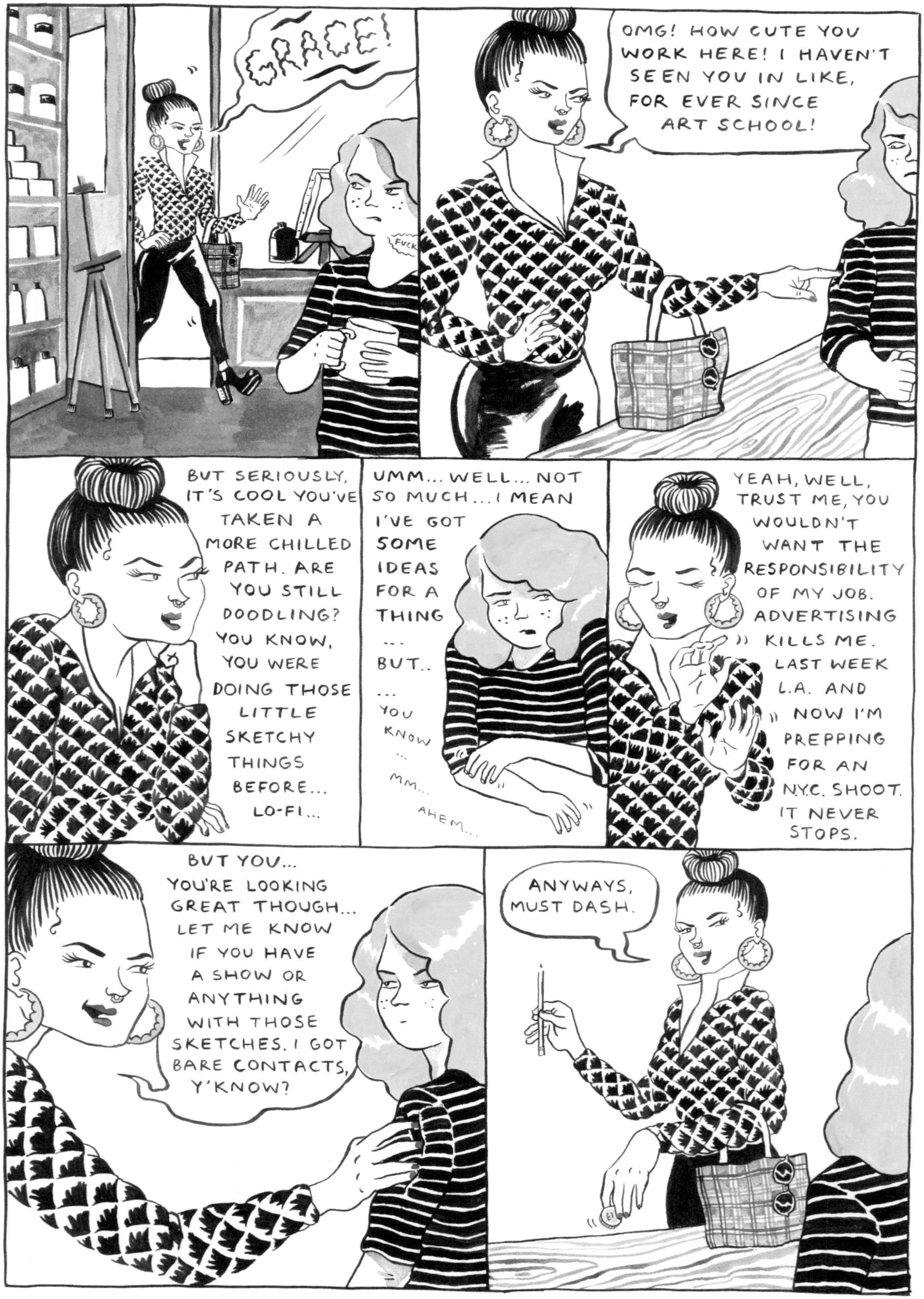
GRACE!
FUCK
OMG! HOW CUTE YOU WORK HERE! I HAVEN'T SEEN YOU IN LIKE, FOR EVER SINCE ART SCHOOL!
BUT SERIOUSLY, IT'S COOL YOU'VE TAKEN A MORE CHILLED PATH. ARE YOU STILL DOODLING? YOU KNOW, YOU WERE DOING THOSE LITTLE SKETCHY THINGS BEFORE... LO-FI...
UMM... WELL... NOT SO MUCH... I MEAN I'VE GOT SOME IDEAS FOR A THING ... BUT.. ... YOU KNOW ... MM... AHEM...
YEAH, WELL, TRUST ME, YOU WOULDN'T WANT THE RESPONSIBILITY OF MY JOB. ADVERTISING KILLS ME. LAST WEEK L.A. AND NOW I'M PREPPING FOR AN N.Y.C. SHOOT. IT NEVER STOPS.
BUT YOU... YOU'RE LOOKING GREAT THOUGH... LET ME KNOW IF YOU HAVE A SHOW OR ANYTHING WITH THOSE SKETCHES. I GOT BARE CONTACTS, Y'KNOW?
ANYWAYS, MUST DASH.

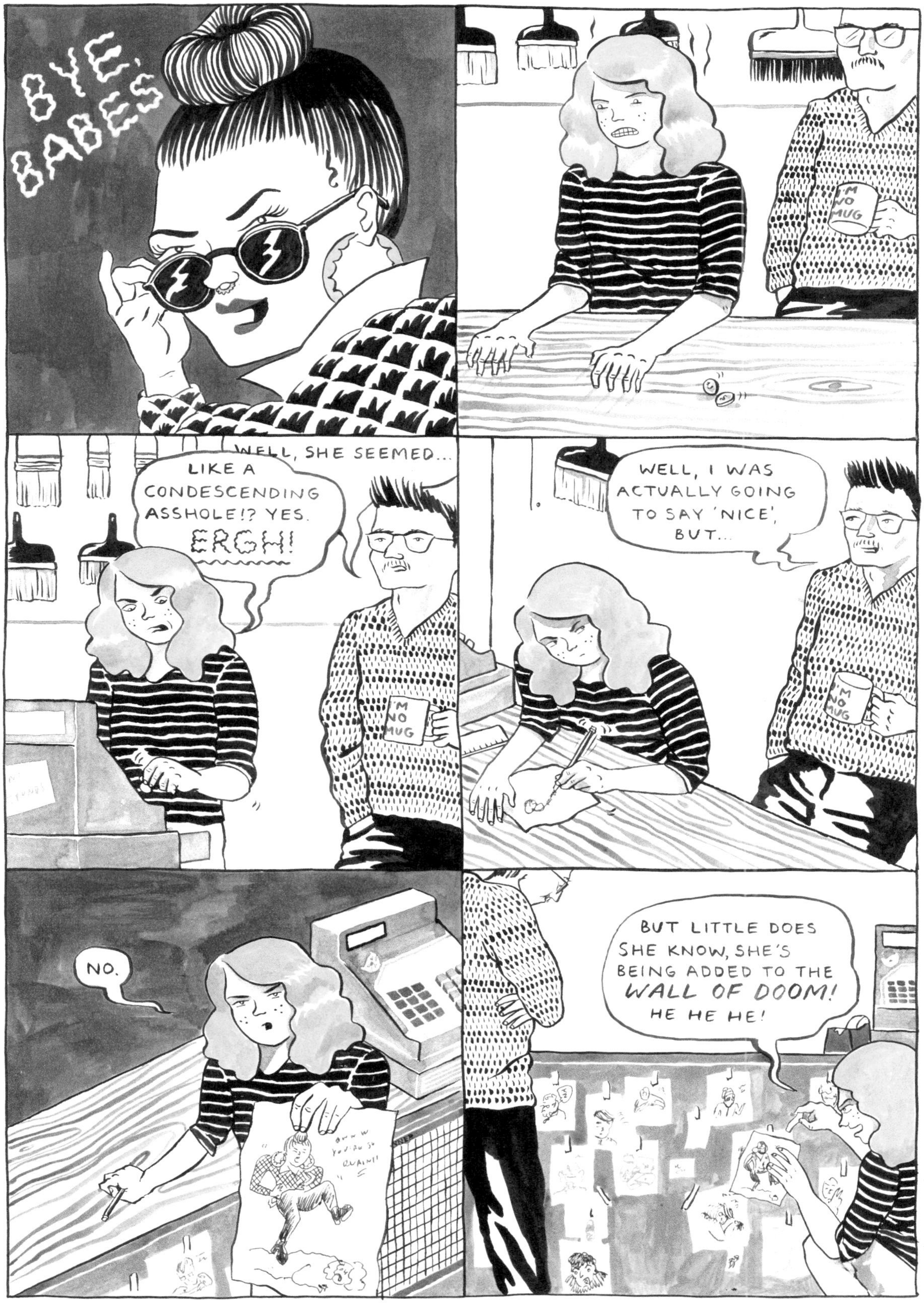
BYE, BABES
WELL, SHE SEEMED...
LIKE A CONDESCENDING ASSHOLE!? YES. ERGH!
I'M NO MUG
WELL, I WAS ACTUALLY GOING TO SAY 'NICE', BUT...
NO.
BUT LITTLE DOES SHE KNOW, SHE'S BEING ADDED TO THE WALL OF DOOM! HE HE HE!

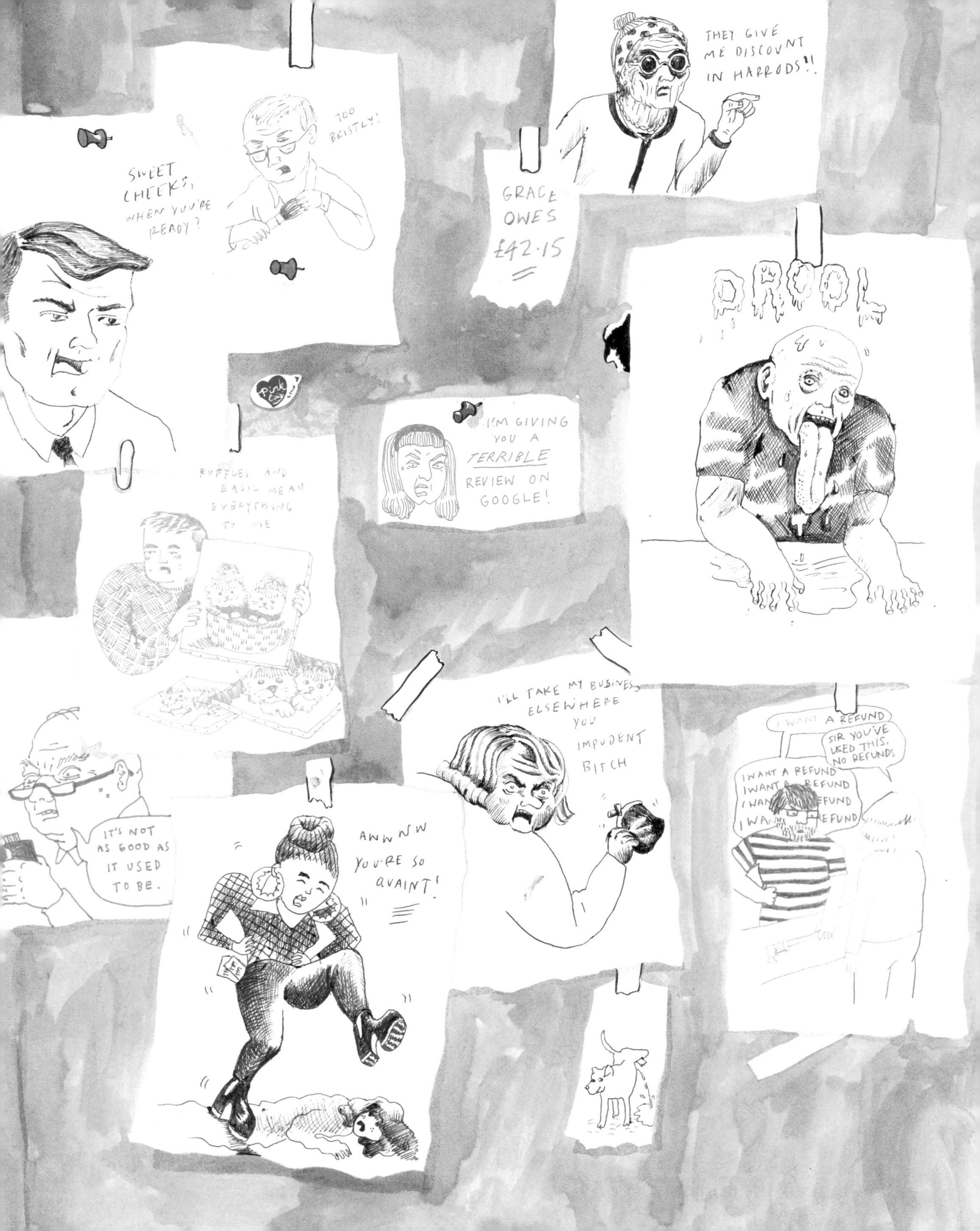
SWEET CHEEKS, WHEN YOU'RE READY?
TOO BRISTLY!
THEY GIVE ME DISCOUNT IN HARRODS!!
GRACE OWES £42.15
DROOL
I'M GIVING YOU A TERRIBLE REVIEW ON GOOGLE!
RUFFLES AND BASIL MEAN EVERYTHING TO ME
I'LL TAKE MY BUSINESS ELSEWHERE YOU IMPUDENT BITCH
I WANT A REFUND
SIR YOU'VE USED THIS. NO REFUNDS
I WANT A REFUND
I WANT A REFUND
IT'S NOT AS GOOD AS IT USED TO BE.
AWWWW YOU'RE SO QUAINT!

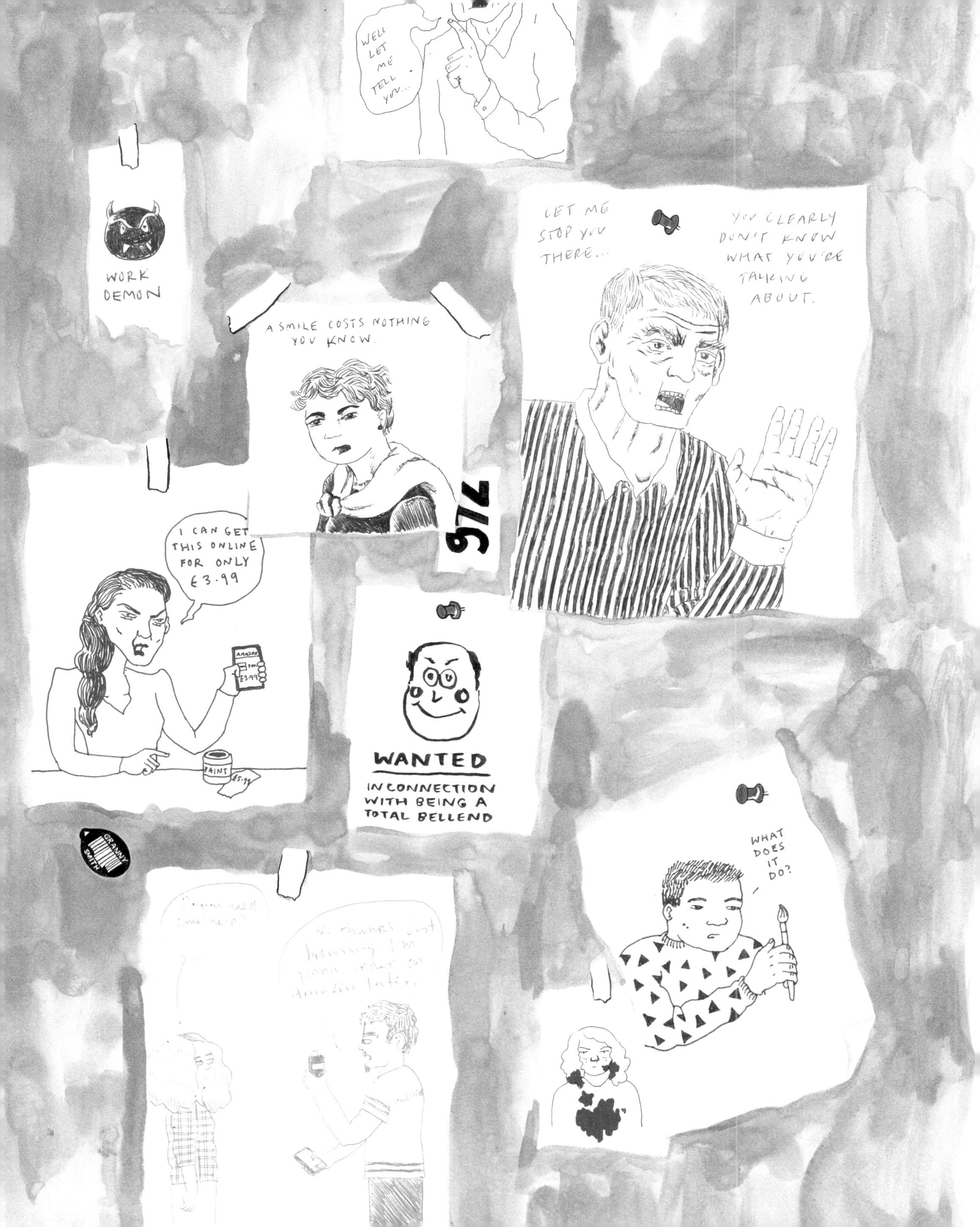
WELL LET ME TELL YOU...
WORK DEMON
A SMILE COSTS NOTHING YOU KNOW.
LET ME STOP YOU THERE...
YOU CLEARLY DON'T KNOW WHAT YOU'RE TALKING ABOUT.
I CAN GET THIS ONLINE FOR ONLY £3.99
AMAZON
PAINT
£3.99
PAINT
£5.99
WANTED
IN CONNECTION WITH BEING A TOTAL BELLEND
GRANNY SMITH
WHAT DOES IT DO?
Do you need some help?
No thanks, just browsing. I'm gonna order on Amazon later.

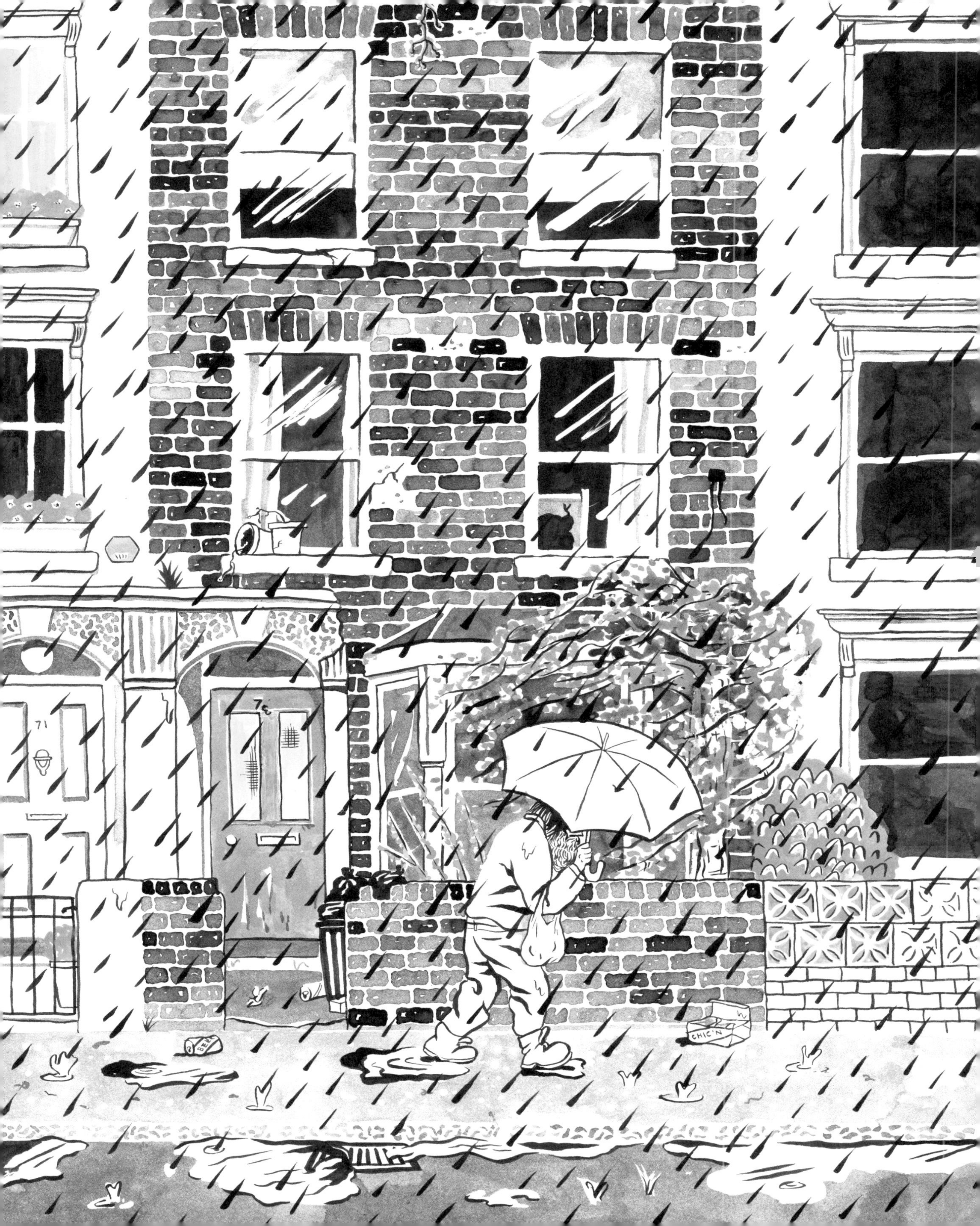
71
CHIC'N

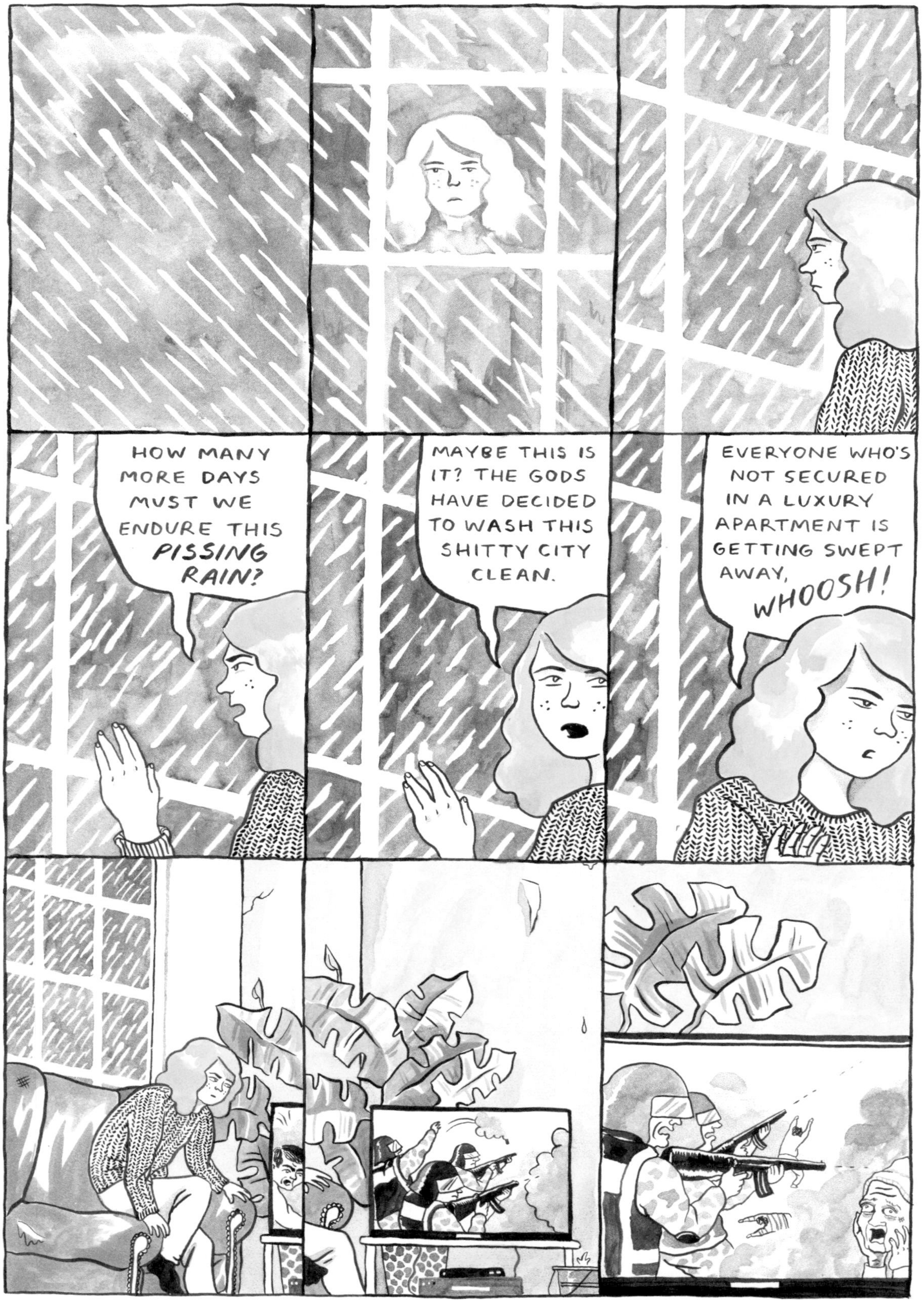
HOW MANY MORE DAYS MUST WE ENDURE THIS PISSING RAIN?
MAYBE THIS IS IT? THE GODS HAVE DECIDED TO WASH THIS SHITTY CITY CLEAN.
EVERYONE WHO'S NOT SECURED IN A LUXURY APARTMENT IS GETTING SWEPT AWAY, WHOOSH!

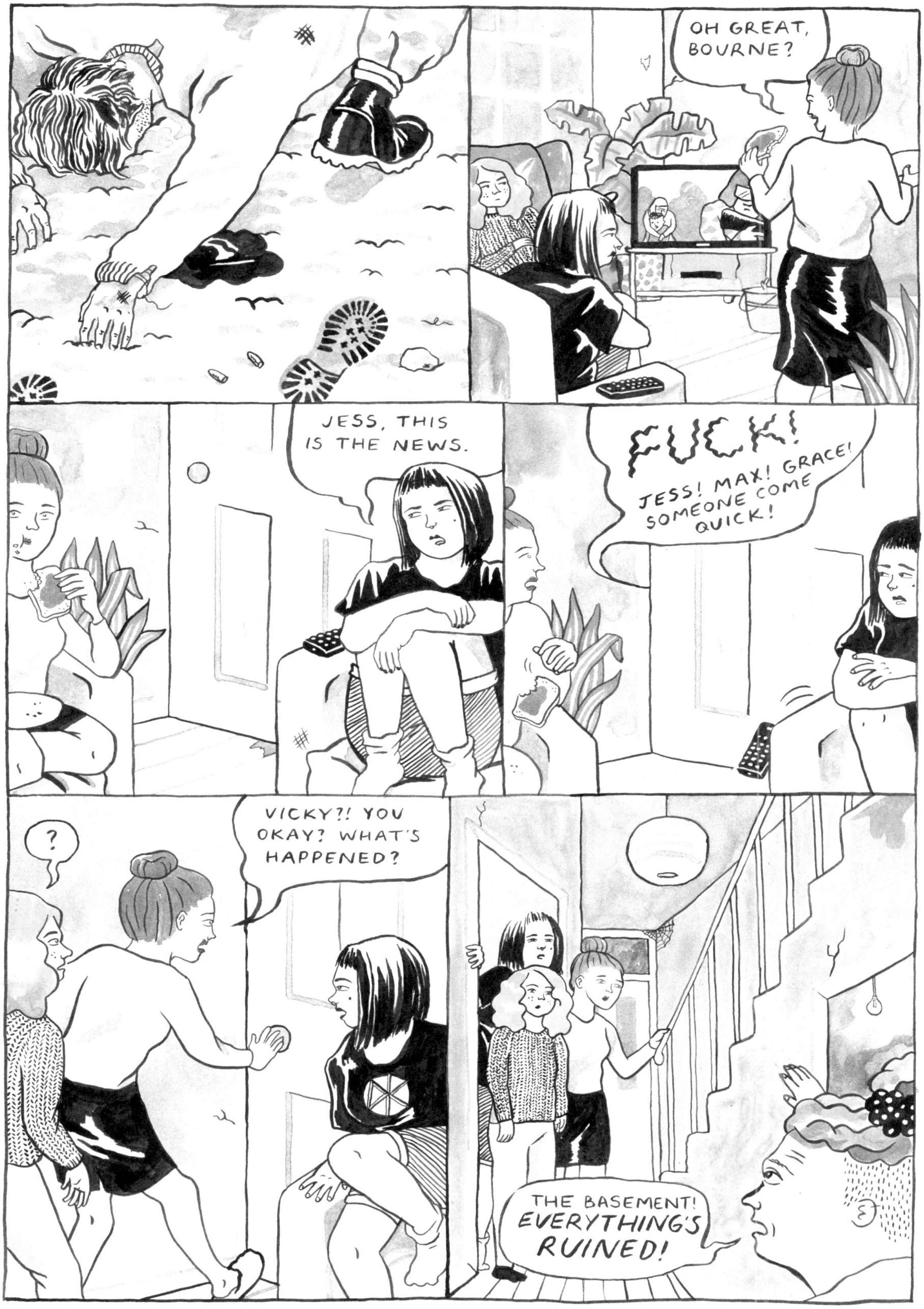
OH GREAT, BOURNE?
JESS, THIS IS THE NEWS.
FUCK!
JESS! MAX! GRACE! SOMEONE COME QUICK!
?
VICKY?! YOU OKAY? WHAT'S HAPPENED?
THE BASEMENT! EVERYTHING'S RUINED!

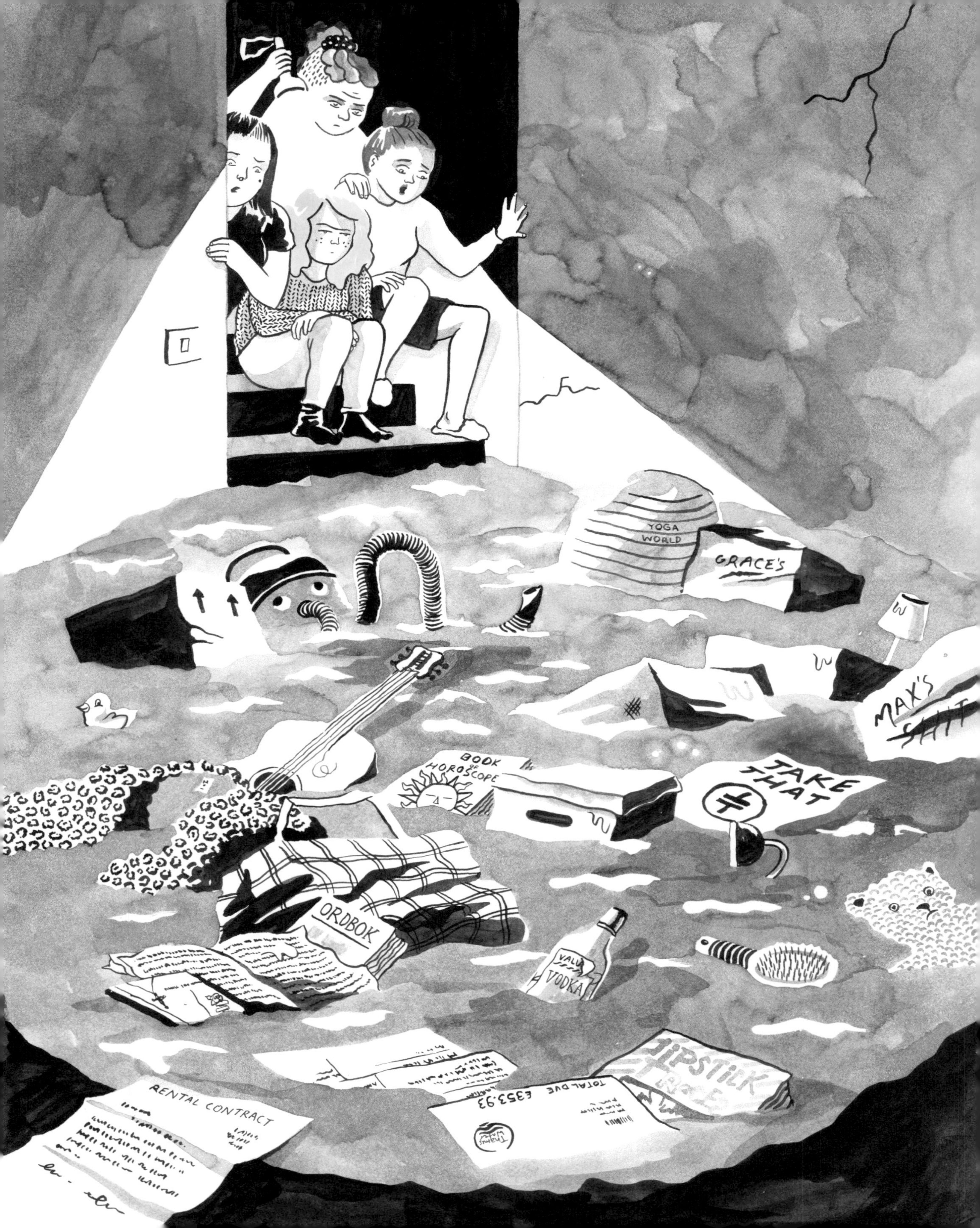
YOGA WORLD
GRACE'S
MAX'S SHIT
BOOK OF HOROSCOPE
TAKE THAT
ORDBOK
VODKA
RENTAL CONTRACT
TOTAL DUE £353.93

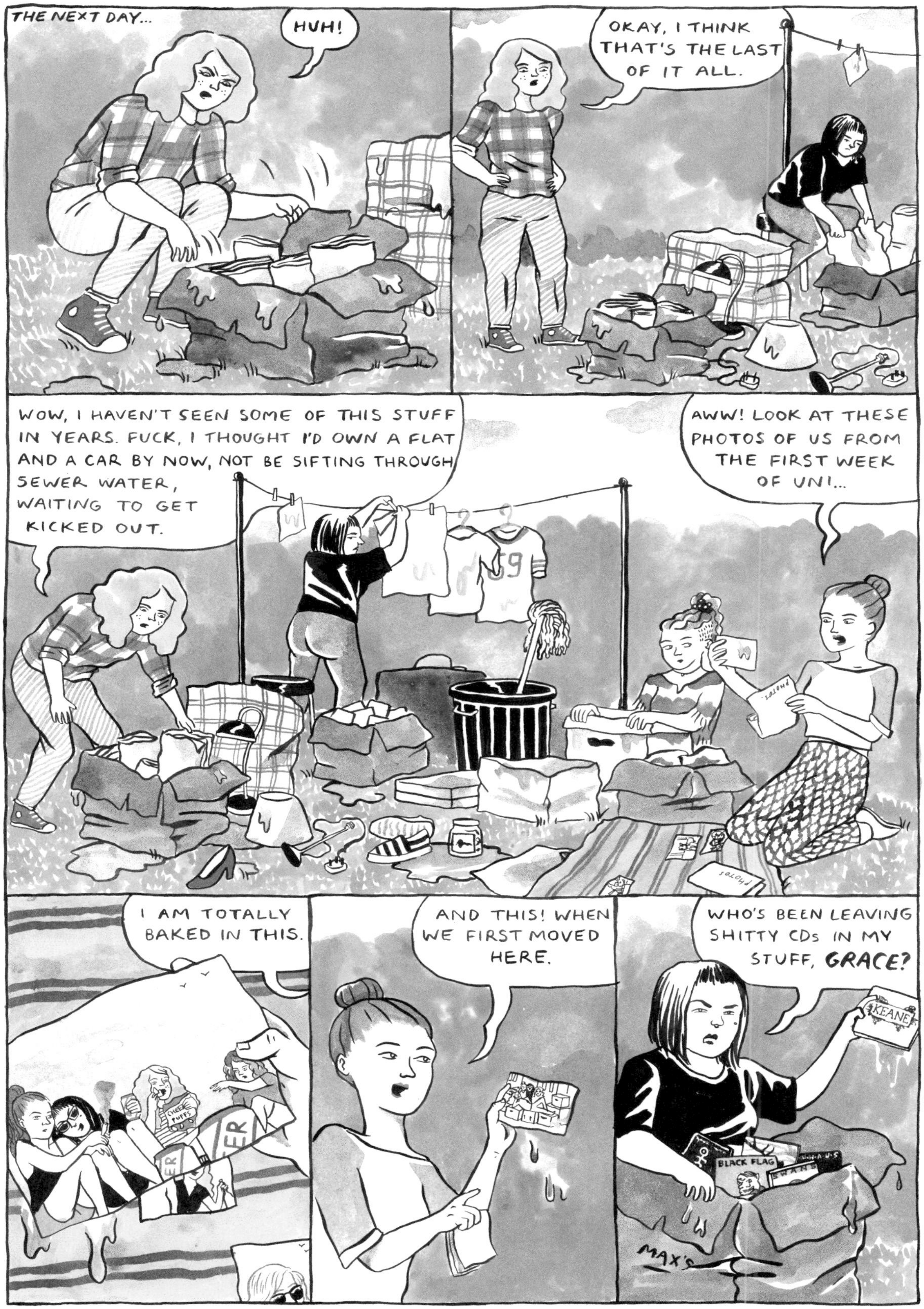
THE NEXT DAY...
HUH!
OKAY, I THINK THAT'S THE LAST OF IT ALL.
WOW, I HAVEN'T SEEN SOME OF THIS STUFF IN YEARS. FUCK, I THOUGHT I'D OWN A FLAT AND A CAR BY NOW, NOT BE SIFTING THROUGH SEWER WATER, WAITING TO GET KICKED OUT.
AWW! LOOK AT THESE PHOTOS OF US FROM THE FIRST WEEK OF UNI!...
I AM TOTALLY BAKED IN THIS.
AND THIS! WHEN WE FIRST MOVED HERE.
WHO'S BEEN LEAVING SHITTY CDs IN MY STUFF, GRACE?
KEANE
BLACK FLAG
SWANS
MAX'S

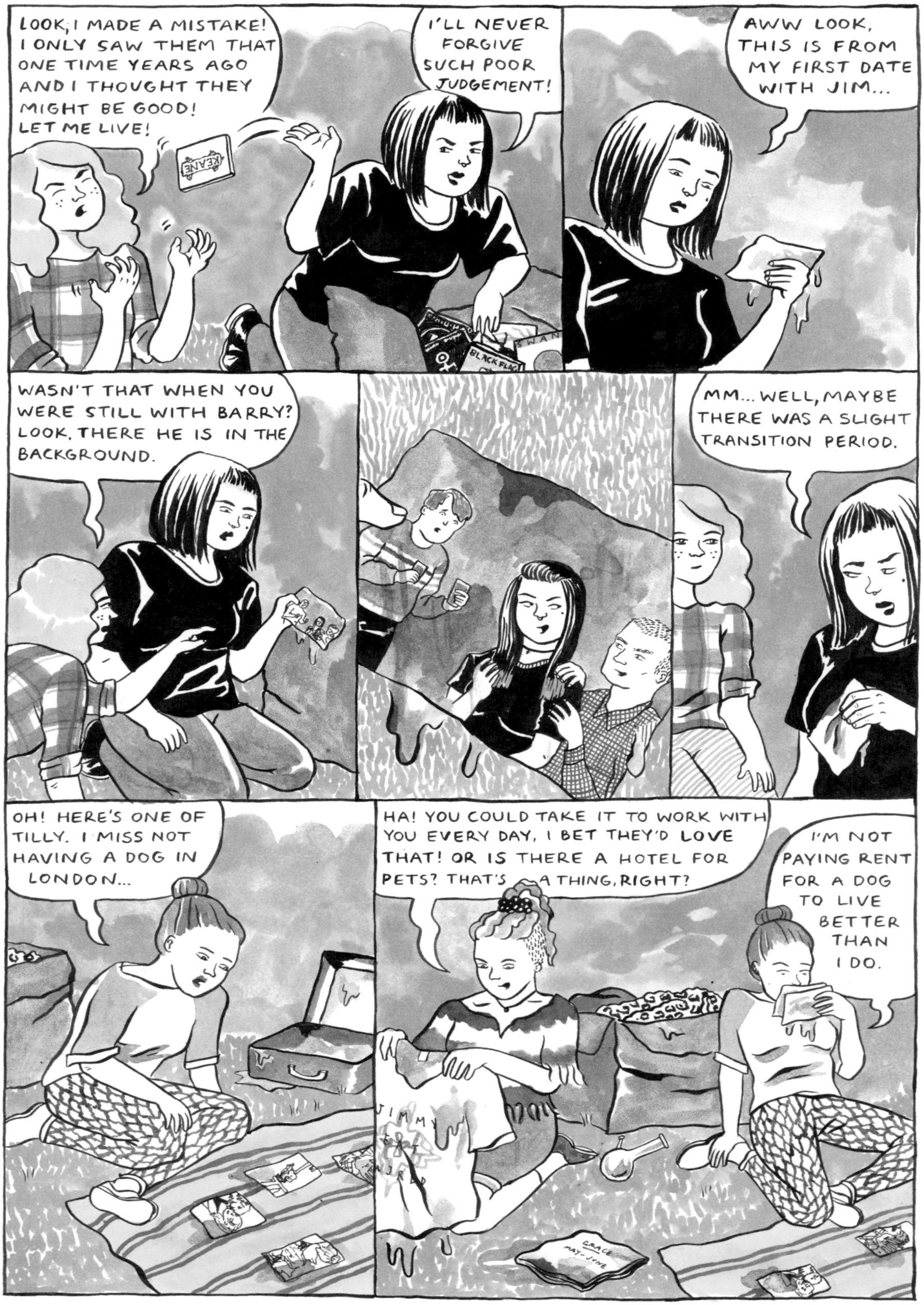
LOOK, I MADE A MISTAKE! I ONLY SAW THEM THAT ONE TIME YEARS AGO AND I THOUGHT THEY MIGHT BE GOOD! LET ME LIVE!
KEANE
I'LL NEVER FORGIVE SUCH POOR JUDGEMENT!
BLACK FLAG
SWAN
AWW LOOK, THIS IS FROM MY FIRST DATE WITH JIM...
WASN'T THAT WHEN YOU WERE STILL WITH BARRY? LOOK, THERE HE IS IN THE BACKGROUND.
MM... WELL, MAYBE THERE WAS A SLIGHT TRANSITION PERIOD.
OH! HERE'S ONE OF TILLY. I MISS NOT HAVING A DOG IN LONDON...
HA! YOU COULD TAKE IT TO WORK WITH YOU EVERY DAY, I BET THEY'D LOVE THAT! OR IS THERE A HOTEL FOR PETS? THAT'S A THING, RIGHT?
I'M NOT PAYING RENT FOR A DOG TO LIVE BETTER THAN I DO.
GRACE
MAY-JUNE

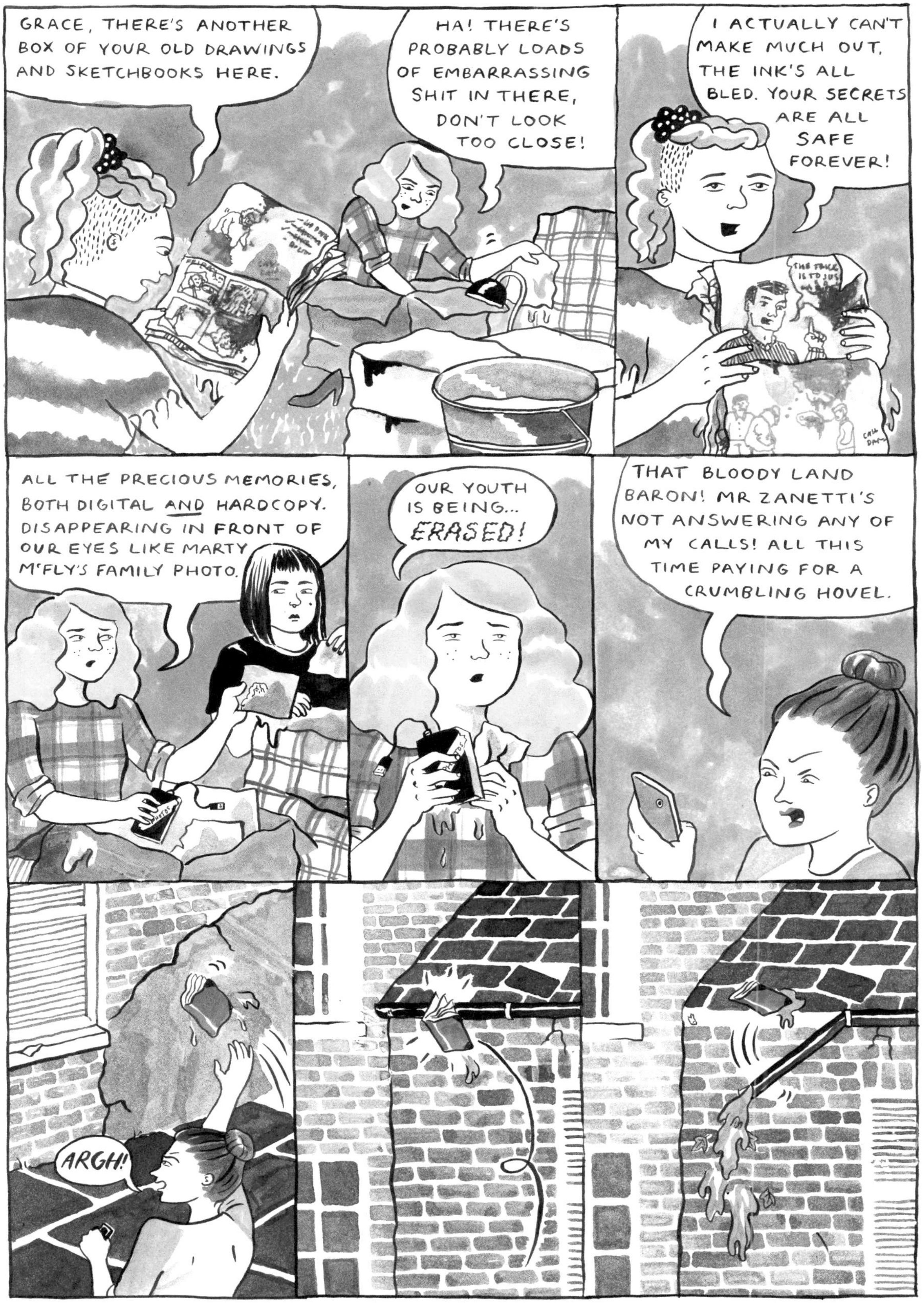
GRACE, THERE'S ANOTHER BOX OF YOUR OLD DRAWINGS AND SKETCHBOOKS HERE.
HA! THERE'S PROBABLY LOADS OF EMBARRASSING SHIT IN THERE, DON'T LOOK TOO CLOSE!
I ACTUALLY CAN'T MAKE MUCH OUT. THE INK'S ALL BLED. YOUR SECRETS ARE ALL SAFE FOREVER!
ALL THE PRECIOUS MEMORIES, BOTH DIGITAL AND HARDCOPY. DISAPPEARING IN FRONT OF OUR EYES LIKE MARTY McFLY'S FAMILY PHOTO.
OUR YOUTH IS BEING... ERASED!
THAT BLOODY LAND BARON! MR ZANETTI'S NOT ANSWERING ANY OF MY CALLS! ALL THIS TIME PAYING FOR A CRUMBLING HOVEL.
ARGH!

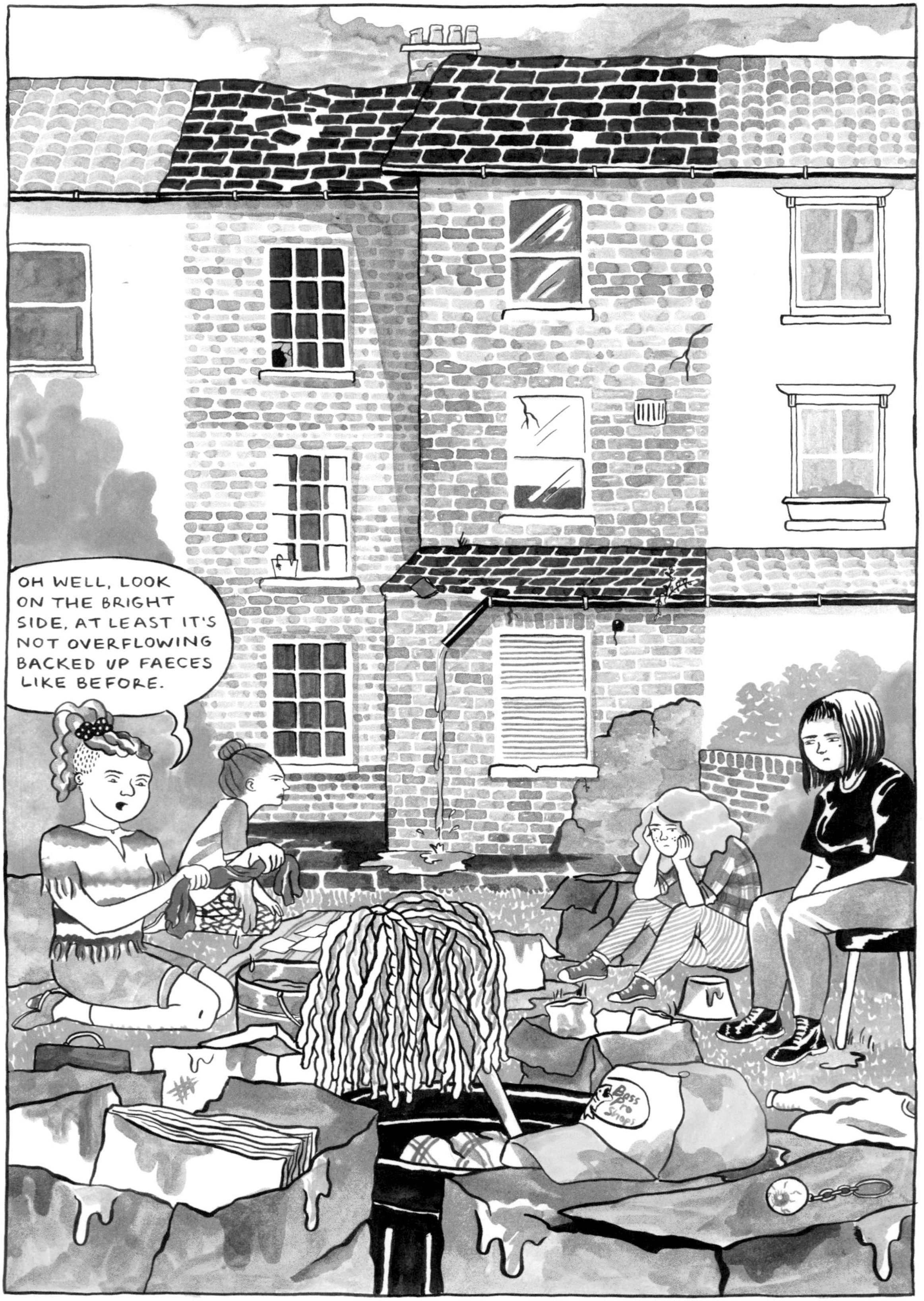
OH WELL, LOOK ON THE BRIGHT SIDE, AT LEAST IT'S NOT OVERFLOWING BACKED UP FAECES LIKE BEFORE.
BOSS PRO SHOPS

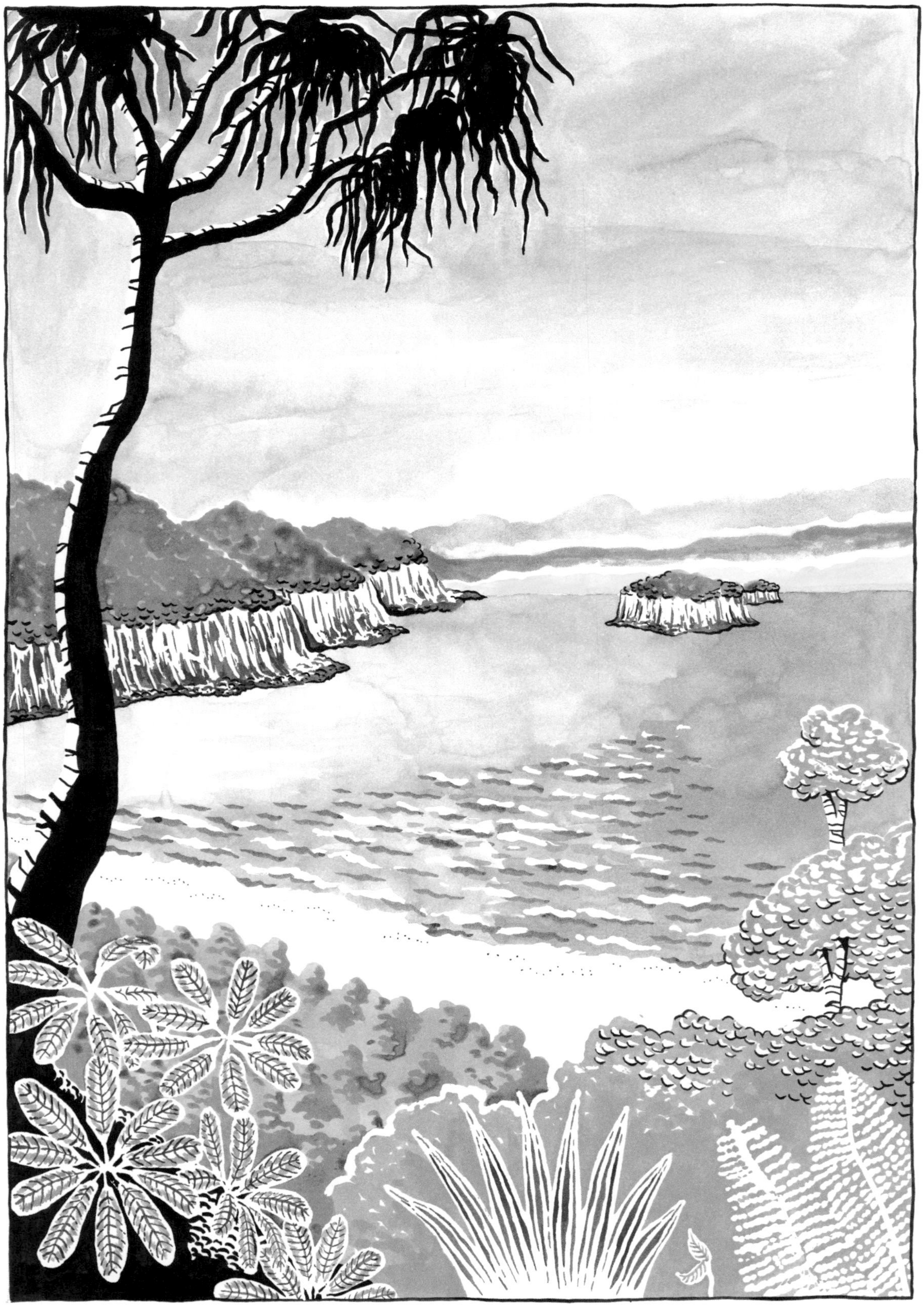

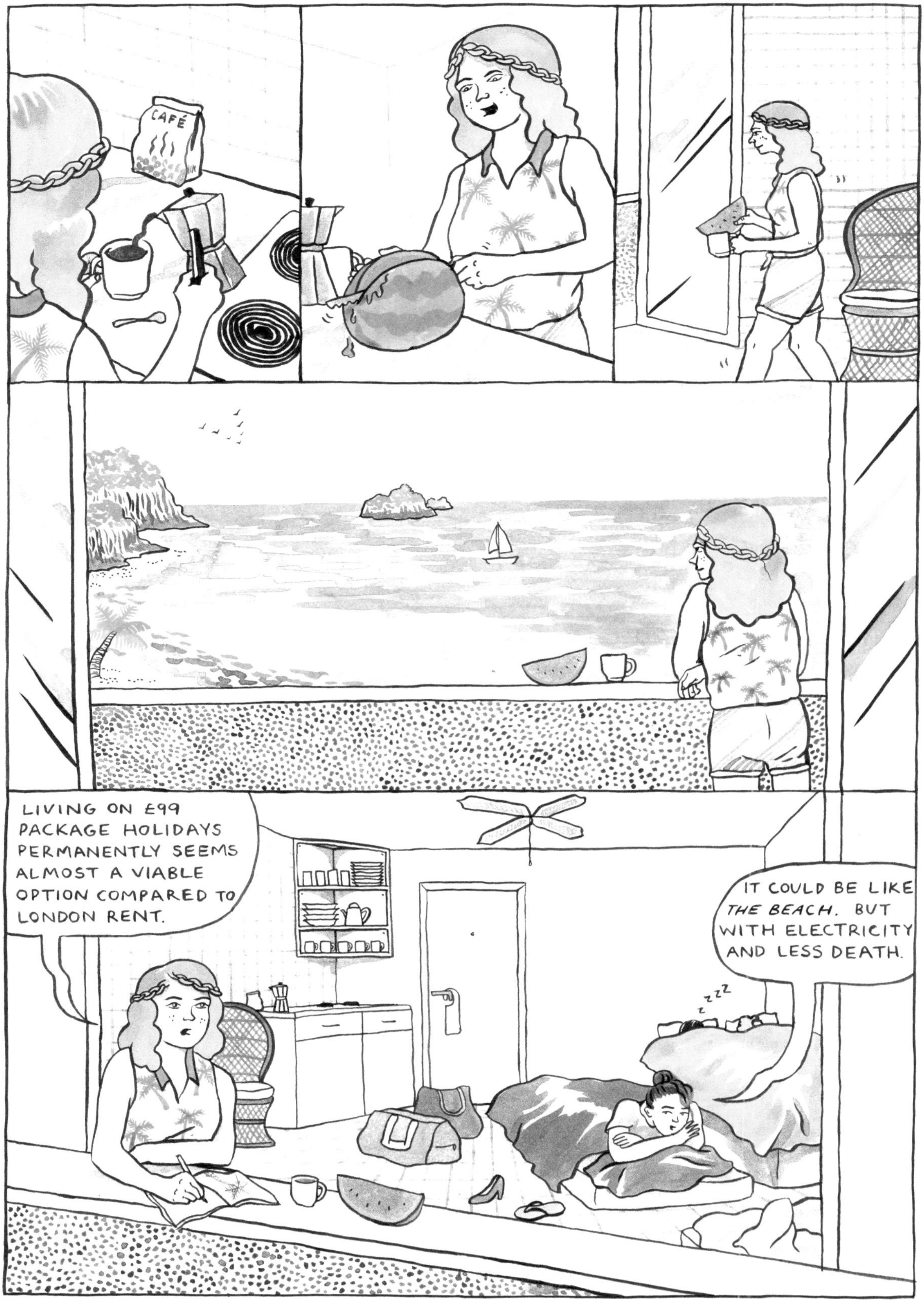
CAFÉ
LIVING ON £99 PACKAGE HOLIDAYS PERMANENTLY SEEMS ALMOST A VIABLE OPTION COMPARED TO LONDON RENT.
IT COULD BE LIKE *THE BEACH*. BUT WITH ELECTRICITY AND LESS DEATH.
Z Z Z Z

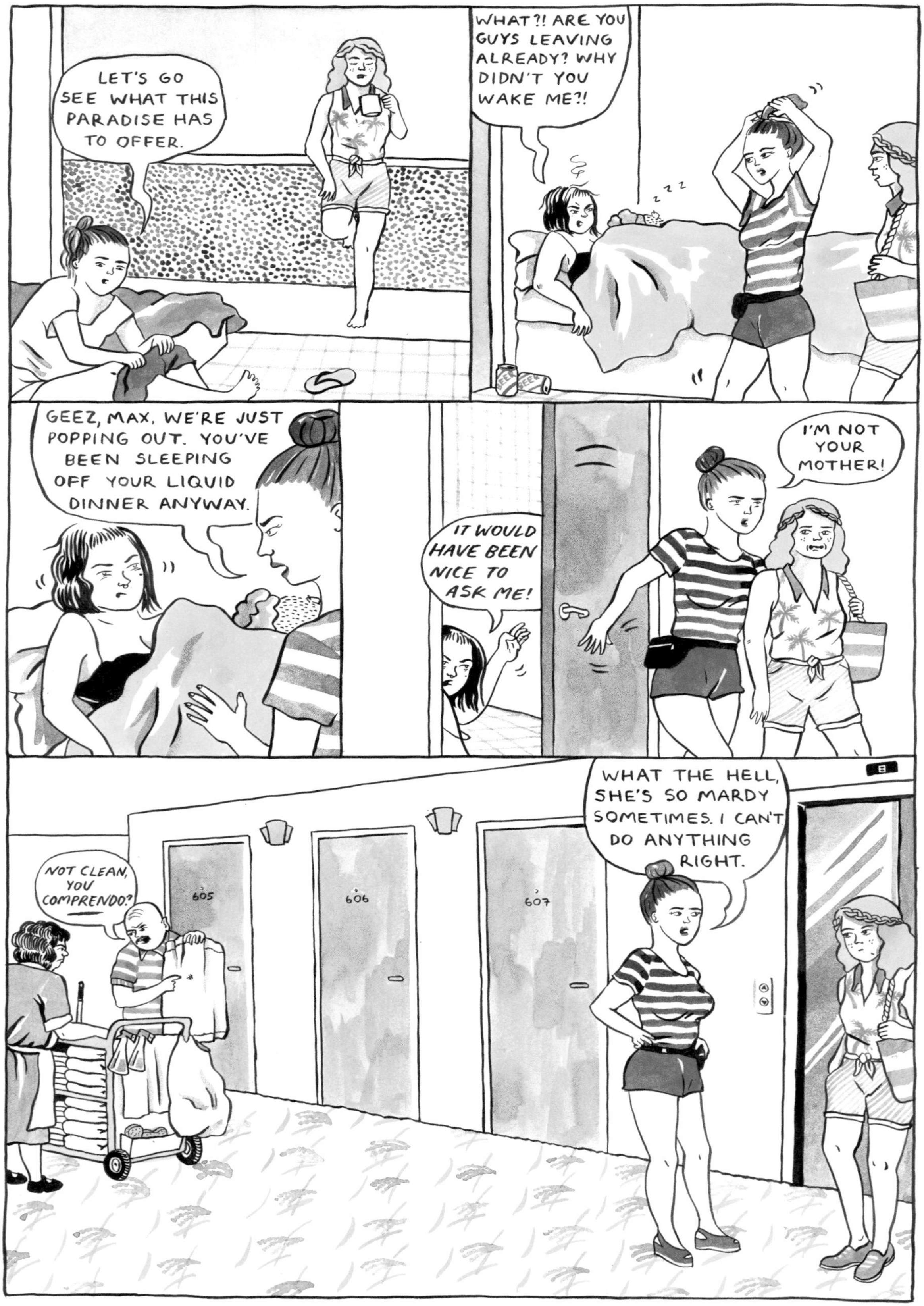
LET'S GO SEE WHAT THIS PARADISE HAS TO OFFER.
WHAT?! ARE YOU GUYS LEAVING ALREADY? WHY DIDN'T YOU WAKE ME?!
Z Z Z
BEER
GEEZ, MAX, WE'RE JUST POPPING OUT. YOU'VE BEEN SLEEPING OFF YOUR LIQUID DINNER ANYWAY.
IT WOULD HAVE BEEN NICE TO ASK ME!
I'M NOT YOUR MOTHER!
NOT CLEAN, YOU COMPRENDO?
605
606
607
WHAT THE HELL, SHE'S SO MARDY SOMETIMES. I CAN'T DO ANYTHING RIGHT.

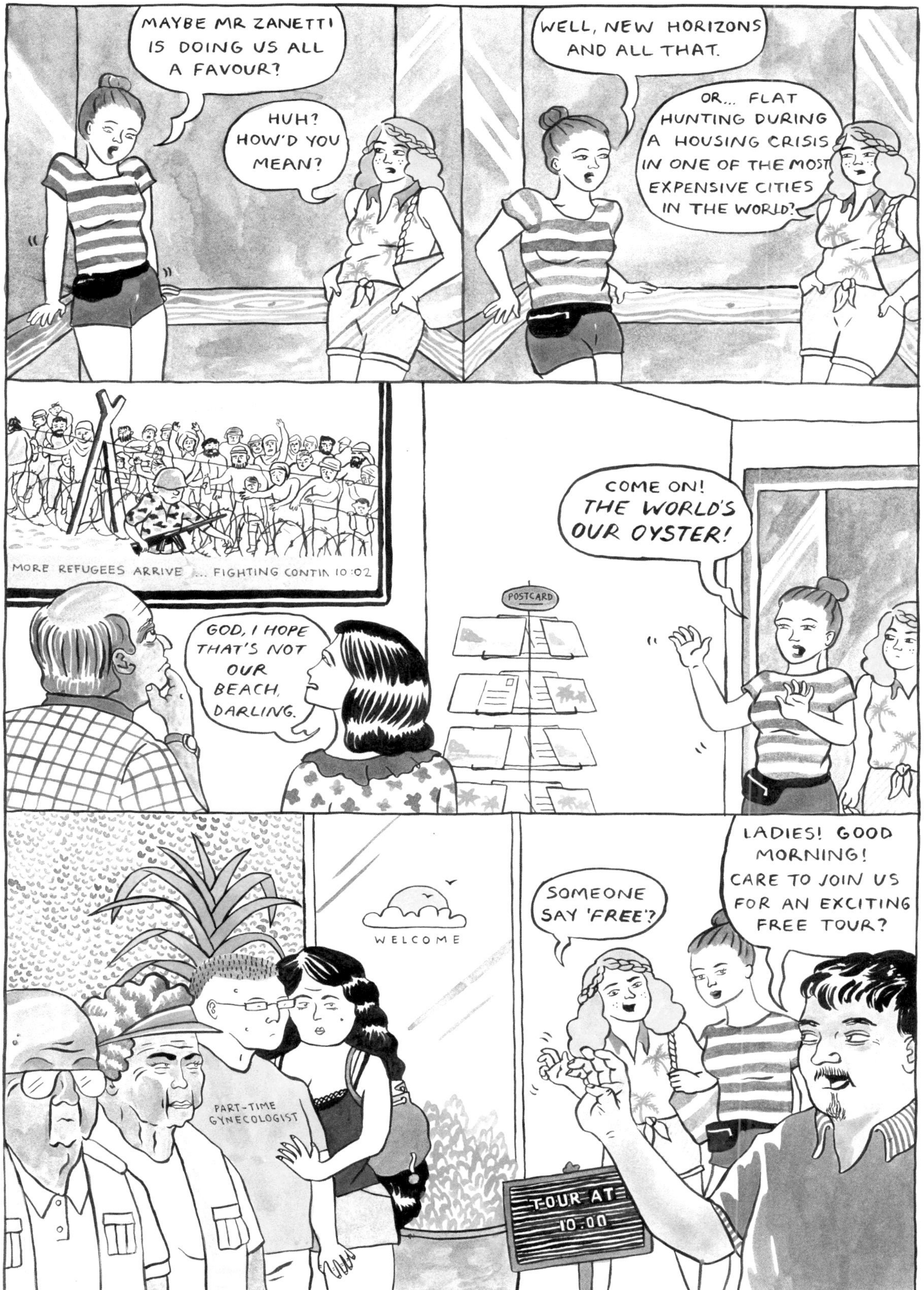
MAYBE MR ZANETTI IS DOING US ALL A FAVOUR?
HUH? HOW'D YOU MEAN?
WELL, NEW HORIZONS AND ALL THAT.
OR... FLAT HUNTING DURING A HOUSING CRISIS IN ONE OF THE MOST EXPENSIVE CITIES IN THE WORLD?
MORE REFUGEES ARRIVE ... FIGHTING CONTIN 10:02
GOD, I HOPE THAT'S NOT OUR BEACH, DARLING.
POSTCARD
COME ON! THE WORLD'S OUR OYSTER!
WELCOME
PART-TIME GYNECOLOGIST
SOMEONE SAY 'FREE'?
LADIES! GOOD MORNING! CARE TO JOIN US FOR AN EXCITING FREE TOUR?
TOUR AT 10:00

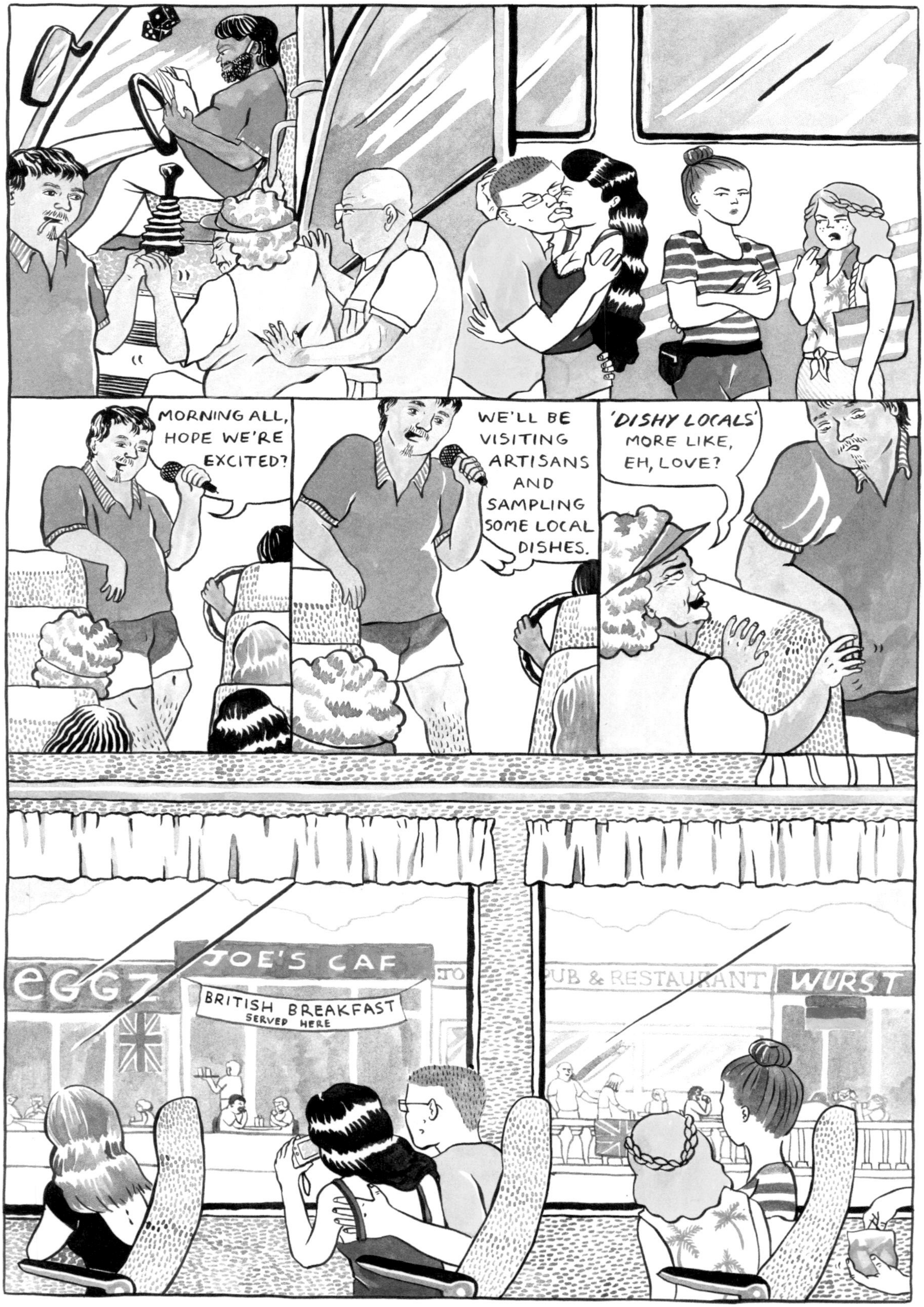
MORNING ALL, HOPE WE'RE EXCITED?
WE'LL BE VISITING ARTISANS AND SAMPLING SOME LOCAL DISHES.
'DISHY LOCALS' MORE LIKE, EH, LOVE?
EGGZ
JOE'S CAF
BRITISH BREAKFAST SERVED HERE
PUB & RESTAURANT
WURST

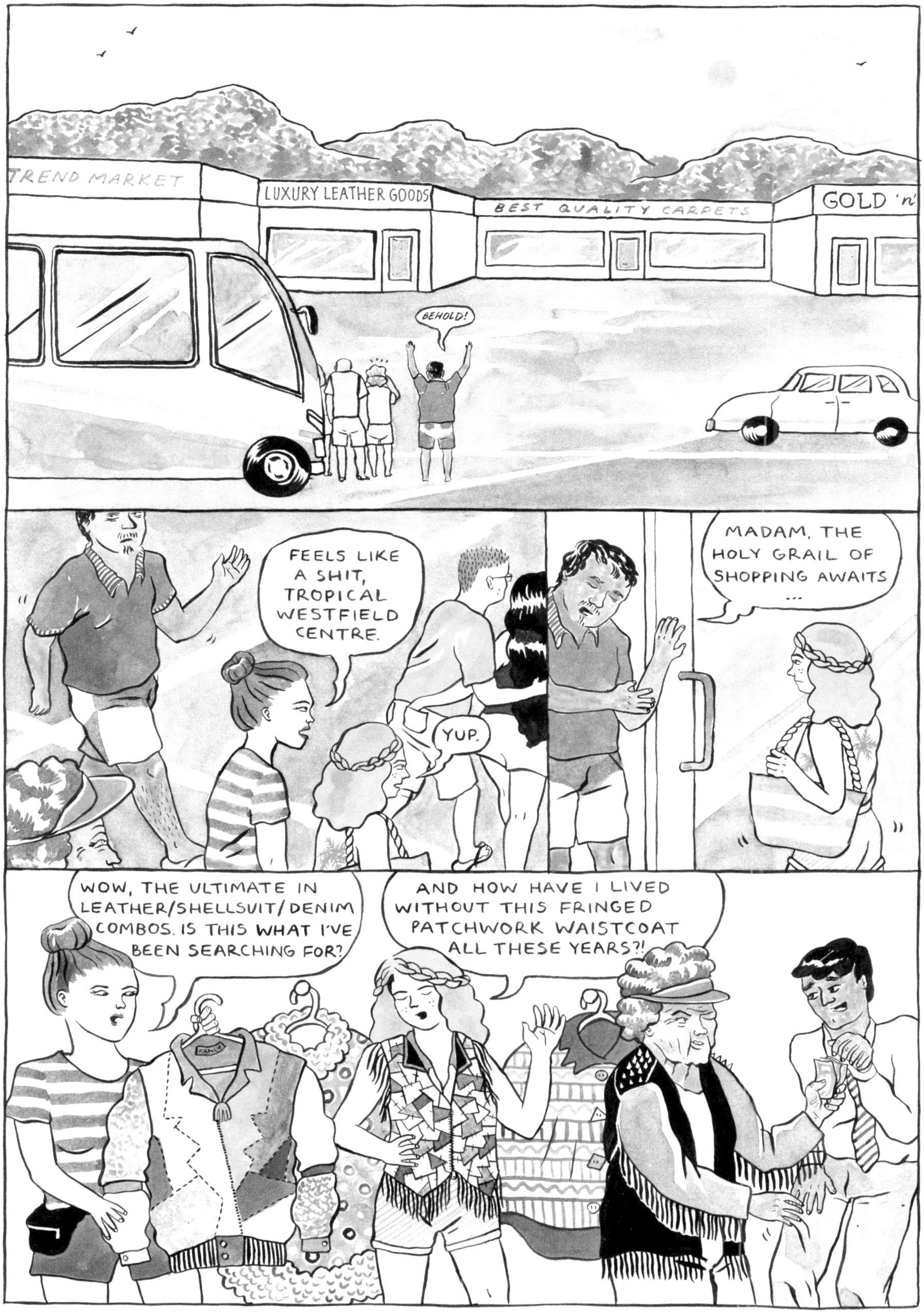

TREND MARKET
LUXURY LEATHER GOODS
BEST QUALITY CARPETS
GOLD 'n'
BEHOLD!
FEELS LIKE A SHIT, TROPICAL WESTFIELD CENTRE.
YUP.
MADAM, THE HOLY GRAIL OF SHOPPING AWAITS ...
WOW, THE ULTIMATE IN LEATHER/SHELLSUIT/DENIM COMBOS. IS THIS WHAT I'VE BEEN SEARCHING FOR?
AND HOW HAVE I LIVED WITHOUT THIS FRINGED PATCHWORK WAISTCOAT ALL THESE YEARS?!

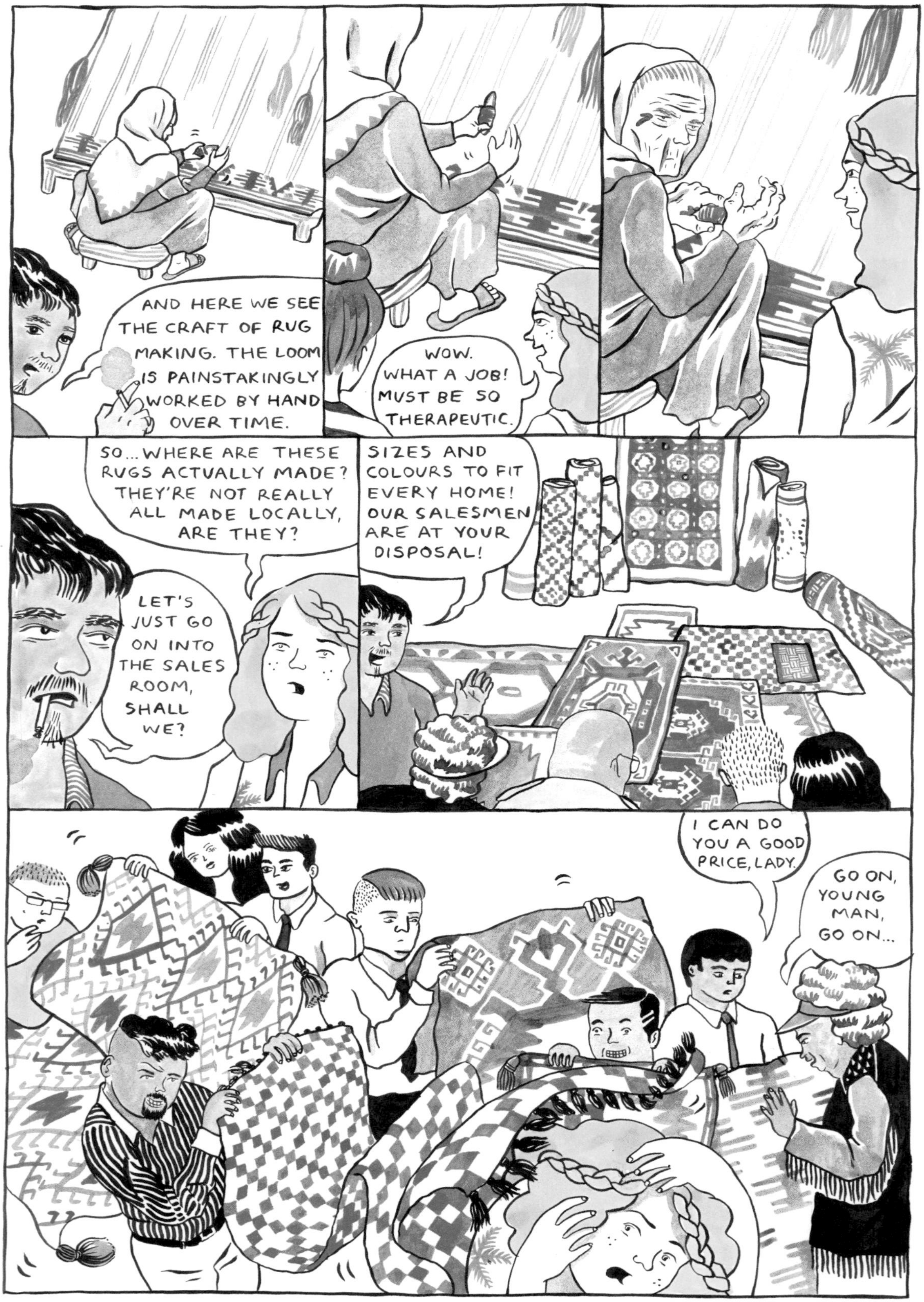
AND HERE WE SEE THE CRAFT OF RUG MAKING. THE LOOM IS PAINSTAKINGLY WORKED BY HAND OVER TIME.
WOW. WHAT A JOB! MUST BE SO THERAPEUTIC.
SO... WHERE ARE THESE RUGS ACTUALLY MADE? THEY'RE NOT REALLY ALL MADE LOCALLY, ARE THEY?
LET'S JUST GO ON INTO THE SALES ROOM, SHALL WE?
SIZES AND COLOURS TO FIT EVERY HOME! OUR SALESMEN ARE AT YOUR DISPOSAL!
I CAN DO YOU A GOOD PRICE, LADY.
GO ON, YOUNG MAN, GO ON...

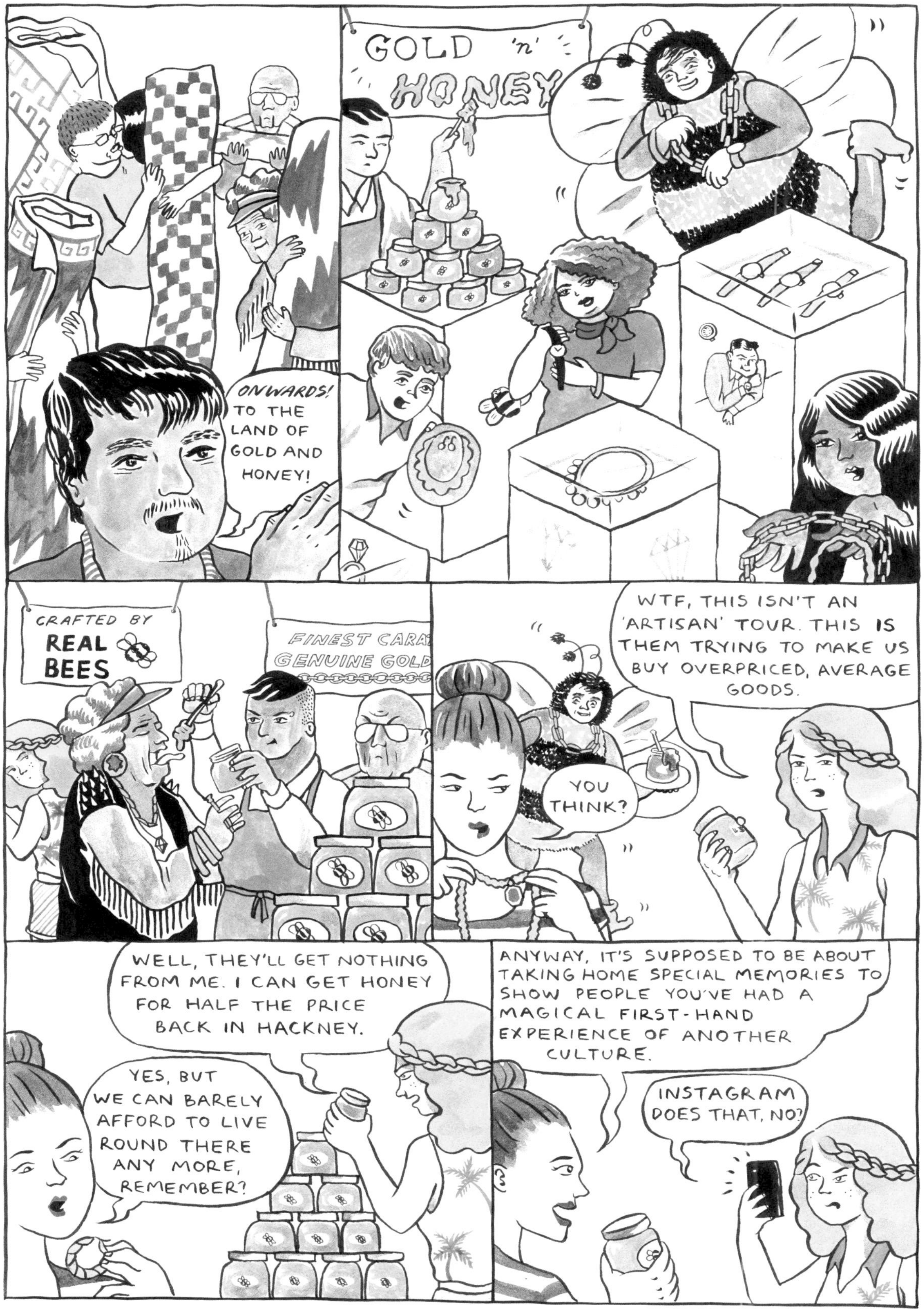
ONWARDS! TO THE LAND OF GOLD AND HONEY!
GOLD 'n' HONEY
CRAFTED BY REAL BEES
FINEST CARA
GENUINE GOLD
WTF, THIS ISN'T AN 'ARTISAN' TOUR. THIS IS THEM TRYING TO MAKE US BUY OVERPRICED, AVERAGE GOODS.
YOU THINK?
WELL, THEY'LL GET NOTHING FROM ME. I CAN GET HONEY FOR HALF THE PRICE BACK IN HACKNEY.
YES, BUT WE CAN BARELY AFFORD TO LIVE ROUND THERE ANY MORE, REMEMBER?
ANYWAY, IT'S SUPPOSED TO BE ABOUT TAKING HOME SPECIAL MEMORIES TO SHOW PEOPLE YOU'VE HAD A MAGICAL FIRST-HAND EXPERIENCE OF ANOTHER CULTURE.
INSTAGRAM DOES THAT, NO?

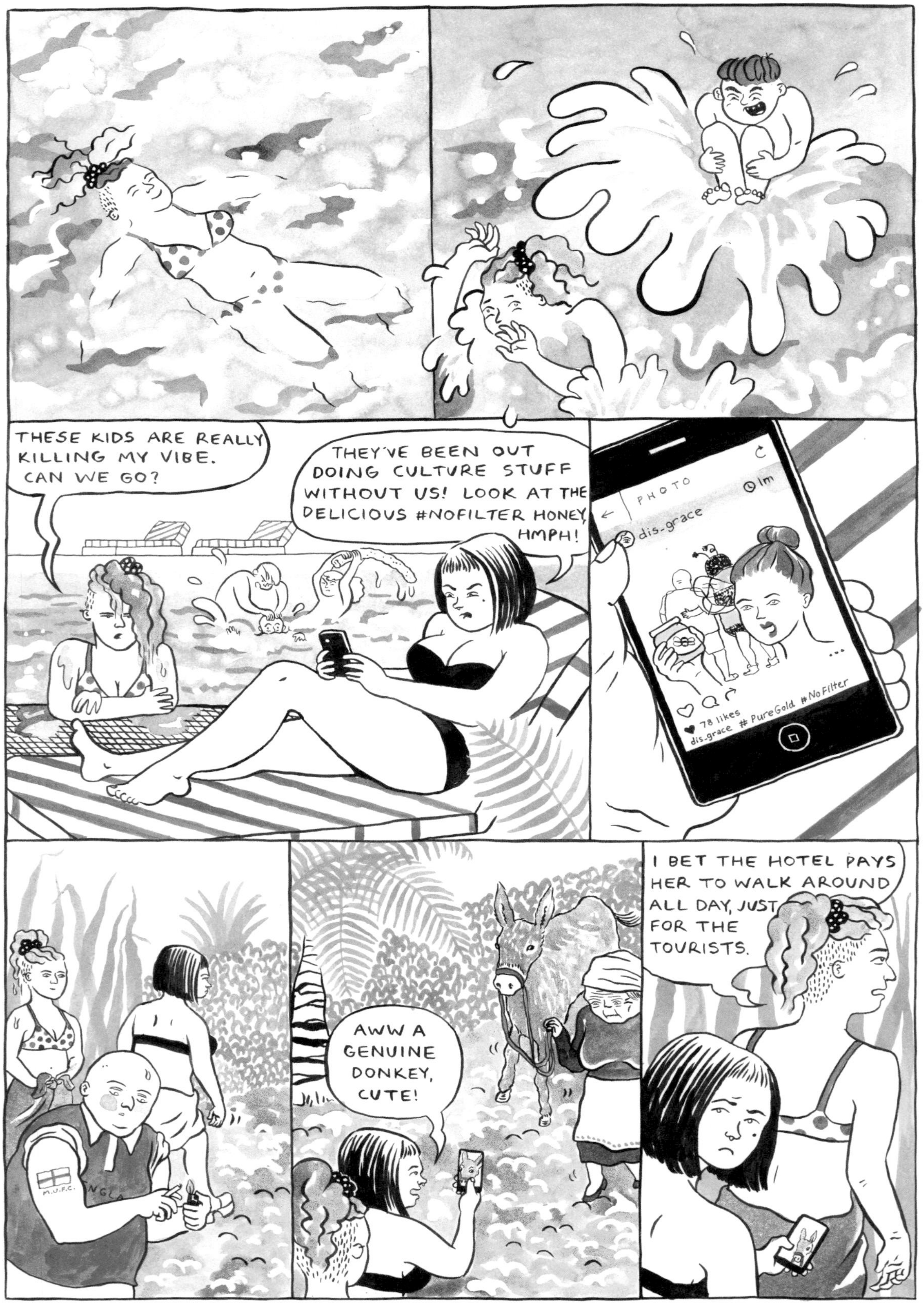
THESE KIDS ARE REALLY KILLING MY VIBE. CAN WE GO?
THEY'VE BEEN OUT DOING CULTURE STUFF WITHOUT US! LOOK AT THE DELICIOUS #NOFILTER HONEY, HMPH!
PHOTO
1m
dis.grace
78 likes
dis.grace # PureGold #NoFilter
M.U.F.C.
AWW A GENUINE DONKEY, CUTE!
I BET THE HOTEL PAYS HER TO WALK AROUND ALL DAY, JUST FOR THE TOURISTS.

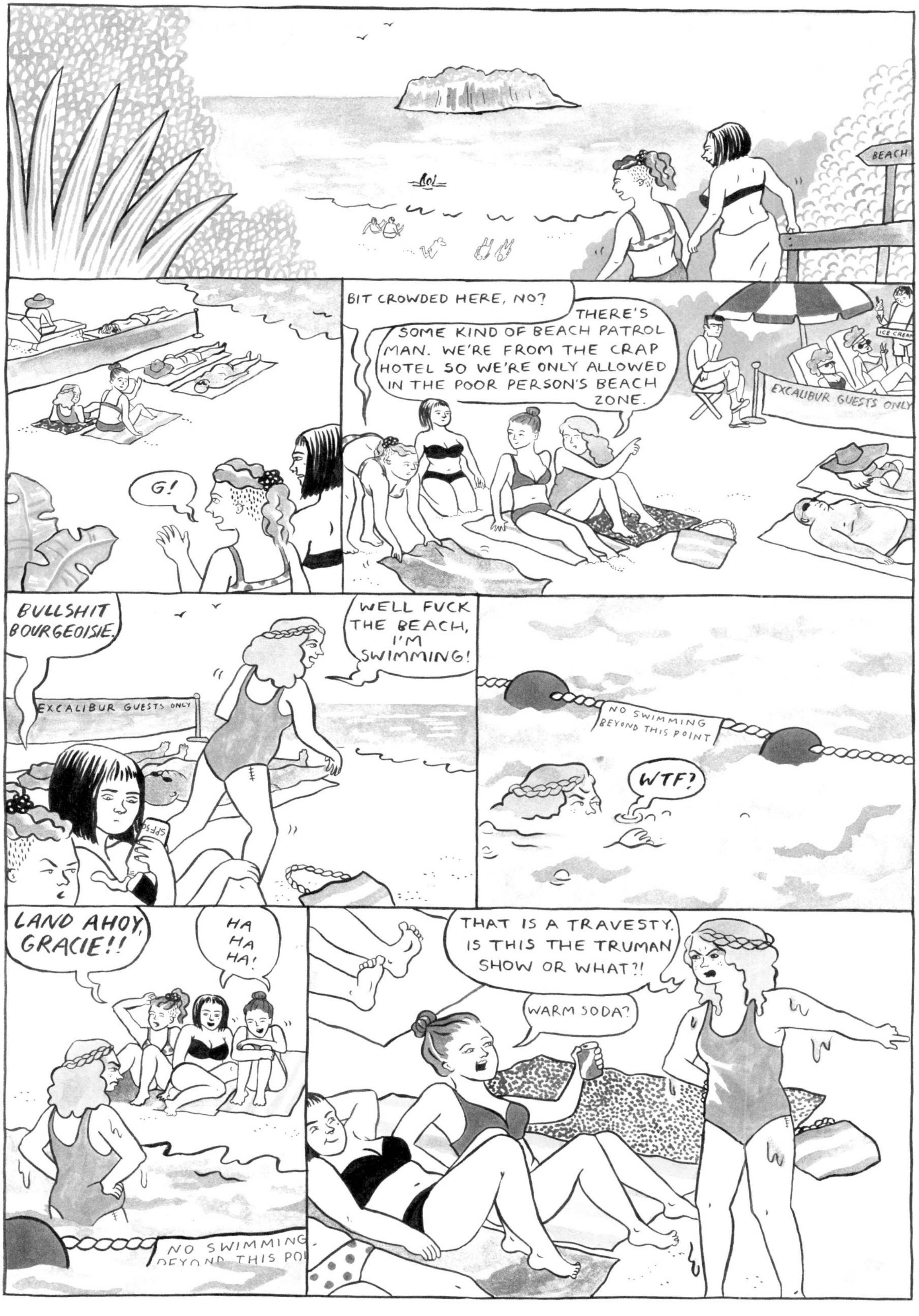
BEACH
G!
BIT CROWDED HERE, NO?
THERE'S SOME KIND OF BEACH PATROL MAN. WE'RE FROM THE CRAP HOTEL SO WE'RE ONLY ALLOWED IN THE POOR PERSON'S BEACH ZONE.
ICE CREAM
EXCALIBUR GUESTS ONLY
BULLSHIT BOURGEOISIE.
WELL FUCK THE BEACH, I'M SWIMMING!
EXCALIBUR GUESTS ONLY
NO SWIMMING BEYOND THIS POINT
WTF?
LAND AHOY, GRACIE!!
HA HA HA!
NO SWIMMING BEYOND THIS PO
THAT IS A TRAVESTY. IS THIS THE TRUMAN SHOW OR WHAT?!
WARM SODA?

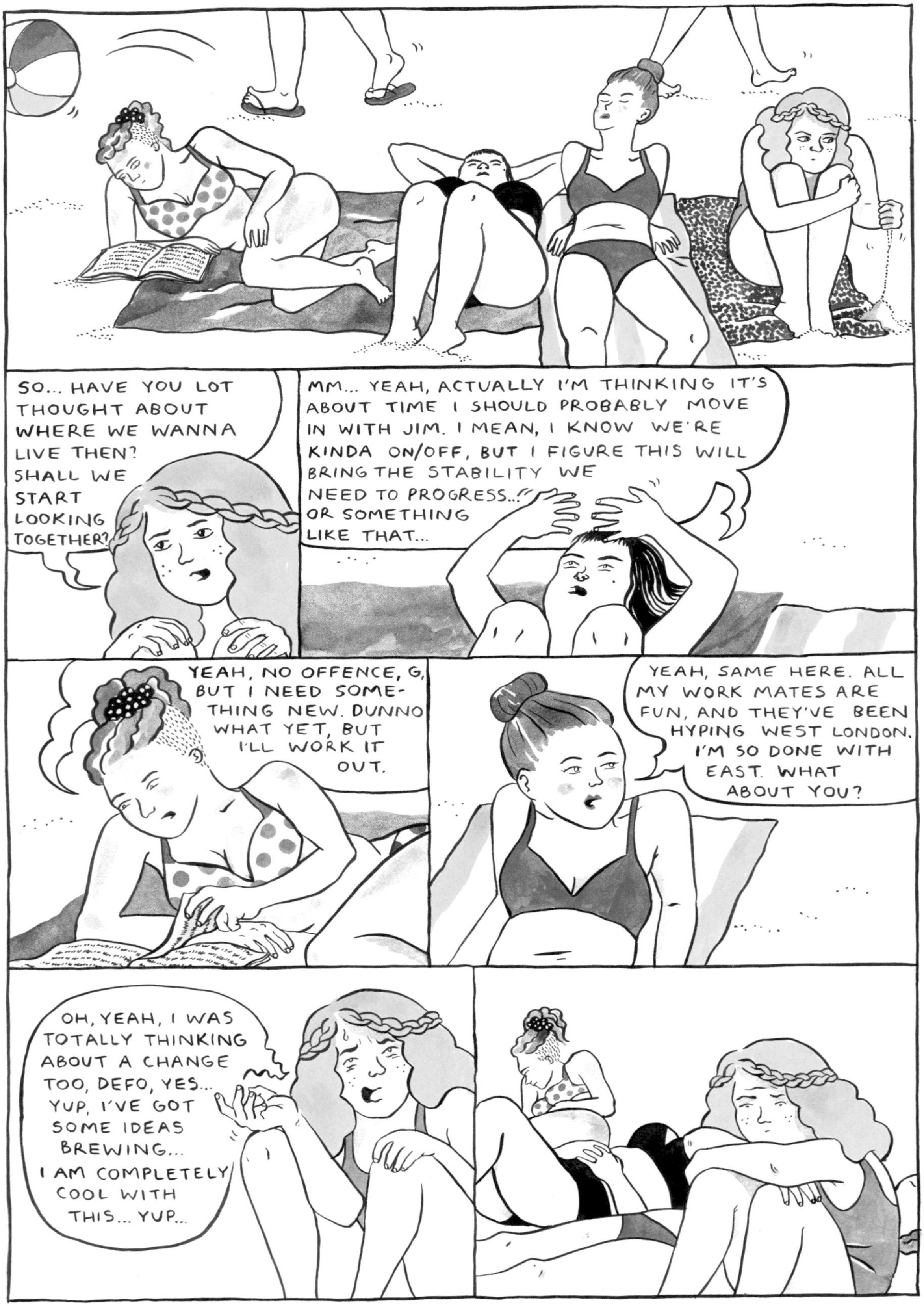
SO... HAVE YOU LOT THOUGHT ABOUT WHERE WE WANNA LIVE THEN? SHALL WE START LOOKING TOGETHER?
MM... YEAH, ACTUALLY I'M THINKING IT'S ABOUT TIME I SHOULD PROBABLY MOVE IN WITH JIM. I MEAN, I KNOW WE'RE KINDA ON/OFF, BUT I FIGURE THIS WILL BRING THE STABILITY WE NEED TO PROGRESS... OR SOMETHING LIKE THAT...
YEAH, NO OFFENCE, G, BUT I NEED SOMETHING NEW. DUNNO WHAT YET, BUT I'LL WORK IT OUT.
YEAH, SAME HERE. ALL MY WORK MATES ARE FUN, AND THEY'VE BEEN HYPING WEST LONDON. I'M SO DONE WITH EAST. WHAT ABOUT YOU?
OH, YEAH, I WAS TOTALLY THINKING ABOUT A CHANGE TOO, DEFO, YES... YUP, I'VE GOT SOME IDEAS BREWING... I AM COMPLETELY COOL WITH THIS... YUP...

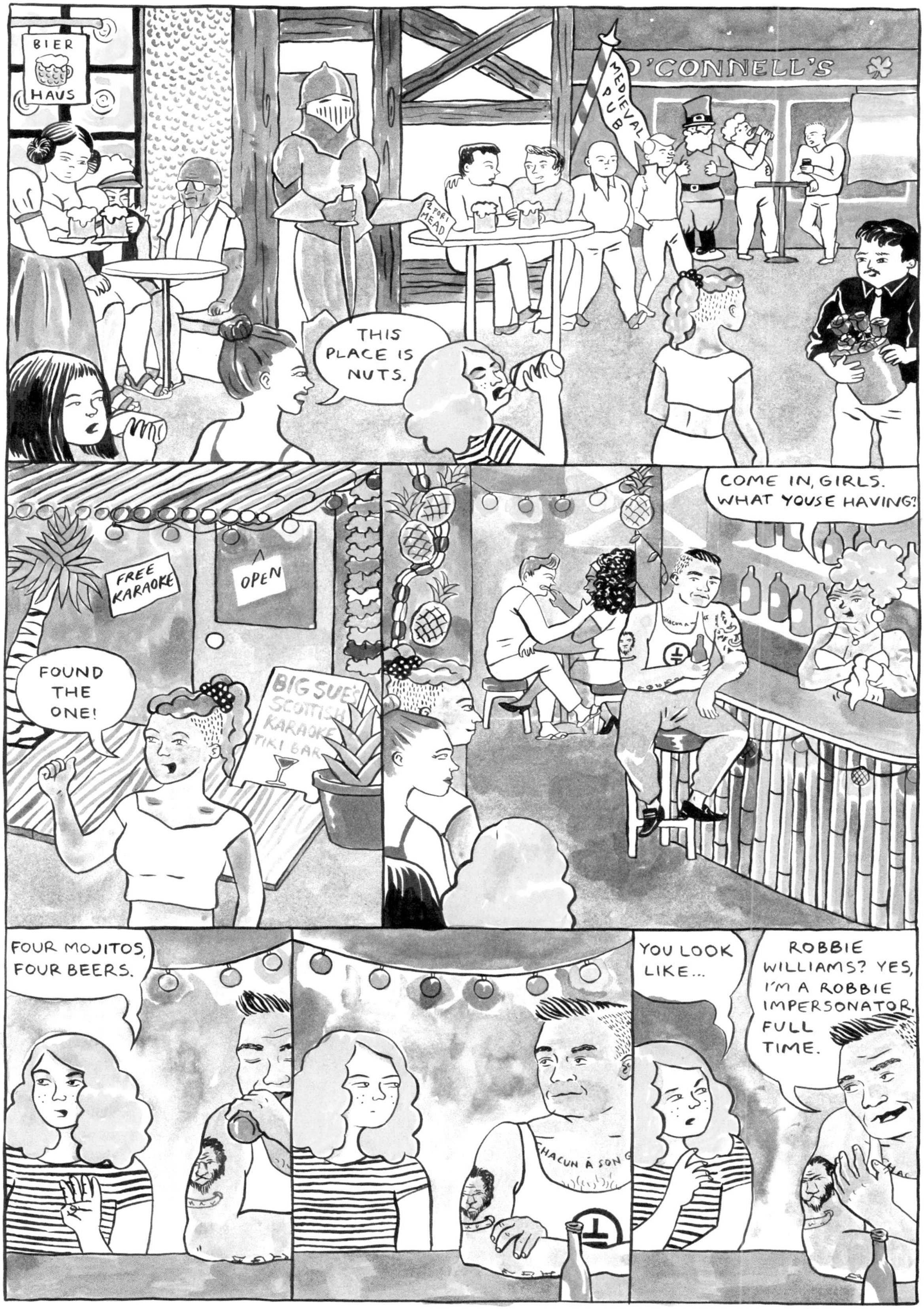
BIER HAUS
MEDIEVAL PUB
O'CONNELL'S
2 FOR 1 MEAD
THIS PLACE IS NUTS.
FREE KARAOKE
OPEN
FOUND THE ONE!
BIG SUE'S SCOTTISH KARAOKE TIKI BAR
COME IN, GIRLS. WHAT YOUSE HAVING?
FOUR MOJITOS, FOUR BEERS.
YOU LOOK LIKE...
ROBBIE WILLIAMS? YES, I'M A ROBBIE IMPERSONATOR, FULL TIME.

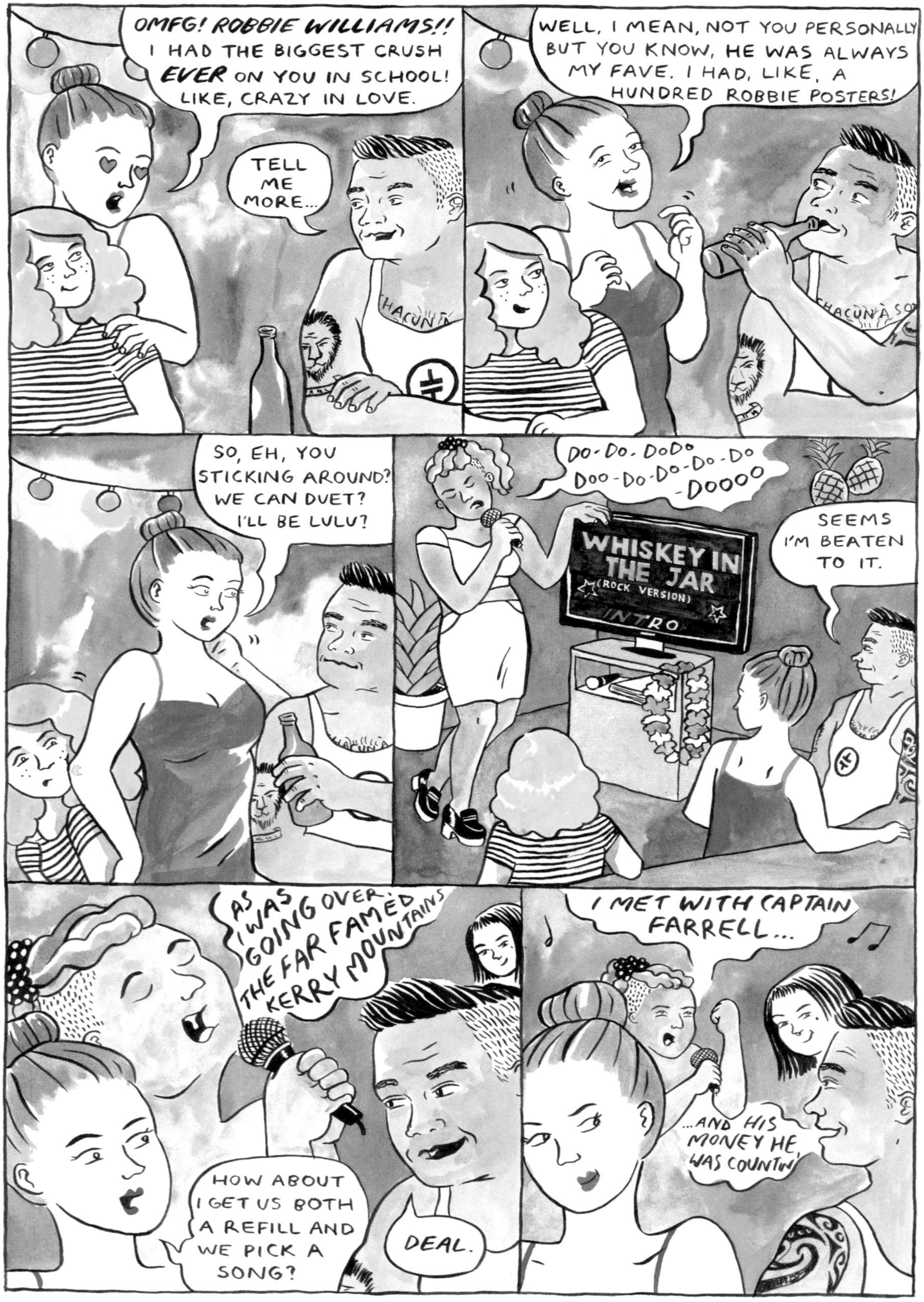
OMFG! ROBBIE WILLIAMS!! I HAD THE BIGGEST CRUSH EVER ON YOU IN SCHOOL! LIKE, CRAZY IN LOVE.
TELL ME MORE...
WELL, I MEAN, NOT YOU PERSONALLY BUT YOU KNOW, HE WAS ALWAYS MY FAVE. I HAD, LIKE, A HUNDRED ROBBIE POSTERS!
SO, EH, YOU STICKING AROUND? WE CAN DUET? I'LL BE LULU?
DO-DO-DODO DOO-DO-DO-DO-DO -DOOOO
WHISKEY IN THE JAR (ROCK VERSION)
INTRO
SEEMS I'M BEATEN TO IT.
AS I WAS GOING OVER THE FAR FAMED KERRY MOUNTAINS
HOW ABOUT I GET US BOTH A REFILL AND WE PICK A SONG?
DEAL.
I MET WITH CAPTAIN FARRELL...
...AND HIS MONEY HE WAS COUNTIN'

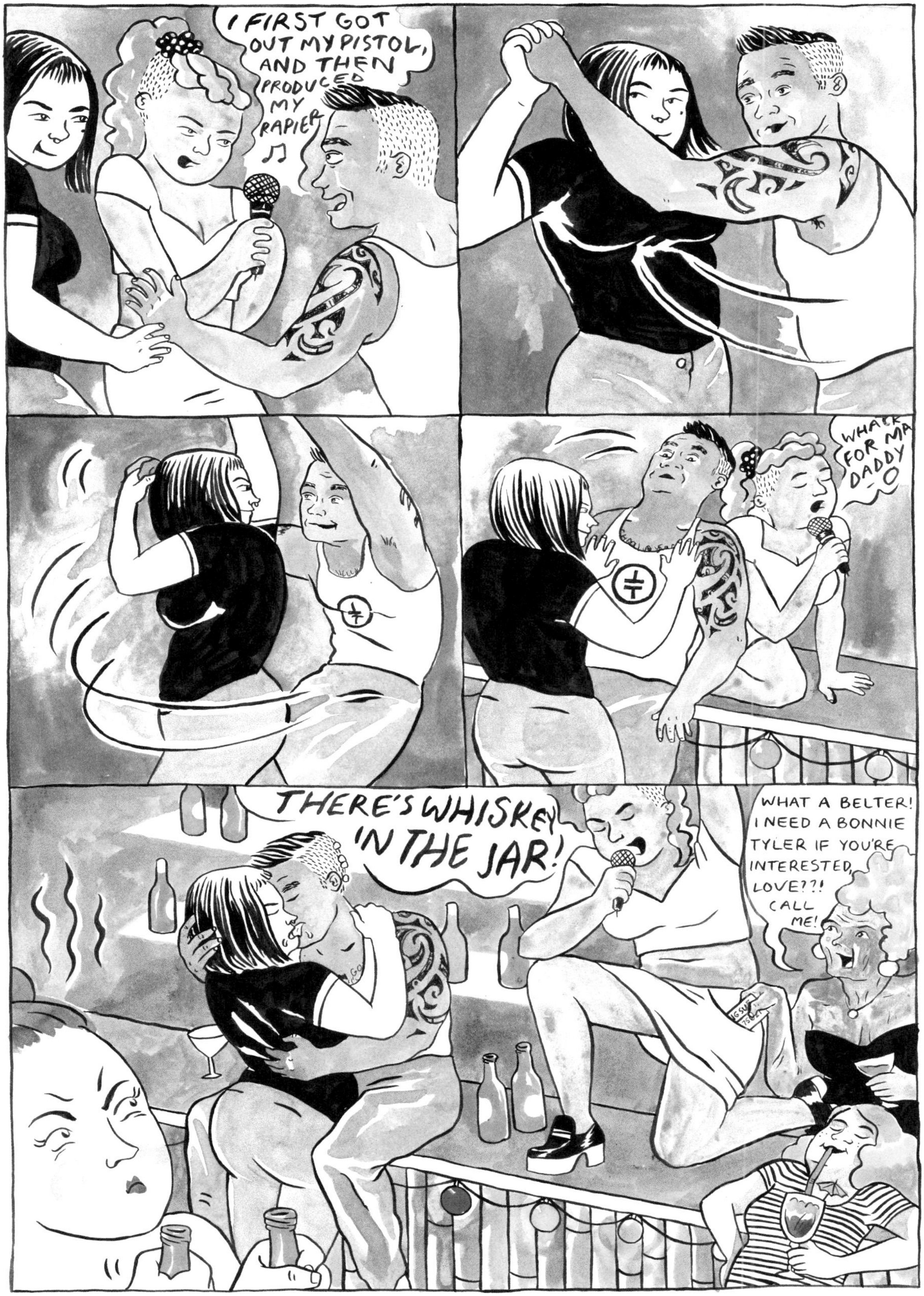
I FIRST GOT OUT MY PISTOL, AND THEN PRODUCED MY RAPIER ♫
WHACK FOR MA DADDY -O
THERE'S WHISKEY IN THE JAR!
WHAT A BELTER! I NEED A BONNIE TYLER IF YOU'RE INTERESTED, LOVE??! CALL ME!

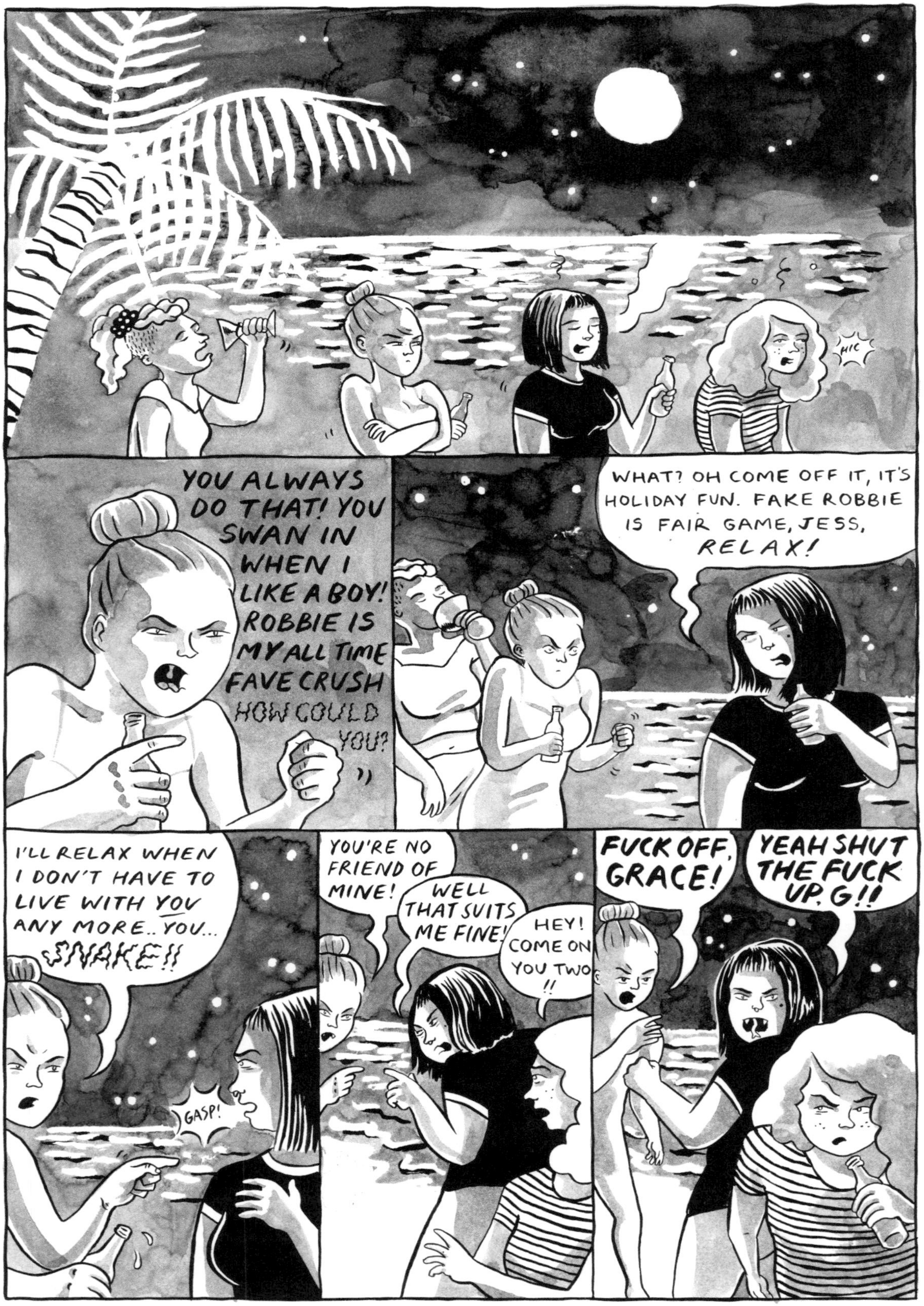
HIC
YOU ALWAYS DO THAT! YOU SWAN IN WHEN I LIKE A BOY! ROBBIE IS MY ALL TIME FAVE CRUSH HOW COULD YOU?
WHAT? OH COME OFF IT, IT'S HOLIDAY FUN. FAKE ROBBIE IS FAIR GAME, JESS, RELAX!
I'LL RELAX WHEN I DON'T HAVE TO LIVE WITH YOU ANY MORE.. YOU... SNAKE!!
GASP!
YOU'RE NO FRIEND OF MINE!
WELL THAT SUITS ME FINE!
HEY! COME ON YOU TWO !!
FUCK OFF, GRACE!
YEAH SHUT THE FUCK UP, G!!

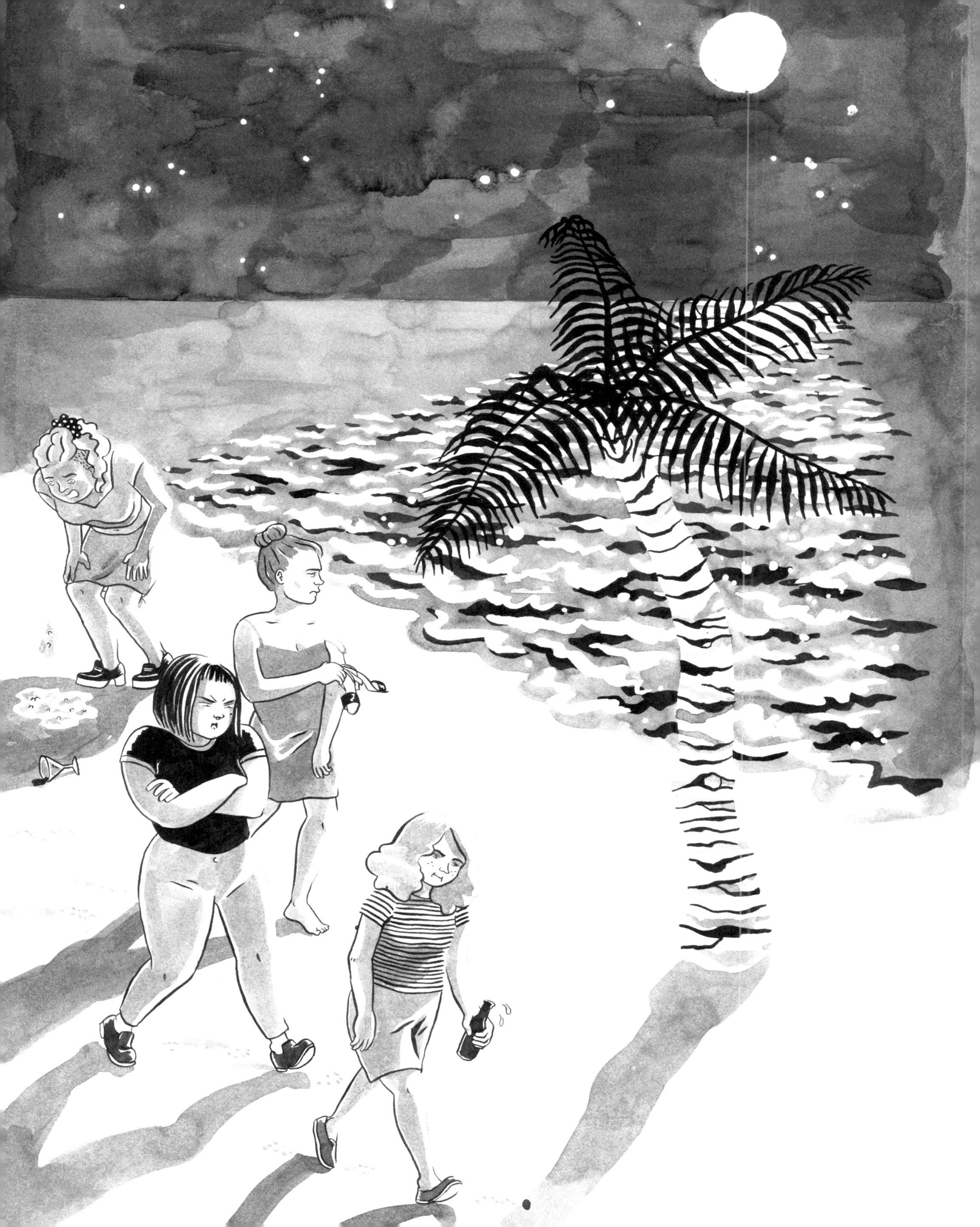

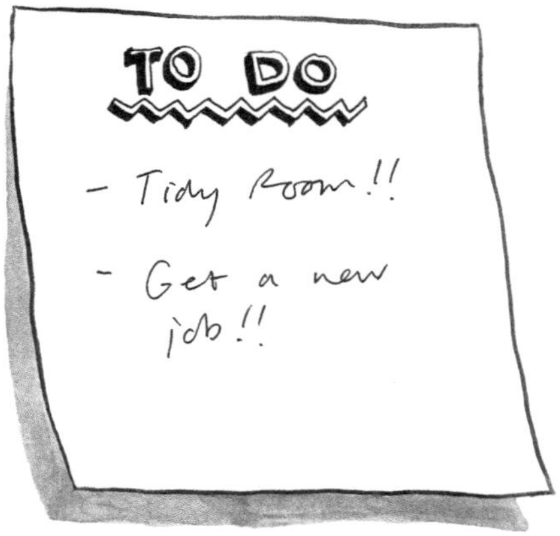
TO DO
- Tidy Room!!
- Get a new job!!

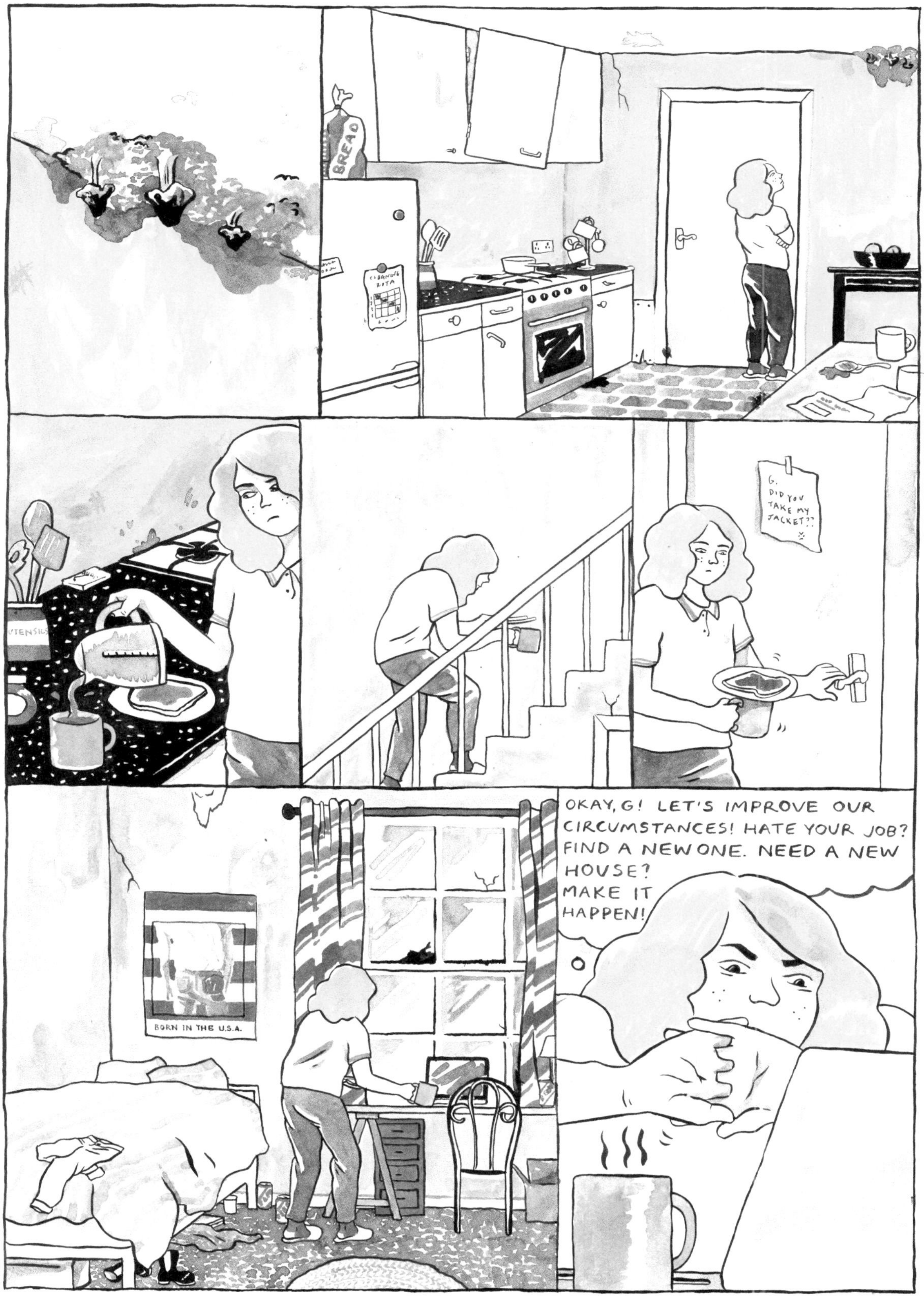
BREAD
UTENSILS
G. DID YOU TAKE MY JACKET??
BORN IN THE U.S.A.
OKAY, G! LET'S IMPROVE OUR CIRCUMSTANCES! HATE YOUR JOB? FIND A NEW ONE. NEED A NEW HOUSE? MAKE IT HAPPEN!

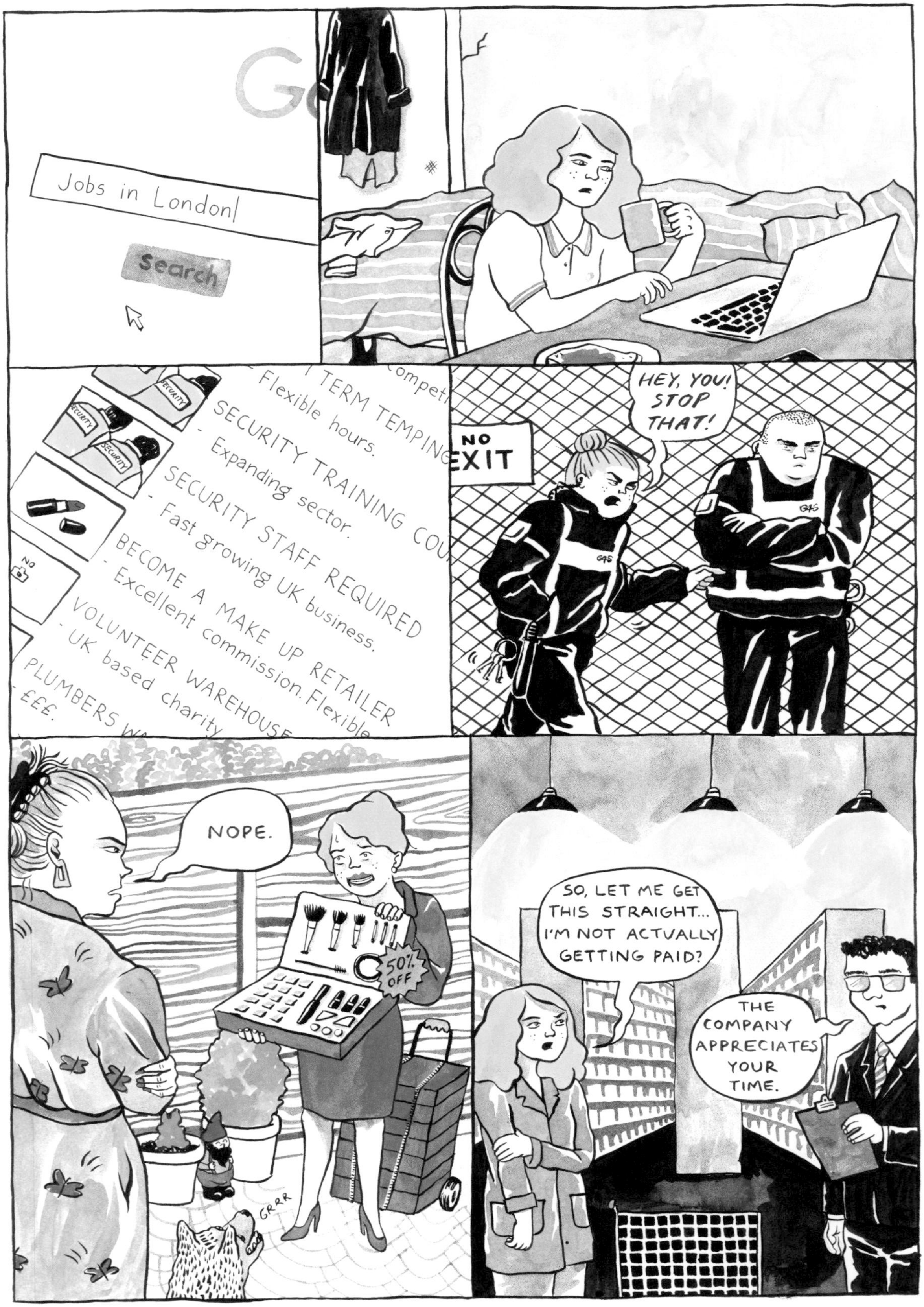

Jobs in London
Search
TERM TEMPING
Flexible hours.
SECURITY TRAINING COU
- Expanding sector.
SECURITY STAFF REQUIRED
- Fast growing UK business.
BECOME A MAKE UP RETAILER
- Excellent commission. Flexible
VOLUNTEER WAREHOUSE
- UK based charity
PLUMBERS
£££.
HEY, YOU! STOP THAT!
NO EXIT
NOPE.
50% OFF
GRRR
SO, LET ME GET THIS STRAIGHT... I'M NOT ACTUALLY GETTING PAID?
THE COMPANY APPRECIATES YOUR TIME.

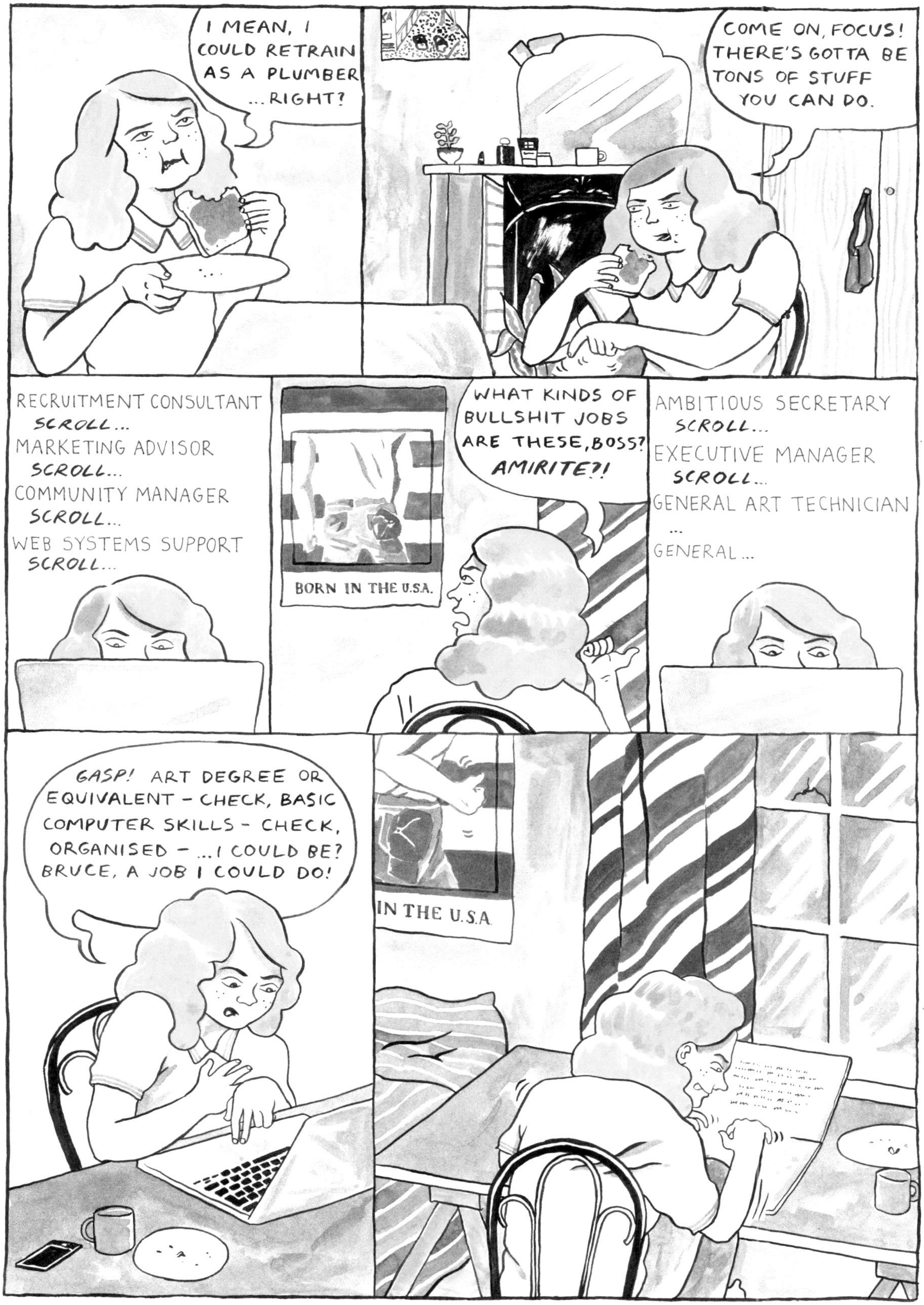
I MEAN, I COULD RETRAIN AS A PLUMBER ...RIGHT?
COME ON, FOCUS! THERE'S GOTTA BE TONS OF STUFF YOU CAN DO.
RECRUITMENT CONSULTANT
SCROLL...
MARKETING ADVISOR
SCROLL...
COMMUNITY MANAGER
SCROLL...
WEB SYSTEMS SUPPORT
SCROLL...
BORN IN THE U.S.A.
WHAT KINDS OF BULLSHIT JOBS ARE THESE, BOSS? AMIRITE?!
AMBITIOUS SECRETARY
SCROLL...
EXECUTIVE MANAGER
SCROLL...
GENERAL ART TECHNICIAN
...
GENERAL...
GASP! ART DEGREE OR EQUIVALENT - CHECK, BASIC COMPUTER SKILLS - CHECK, ORGANISED - ...I COULD BE? BRUCE, A JOB I COULD DO!
IN THE U.S.A

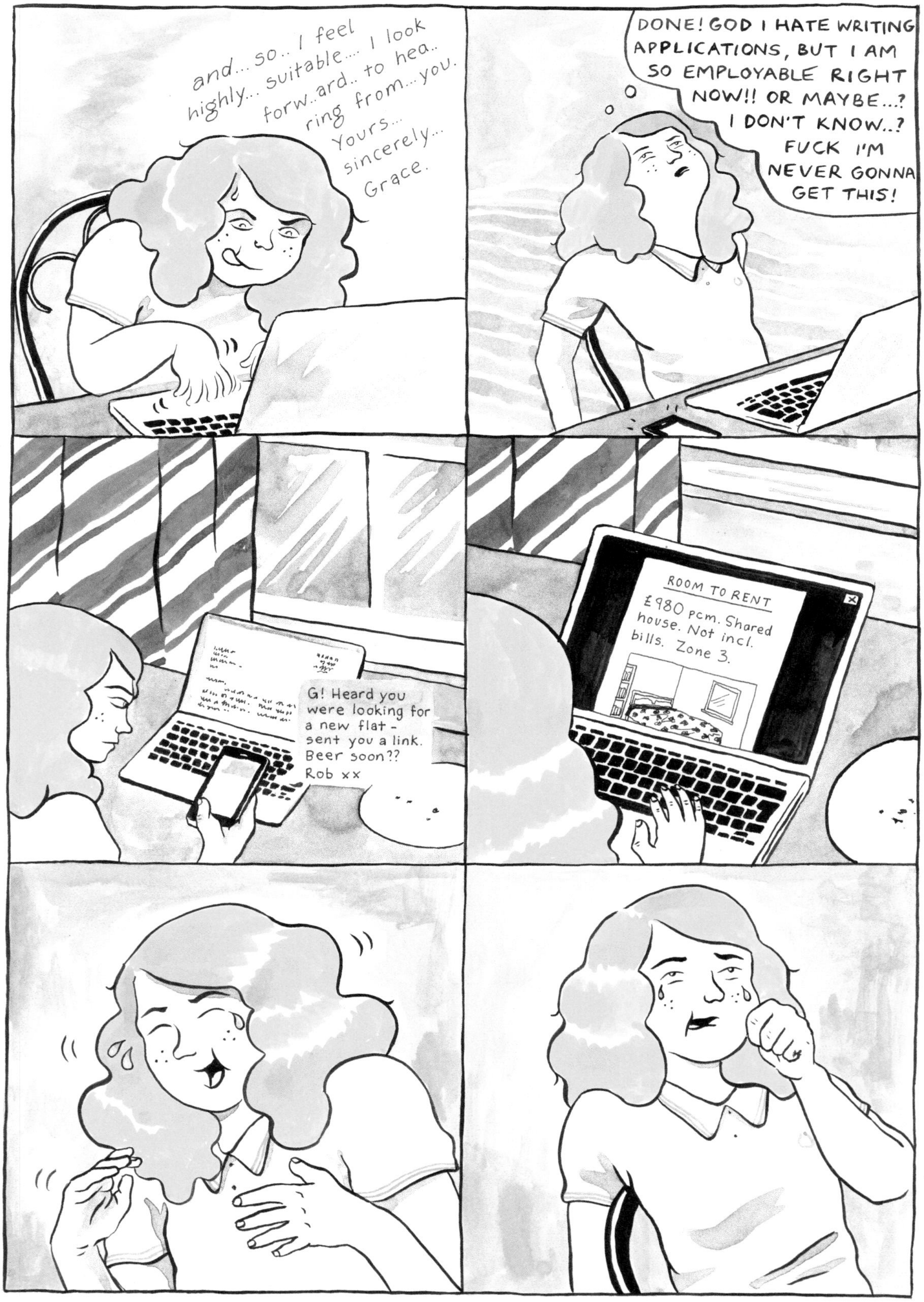
and... so.. I feel highly... suitable... I look forw..ard.. to hea..ring from... you. Yours... sincerely... Grace.
DONE! GOD I HATE WRITING APPLICATIONS, BUT I AM SO EMPLOYABLE RIGHT NOW!! OR MAYBE...? I DON'T KNOW..? FUCK I'M NEVER GONNA GET THIS!
G! Heard you were looking for a new flat - sent you a link. Beer soon?? Rob xx
ROOM TO RENT
£980 pcm. Shared house. Not incl. bills. Zone 3.

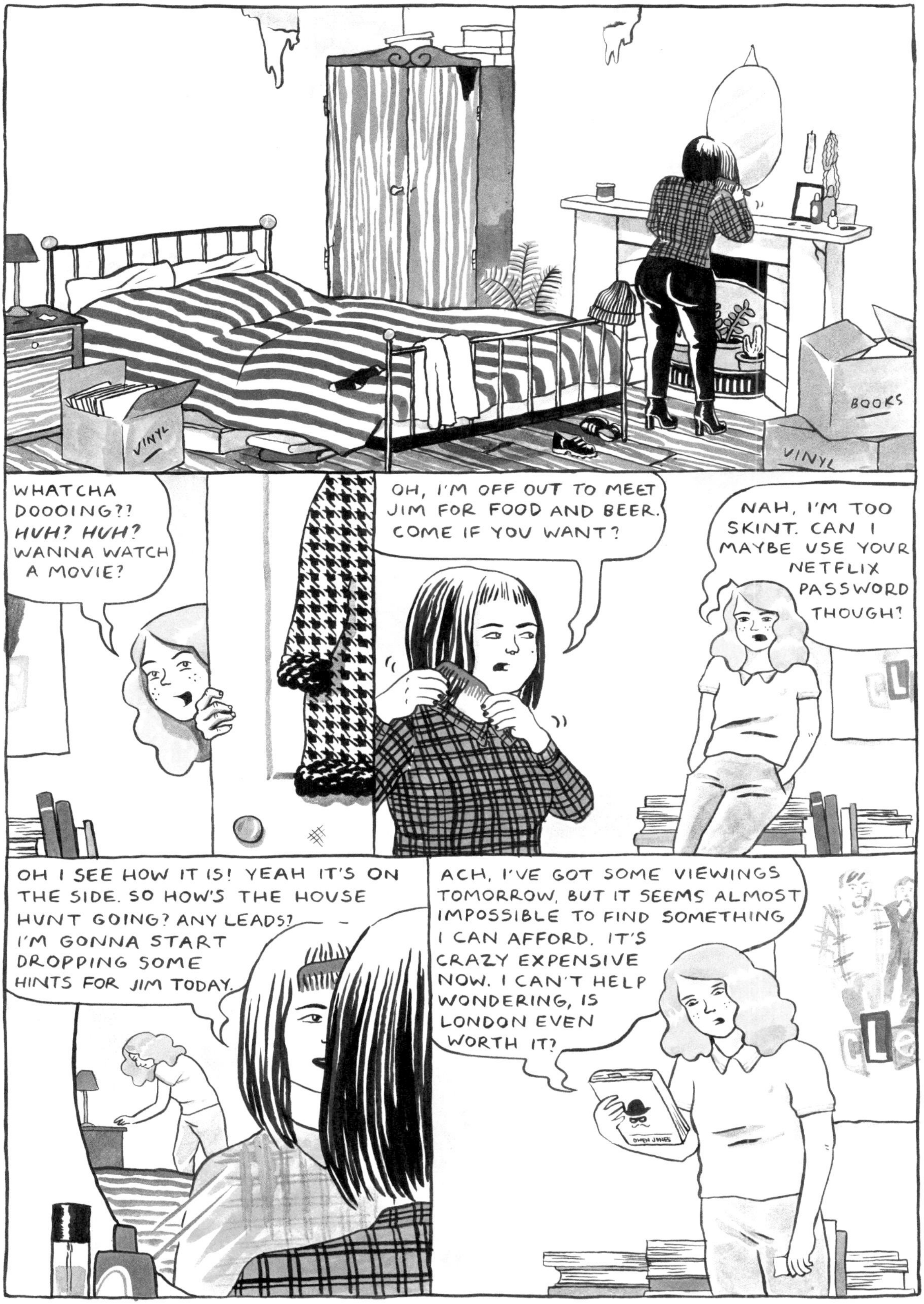
VINYL
BOOKS
VINYL
WHATCHA DOOOING?? *HUH? HUH?* WANNA WATCH A MOVIE?
OH, I'M OFF OUT TO MEET JIM FOR FOOD AND BEER. COME IF YOU WANT?
NAH, I'M TOO SKINT. CAN I MAYBE USE YOUR NETFLIX PASSWORD THOUGH?
OH I SEE HOW IT IS! YEAH IT'S ON THE SIDE. SO HOW'S THE HOUSE HUNT GOING? ANY LEADS? — – I'M GONNA START DROPPING SOME HINTS FOR JIM TODAY.
ACH, I'VE GOT SOME VIEWINGS TOMORROW, BUT IT SEEMS ALMOST IMPOSSIBLE TO FIND SOMETHING I CAN AFFORD. IT'S CRAZY EXPENSIVE NOW. I CAN'T HELP WONDERING, IS LONDON EVEN WORTH IT?
OWEN JONES

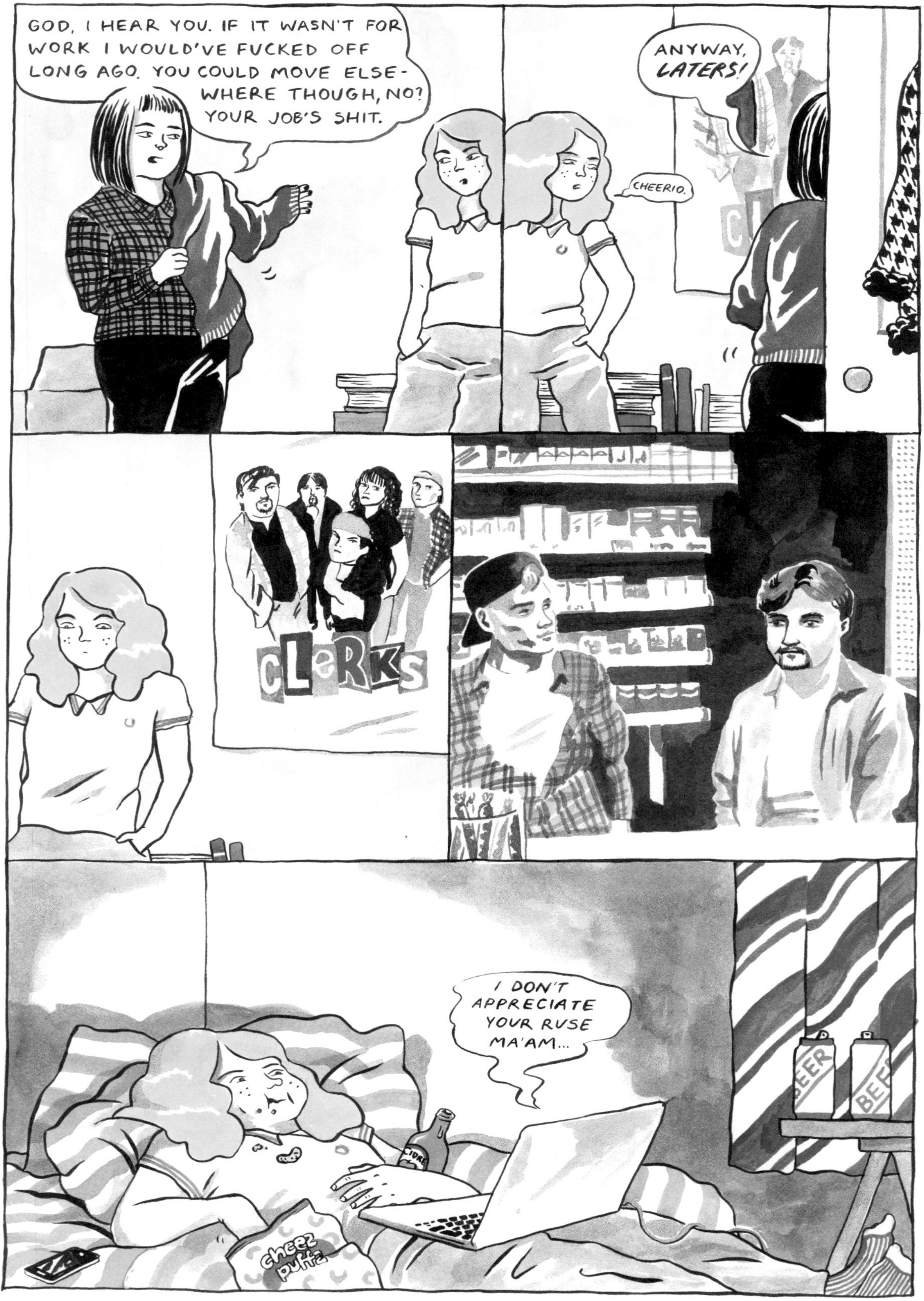
GOD, I HEAR YOU. IF IT WASN'T FOR WORK I WOULD'VE FUCKED OFF LONG AGO. YOU COULD MOVE ELSE-WHERE THOUGH, NO? YOUR JOB'S SHIT.
ANYWAY, LATERS!
CHEERIO.
CLERKS
I DON'T APPRECIATE YOUR RUSE MA'AM...
BEER
BEER
cheez puffz

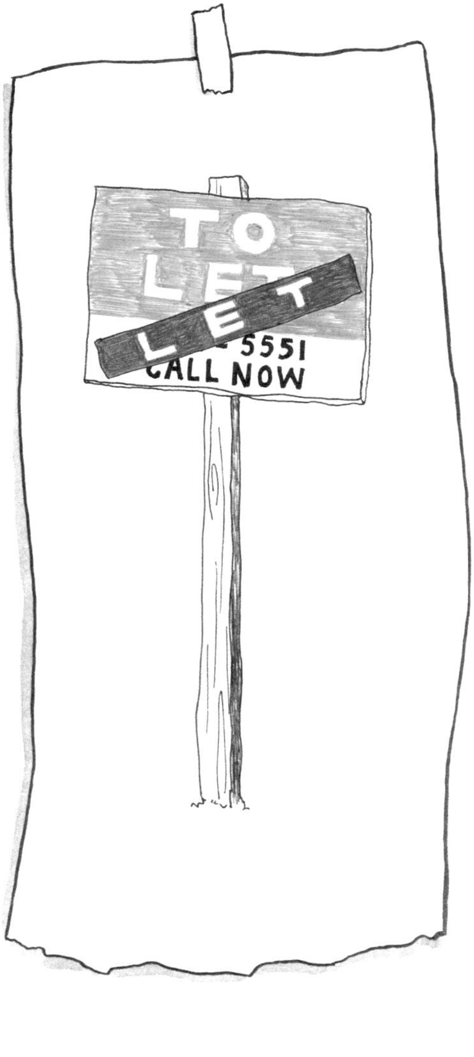
TO
LET
5551
CALL NOW

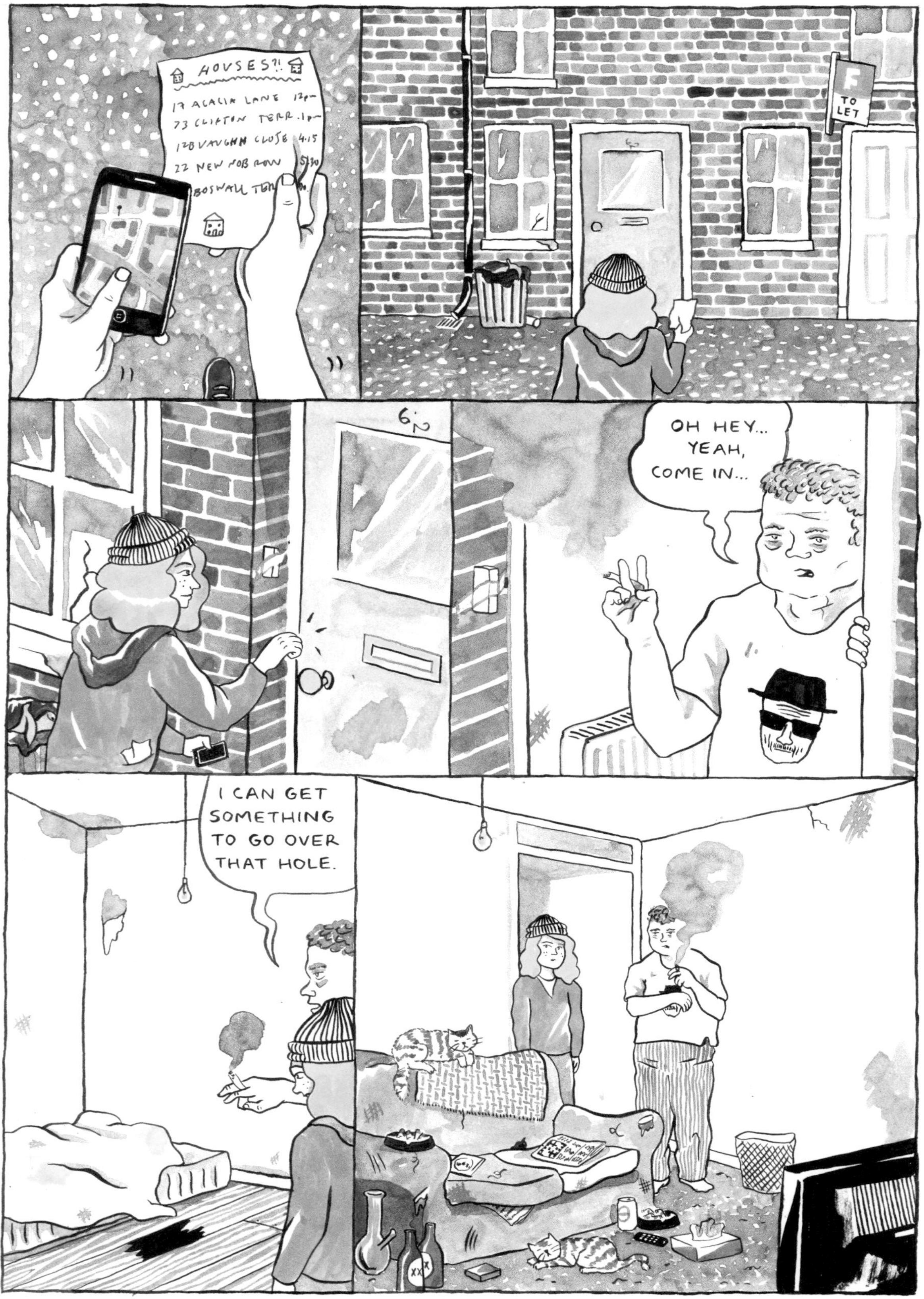
HOUSES?!
17 ACACIA LANE 12pm
73 CLIFTON TERR. 1pm
12B VAUGHN CLOSE 4.15
22 NEW NOB ROW 5.30
BOSWALL
TO LET
OH HEY... YEAH, COME IN...
I CAN GET SOMETHING TO GO OVER THAT HOLE.

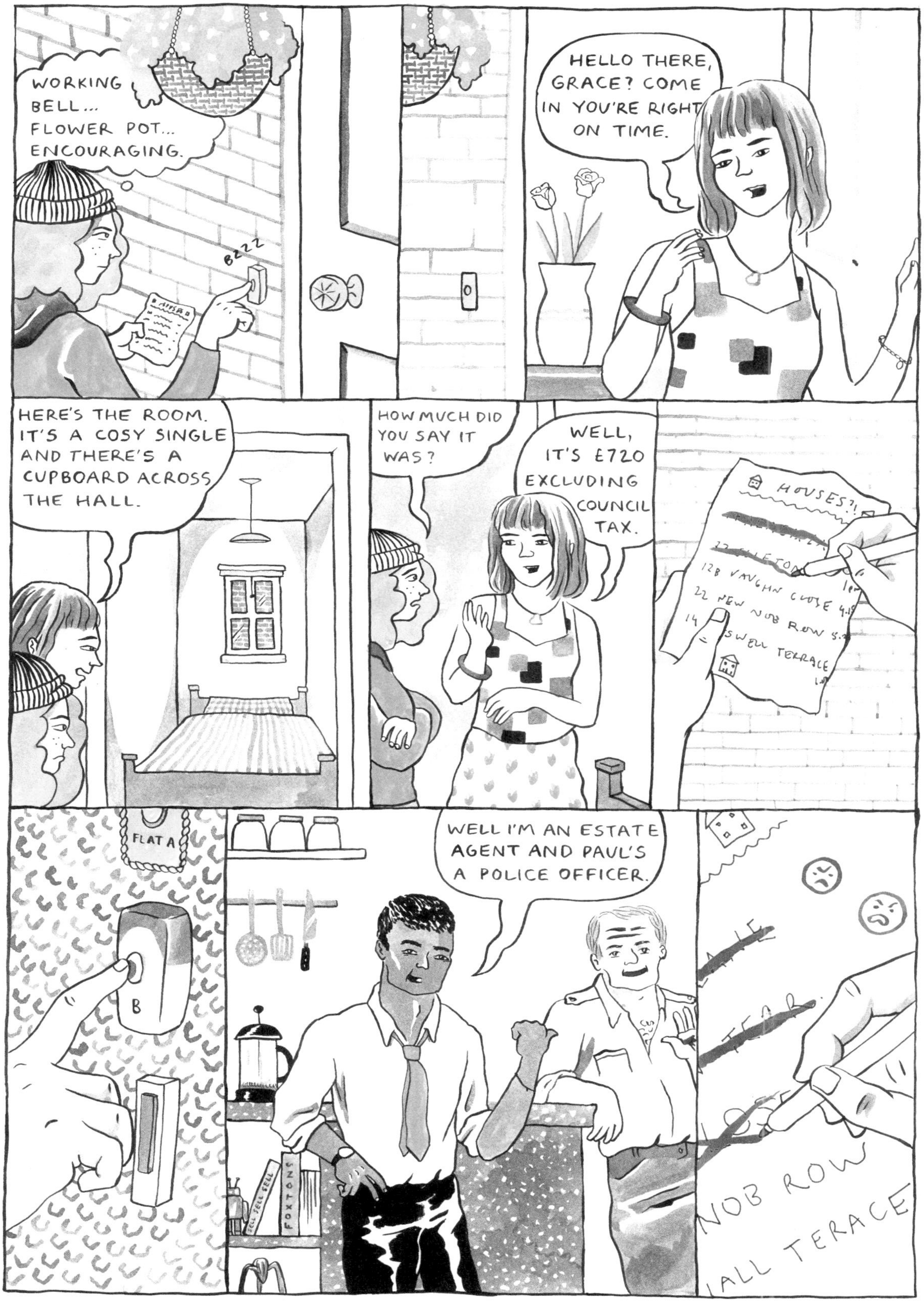
WORKING BELL... FLOWER POT... ENCOURAGING.
BZZZ
HELLO THERE, GRACE? COME IN YOU'RE RIGHT ON TIME.
HERE'S THE ROOM. IT'S A COSY SINGLE AND THERE'S A CUPBOARD ACROSS THE HALL.
HOW MUCH DID YOU SAY IT WAS?
WELL, IT'S £720 EXCLUDING COUNCIL TAX.
HOUSES?!
128 VAUGHN CLOSE
22 NEW NOB ROW
FLAT A
B
WELL I'M AN ESTATE AGENT AND PAUL'S A POLICE OFFICER.
FOXTONS
NOB ROW

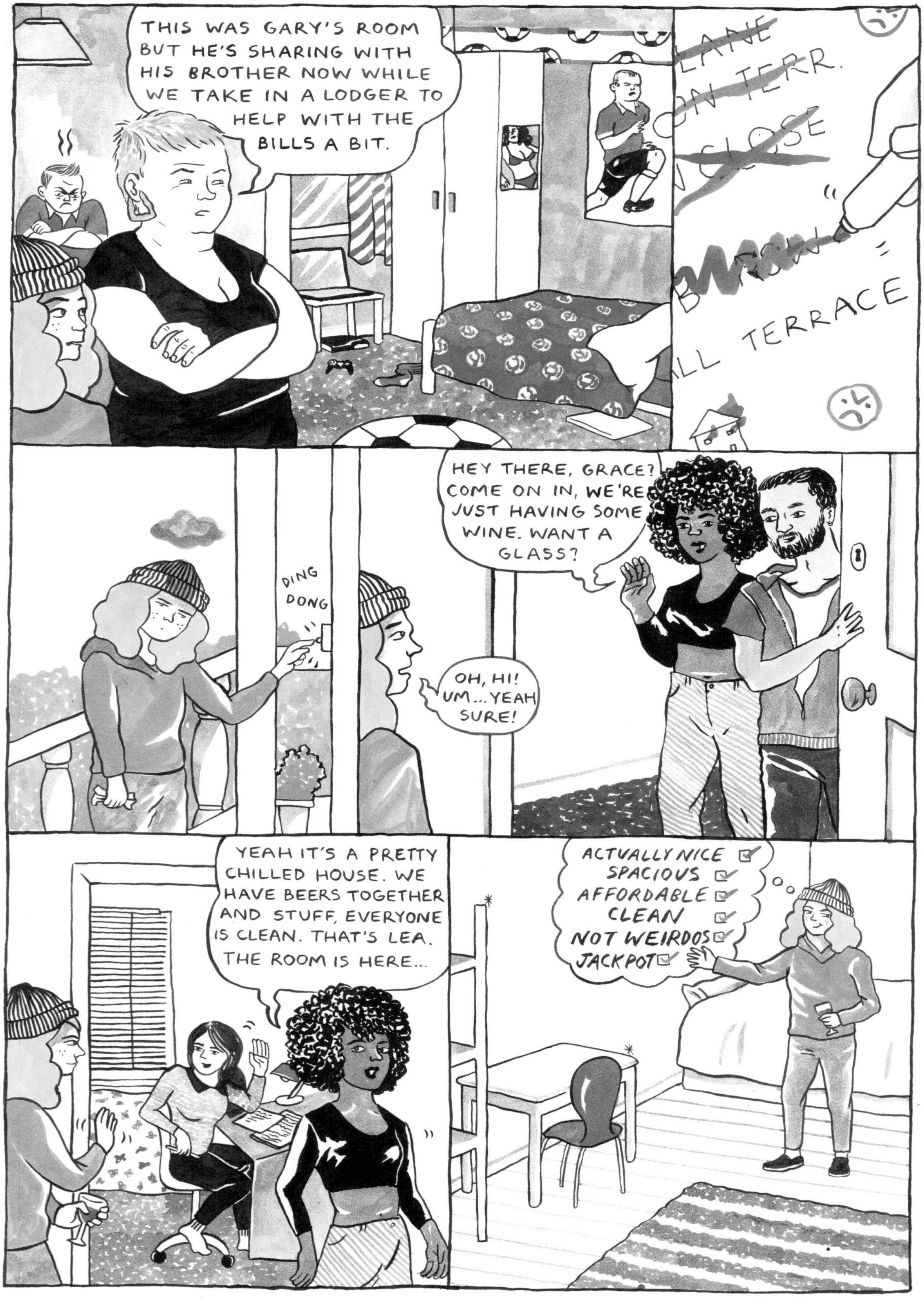
THIS WAS GARY'S ROOM BUT HE'S SHARING WITH HIS BROTHER NOW WHILE WE TAKE IN A LODGER TO HELP WITH THE BILLS A BIT.
LL TERRACE
DING DONG
HEY THERE, GRACE? COME ON IN, WE'RE JUST HAVING SOME WINE. WANT A GLASS?
OH, HI! UM... YEAH SURE!
YEAH IT'S A PRETTY CHILLED HOUSE. WE HAVE BEERS TOGETHER AND STUFF, EVERYONE IS CLEAN. THAT'S LEA. THE ROOM IS HERE...
ACTUALLY NICE
SPACIOUS
AFFORDABLE
CLEAN
NOT WEIRDOS
JACKPOT

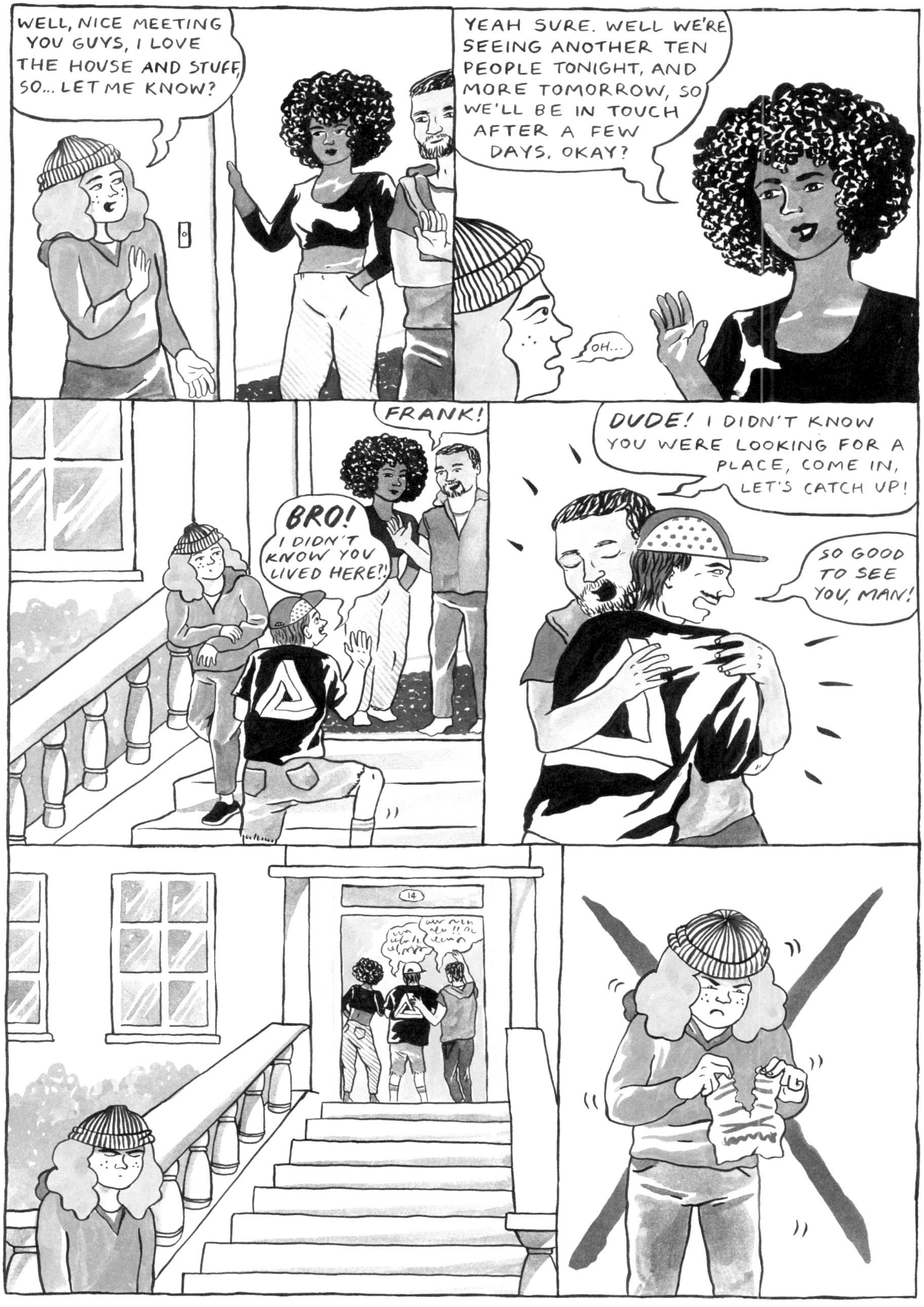

WELL, NICE MEETING YOU GUYS, I LOVE THE HOUSE AND STUFF, SO... LET ME KNOW?
YEAH SURE. WELL WE'RE SEEING ANOTHER TEN PEOPLE TONIGHT, AND MORE TOMORROW, SO WE'LL BE IN TOUCH AFTER A FEW DAYS, OKAY?
OH...
FRANK!
BRO! I DIDN'T KNOW YOU LIVED HERE?!
DUDE! I DIDN'T KNOW YOU WERE LOOKING FOR A PLACE, COME IN, LET'S CATCH UP!
SO GOOD TO SEE YOU, MAN!
14

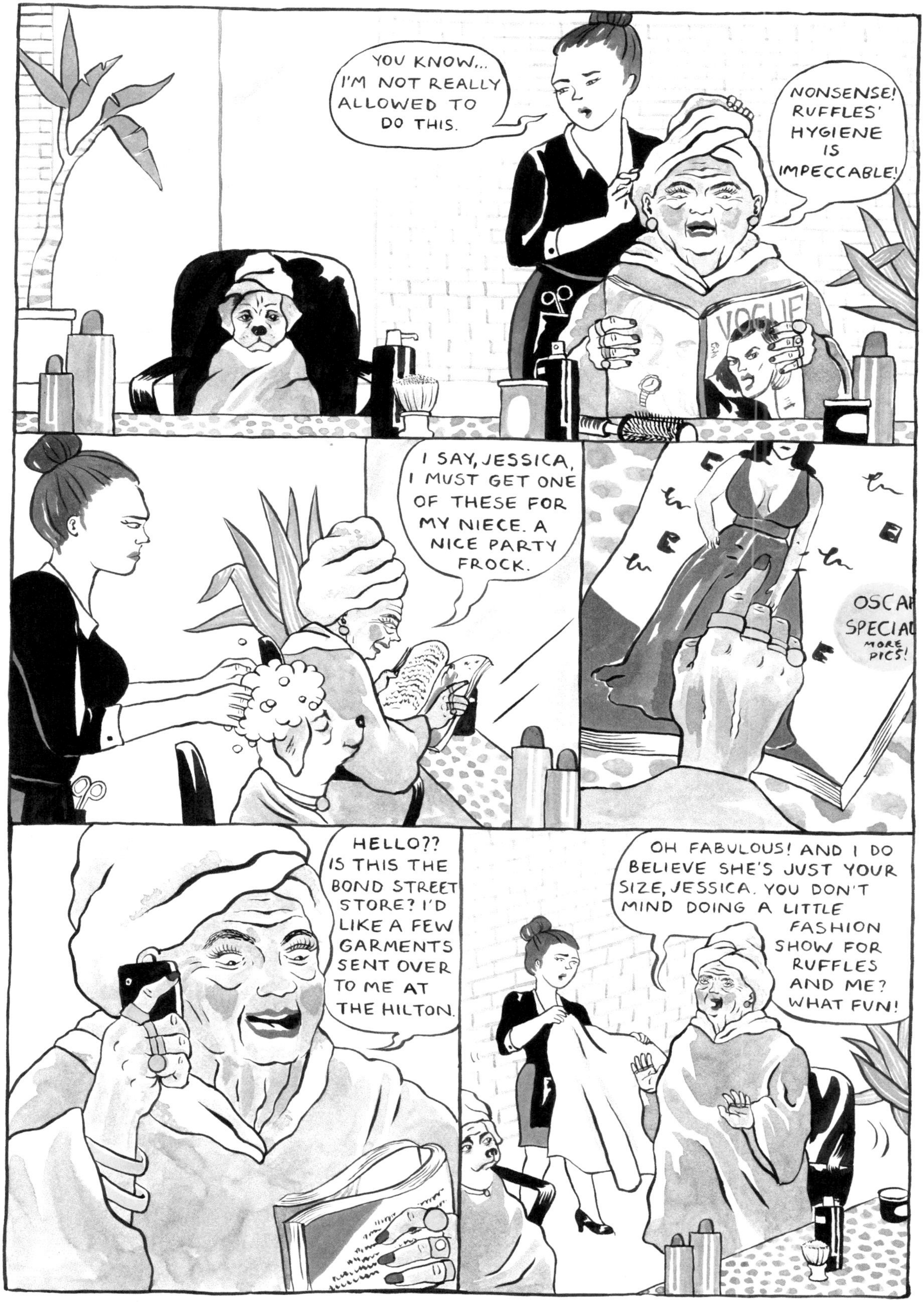
YOU KNOW... I'M NOT REALLY ALLOWED TO DO THIS.
NONSENSE! RUFFLES' HYGIENE IS IMPECCABLE!
VOGUE
I SAY, JESSICA, I MUST GET ONE OF THESE FOR MY NIECE. A NICE PARTY FROCK.
OSCAR SPECIAL MORE PICS!
HELLO?? IS THIS THE BOND STREET STORE? I'D LIKE A FEW GARMENTS SENT OVER TO ME AT THE HILTON.
OH FABULOUS! AND I DO BELIEVE SHE'S JUST YOUR SIZE, JESSICA. YOU DON'T MIND DOING A LITTLE FASHION SHOW FOR RUFFLES AND ME? WHAT FUN!

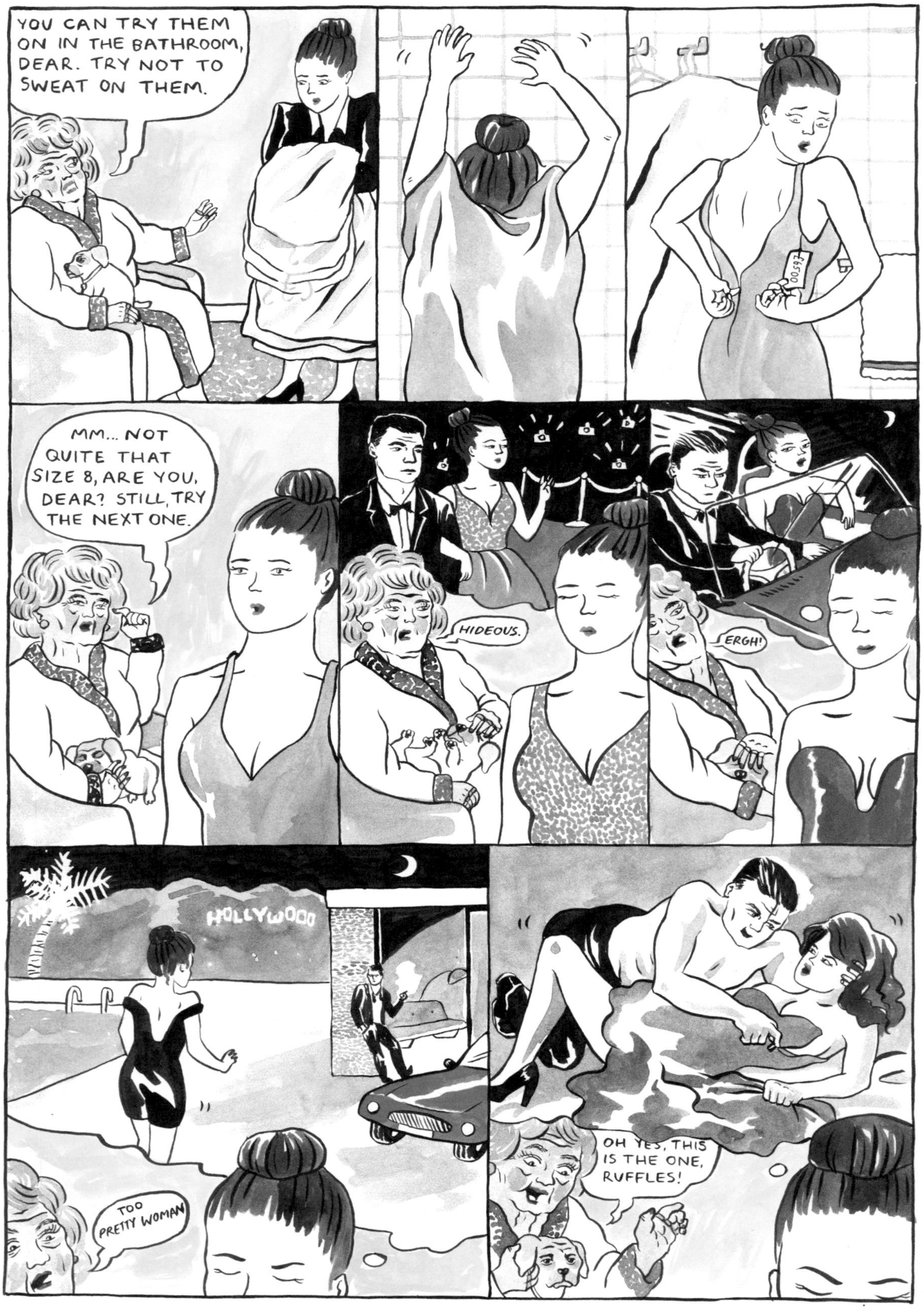
YOU CAN TRY THEM ON IN THE BATHROOM, DEAR. TRY NOT TO SWEAT ON THEM.
MM... NOT QUITE THAT SIZE 8, ARE YOU, DEAR? STILL, TRY THE NEXT ONE.
HIDEOUS.
ERGH!
HOLLYWOOD
TOO PRETTY WOMAN
OH YES, THIS IS THE ONE, RUFFLES!

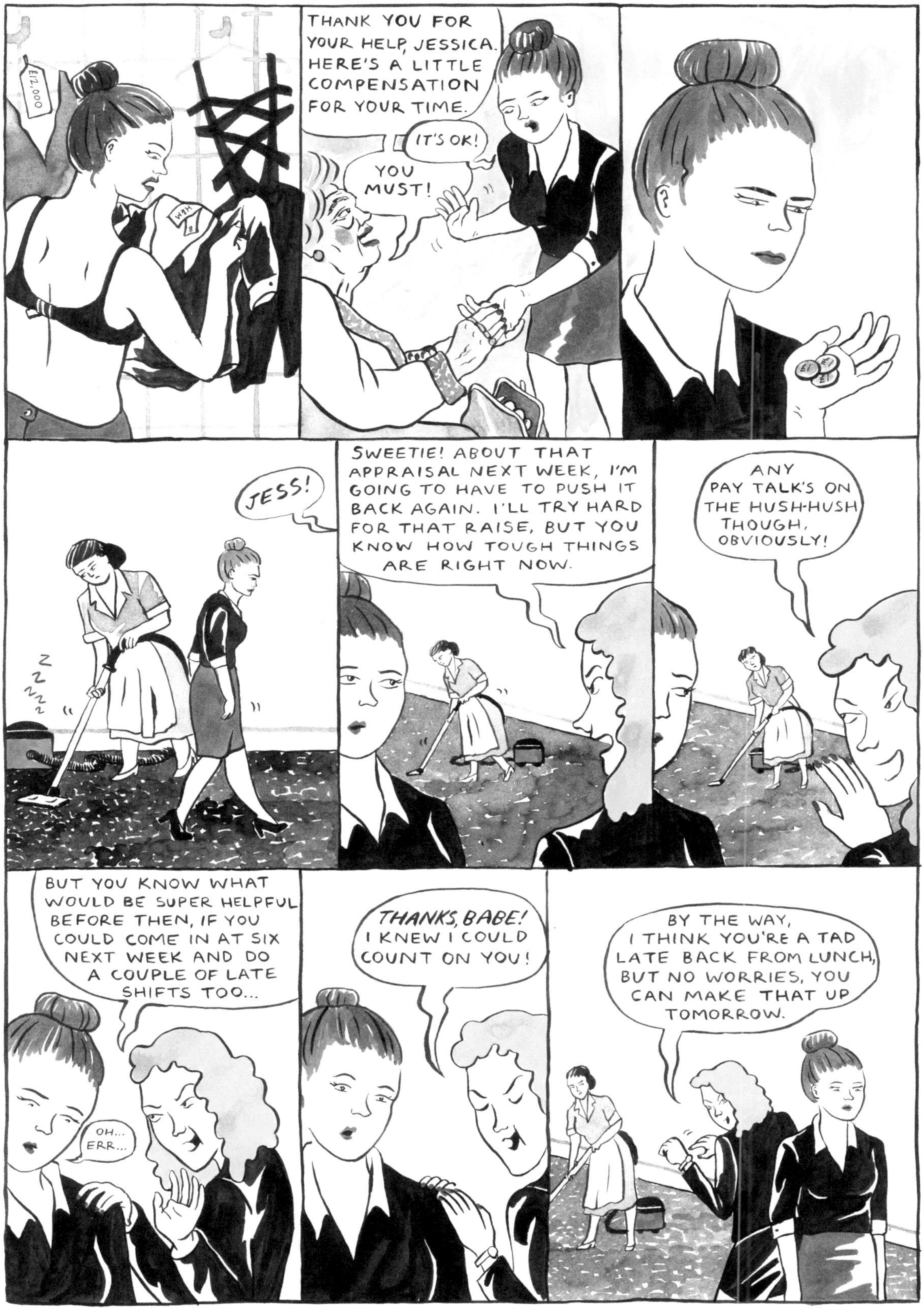
£12,000
THANK YOU FOR YOUR HELP, JESSICA. HERE'S A LITTLE COMPENSATION FOR YOUR TIME.
IT'S OK!
YOU MUST!
JESS!
SWEETIE! ABOUT THAT APPRAISAL NEXT WEEK, I'M GOING TO HAVE TO PUSH IT BACK AGAIN. I'LL TRY HARD FOR THAT RAISE, BUT YOU KNOW HOW TOUGH THINGS ARE RIGHT NOW.
ANY PAY TALK'S ON THE HUSH-HUSH THOUGH, OBVIOUSLY!
BUT YOU KNOW WHAT WOULD BE SUPER HELPFUL BEFORE THEN, IF YOU COULD COME IN AT SIX NEXT WEEK AND DO A COUPLE OF LATE SHIFTS TOO...
OH... ERR...
THANKS, BABE! I KNEW I COULD COUNT ON YOU!
BY THE WAY, I THINK YOU'RE A TAD LATE BACK FROM LUNCH, BUT NO WORRIES, YOU CAN MAKE THAT UP TOMORROW.

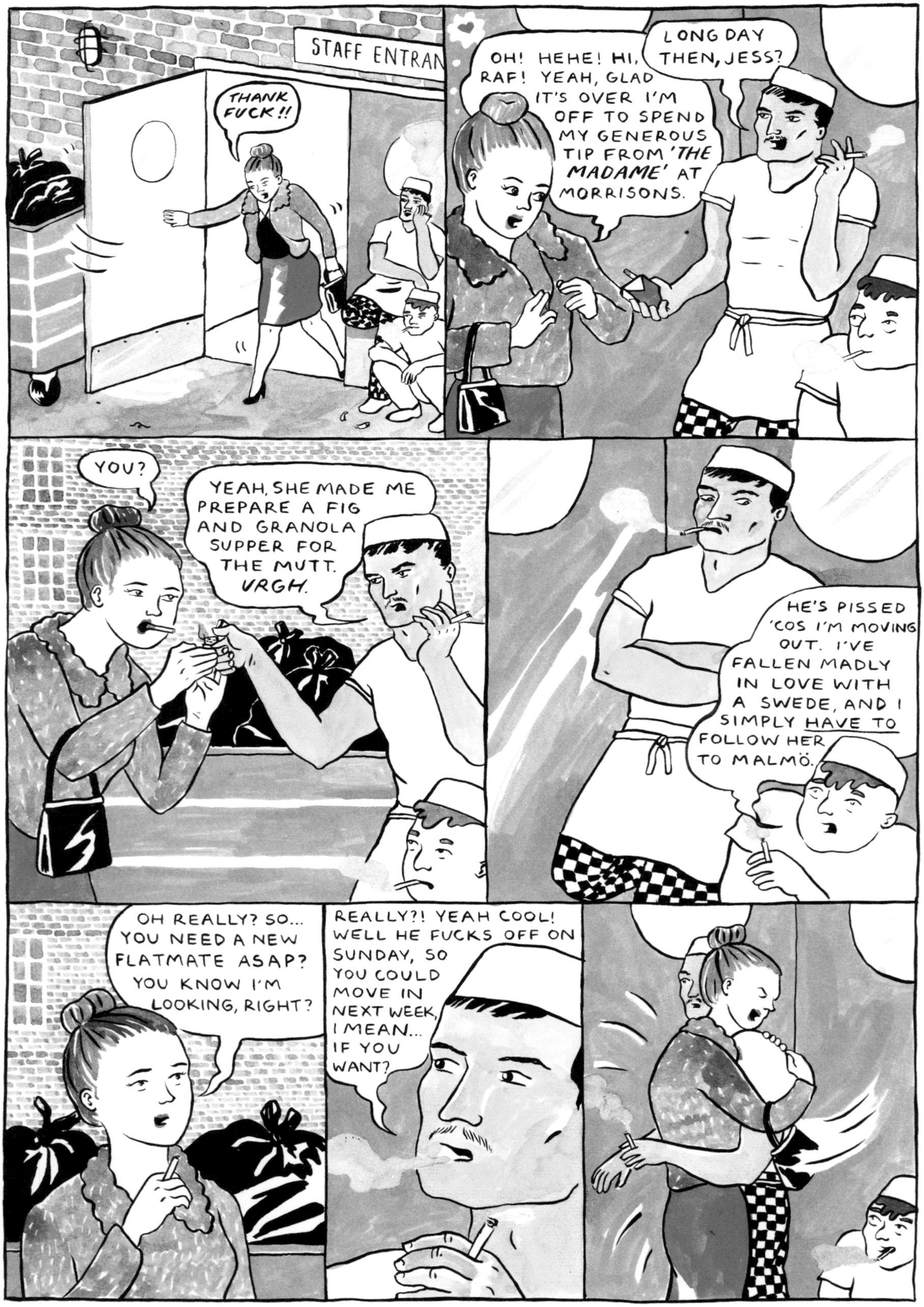
STAFF ENTRAN
THANK FUCK!!
LONG DAY THEN, JESS?
OH! HEHE! HI, RAF! YEAH, GLAD IT'S OVER I'M OFF TO SPEND MY GENEROUS TIP FROM 'THE MADAME' AT MORRISONS.
YOU?
YEAH, SHE MADE ME PREPARE A FIG AND GRANOLA SUPPER FOR THE MUTT. URGH.
HE'S PISSED 'COS I'M MOVING OUT. I'VE FALLEN MADLY IN LOVE WITH A SWEDE, AND I SIMPLY HAVE TO FOLLOW HER TO MALMÖ.
OH REALLY? SO... YOU NEED A NEW FLATMATE ASAP? YOU KNOW I'M LOOKING, RIGHT?
REALLY?! YEAH COOL! WELL HE FUCKS OFF ON SUNDAY, SO YOU COULD MOVE IN NEXT WEEK, I MEAN... IF YOU WANT?

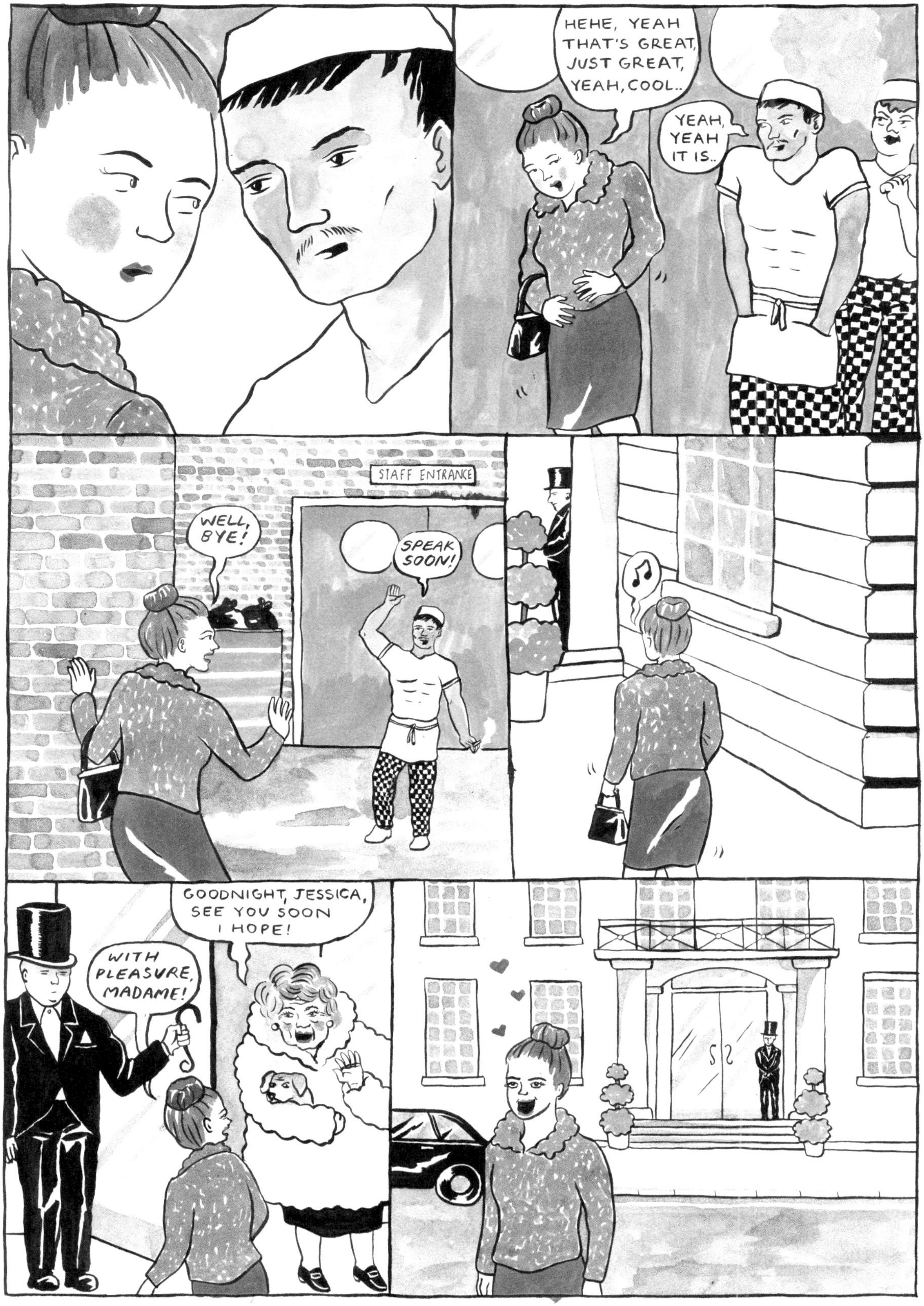
HEHE, YEAH THAT'S GREAT, JUST GREAT, YEAH, COOL..
YEAH, YEAH IT IS..
STAFF ENTRANCE
WELL, BYE!
SPEAK SOON!
♪
WITH PLEASURE, MADAME!
GOODNIGHT, JESSICA, SEE YOU SOON I HOPE!

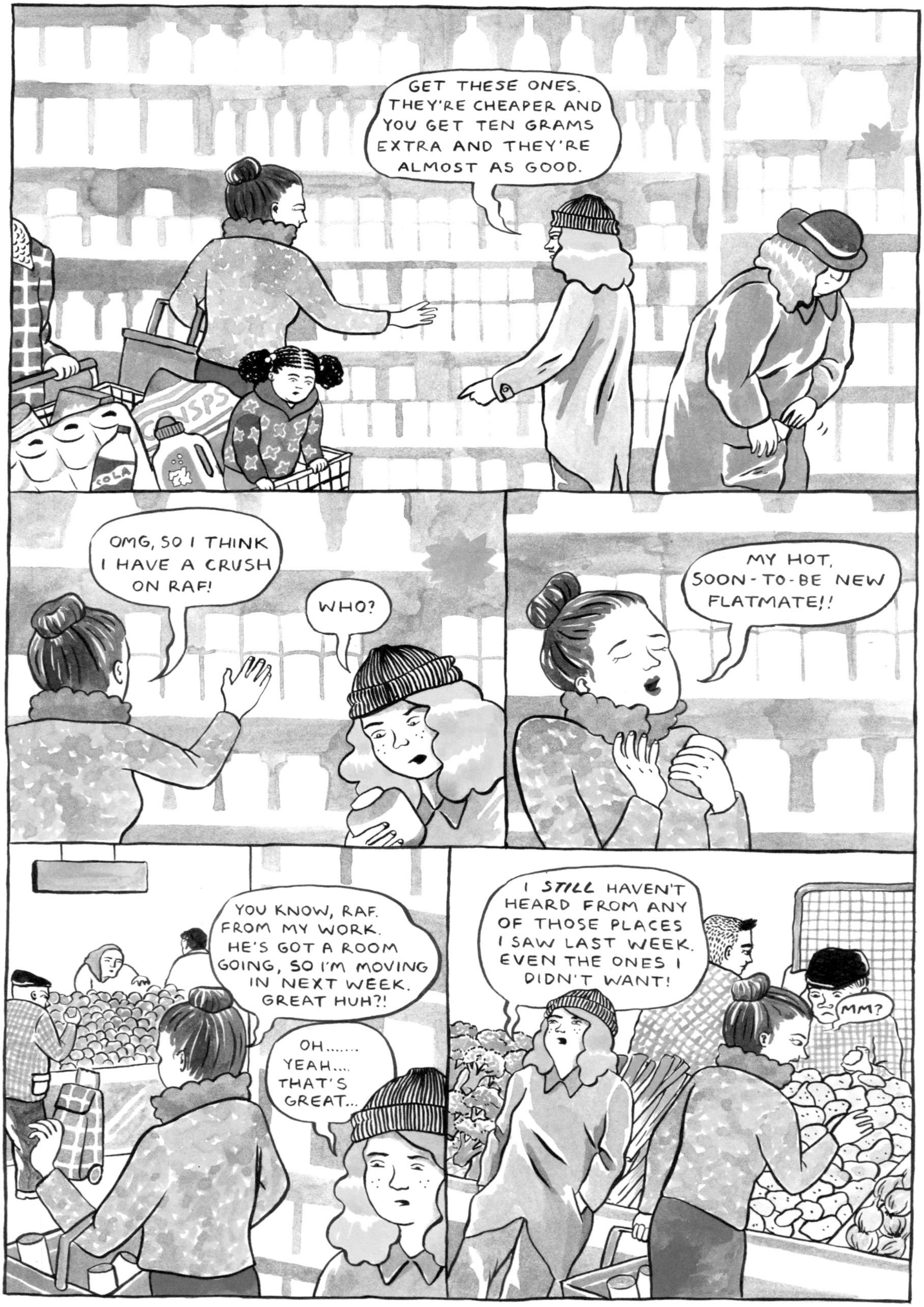
GET THESE ONES. THEY'RE CHEAPER AND YOU GET TEN GRAMS EXTRA AND THEY'RE ALMOST AS GOOD.
OMG, SO I THINK I HAVE A CRUSH ON RAF!
WHO?
MY HOT, SOON-TO-BE NEW FLATMATE!!
YOU KNOW, RAF. FROM MY WORK. HE'S GOT A ROOM GOING, SO I'M MOVING IN NEXT WEEK. GREAT HUH?!
OH...... YEAH.... THAT'S GREAT...
I *STILL* HAVEN'T HEARD FROM ANY OF THOSE PLACES I SAW LAST WEEK. EVEN THE ONES I DIDN'T WANT!
MM?

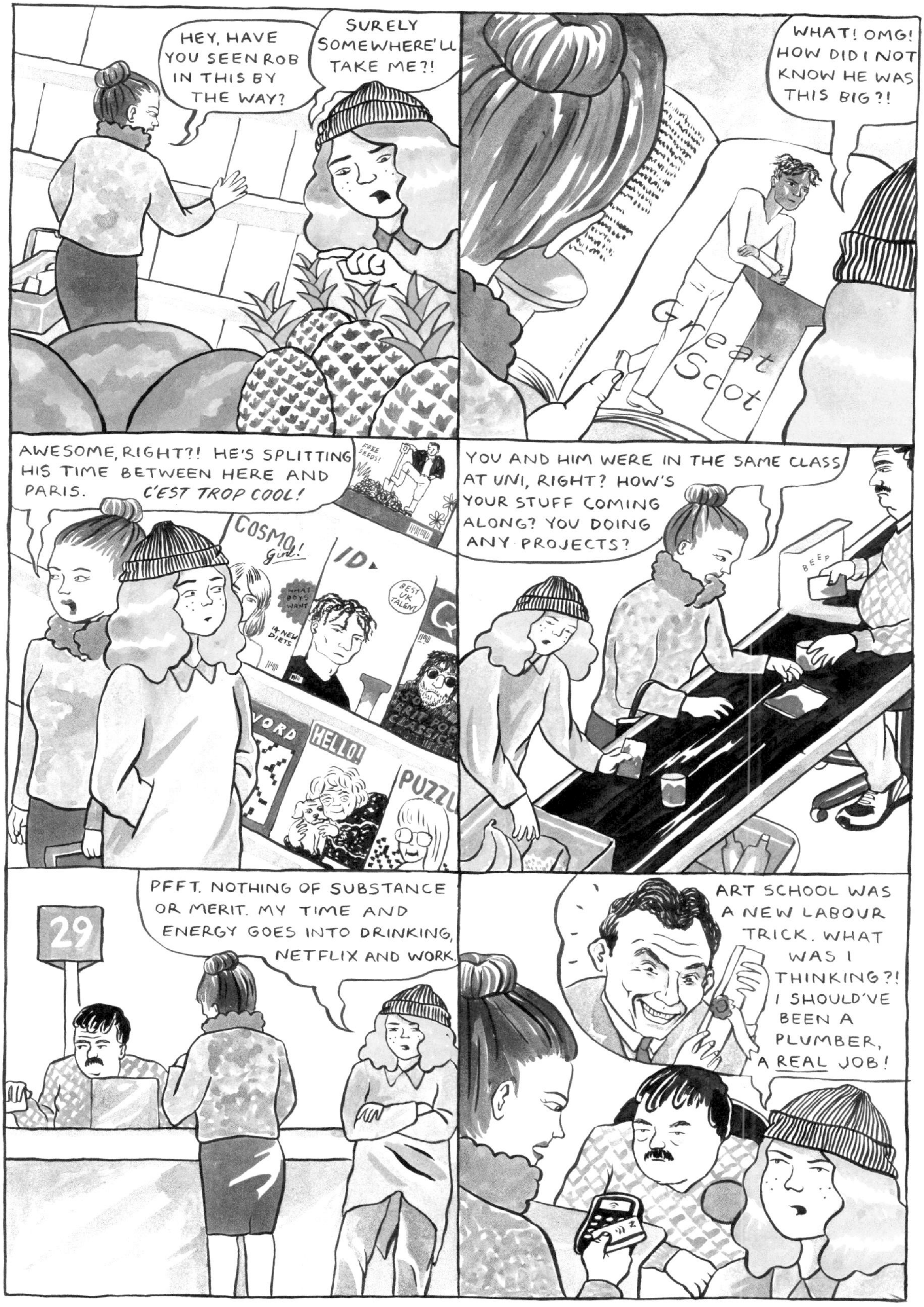

HEY, HAVE YOU SEEN ROB IN THIS BY THE WAY?
SURELY SOMEWHERE'LL TAKE ME?!
WHAT! OMG! HOW DID I NOT KNOW HE WAS THIS BIG?!
Great Scot
AWESOME, RIGHT?! HE'S SPLITTING HIS TIME BETWEEN HERE AND PARIS. C'EST TROP COOL!
FREE SEEDS!
COSMO Girl!
WHAT BOYS WANT
14 NEW DIETS
ID
BEST UK TALENT
WORD
HELLO!
PUZZL
BRIT POP CLASSICS
YOU AND HIM WERE IN THE SAME CLASS AT UNI, RIGHT? HOW'S YOUR STUFF COMING ALONG? YOU DOING ANY PROJECTS?
BEEP
29
PFFT. NOTHING OF SUBSTANCE OR MERIT. MY TIME AND ENERGY GOES INTO DRINKING, NETFLIX AND WORK.
ART SCHOOL WAS A NEW LABOUR TRICK. WHAT WAS I THINKING?! I SHOULD'VE BEEN A PLUMBER, A REAL JOB!

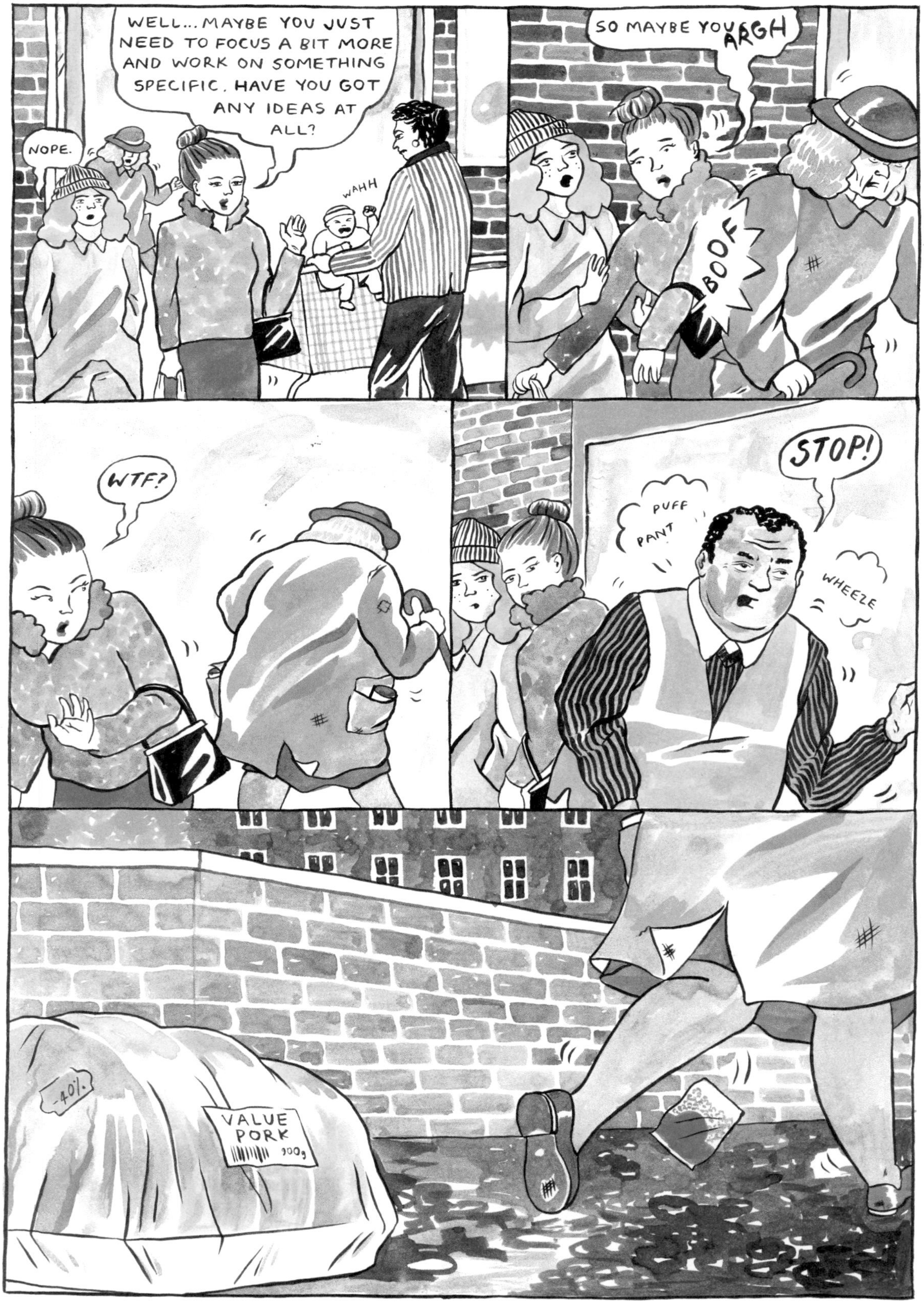
WELL... MAYBE YOU JUST NEED TO FOCUS A BIT MORE AND WORK ON SOMETHING SPECIFIC. HAVE YOU GOT ANY IDEAS AT ALL?
NOPE.
WAHH
SO MAYBE YOU ARGH
BOOF
WTF?
STOP!
PUFF
PANT
WHEEZE
-40%
VALUE PORK
900g

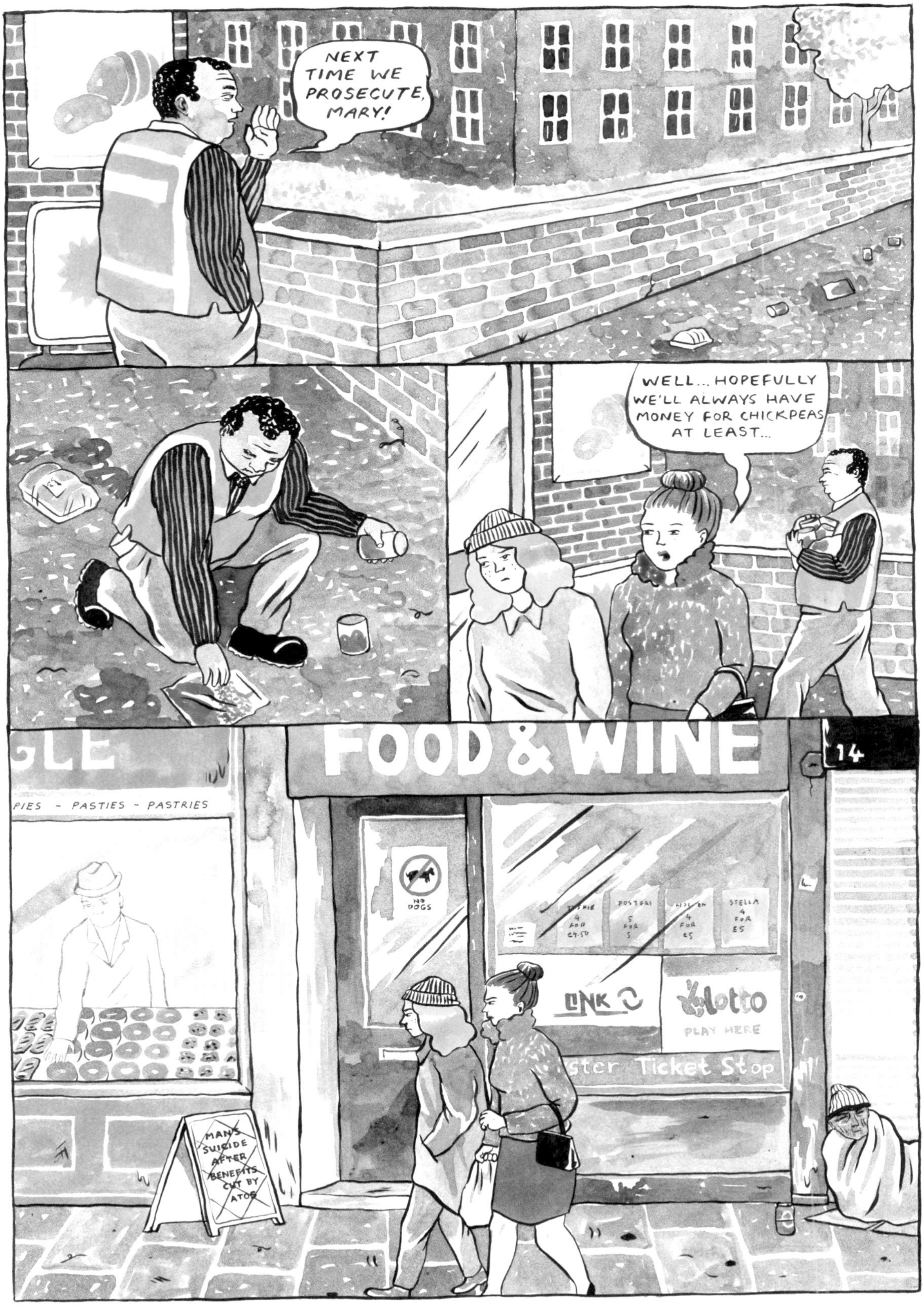
NEXT TIME WE PROSECUTE, MARY!
WELL... HOPEFULLY WE'LL ALWAYS HAVE MONEY FOR CHICKPEAS AT LEAST...
GLE
PIES - PASTIES - PASTRIES
FOOD & WINE
14
NO DOGS
LINK
lotto
PLAY HERE
ster Ticket Stop
MAN'S SUICIDE AFTER BENEFITS CUT BY ATOS

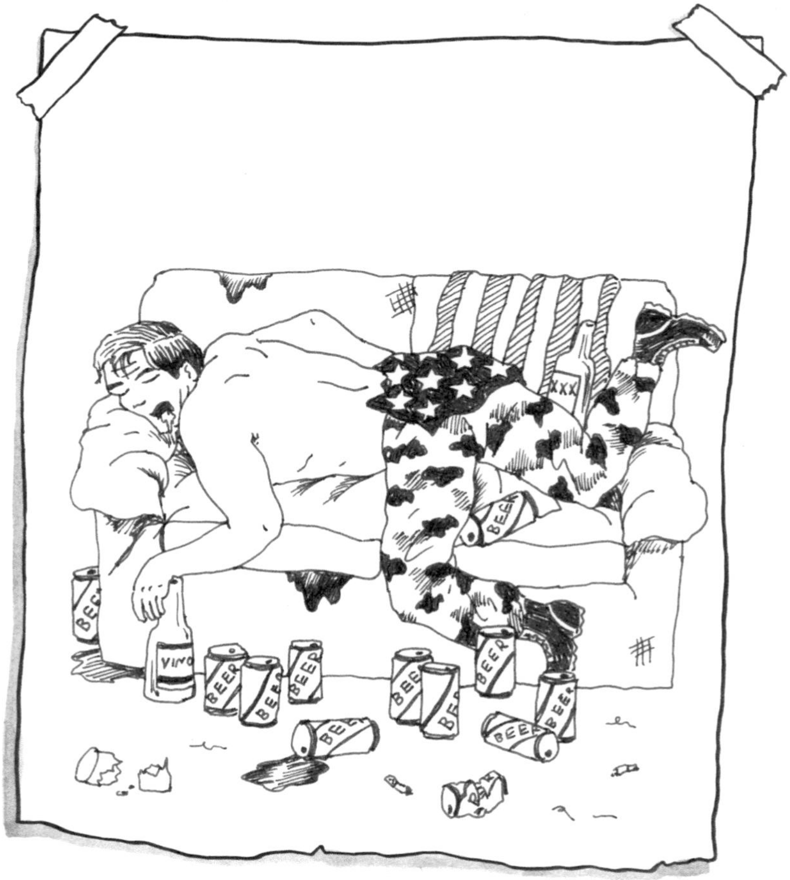
XXX
BEER
VINO
BEER
BEER
BEER
BEER
BEER
BEER
BEER
BEER
BEER

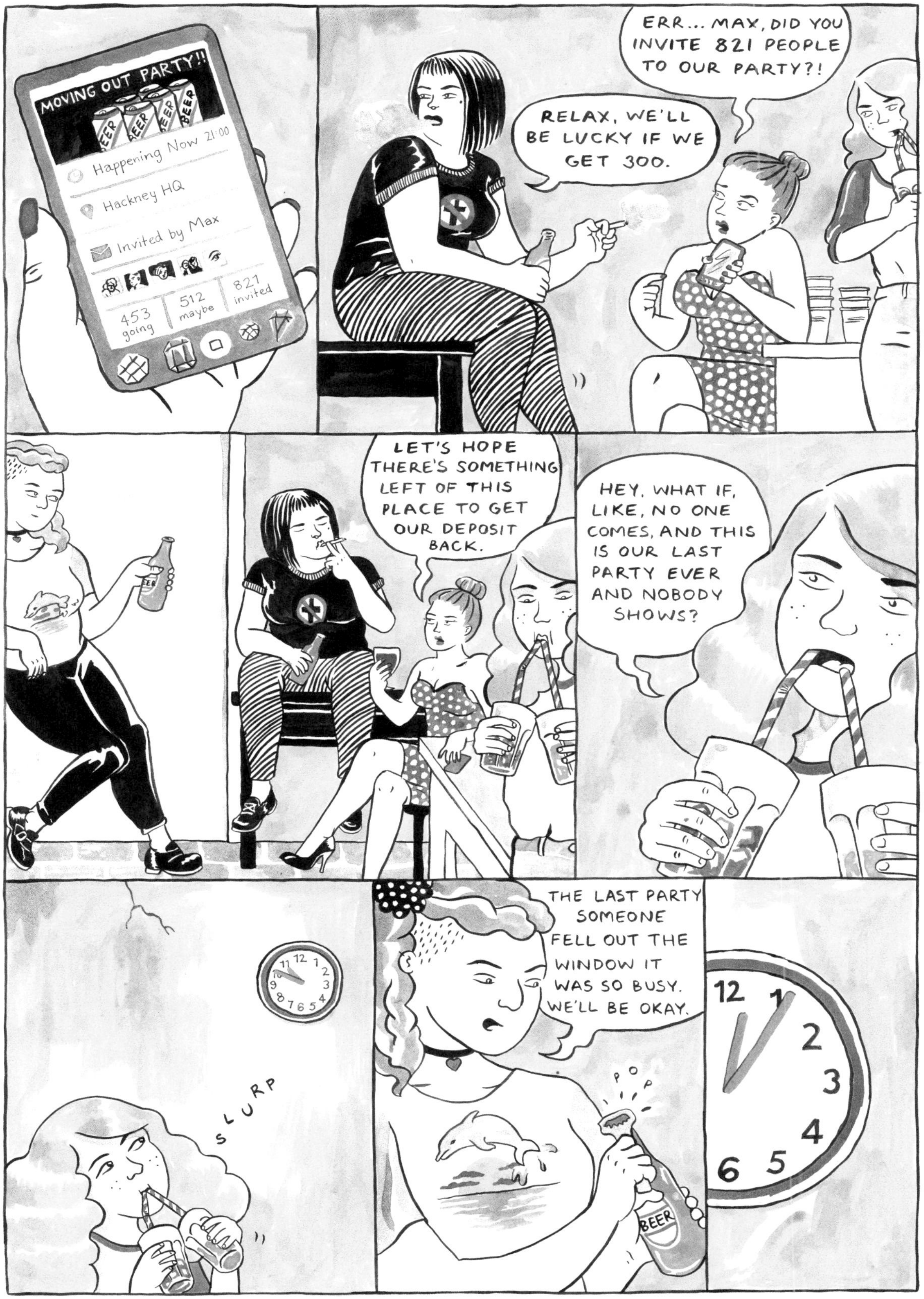
MOVING OUT PARTY!!
BEER
Happening Now 21:00
Hackney HQ
Invited by Max
453 going
512 maybe
821 invited
ERR... MAX, DID YOU INVITE 821 PEOPLE TO OUR PARTY?!
RELAX, WE'LL BE LUCKY IF WE GET 300.
LET'S HOPE THERE'S SOMETHING LEFT OF THIS PLACE TO GET OUR DEPOSIT BACK.
HEY, WHAT IF, LIKE, NO ONE COMES, AND THIS IS OUR LAST PARTY EVER AND NOBODY SHOWS?
SLURP
THE LAST PARTY SOMEONE FELL OUT THE WINDOW IT WAS SO BUSY. WE'LL BE OKAY.
POP
BEER

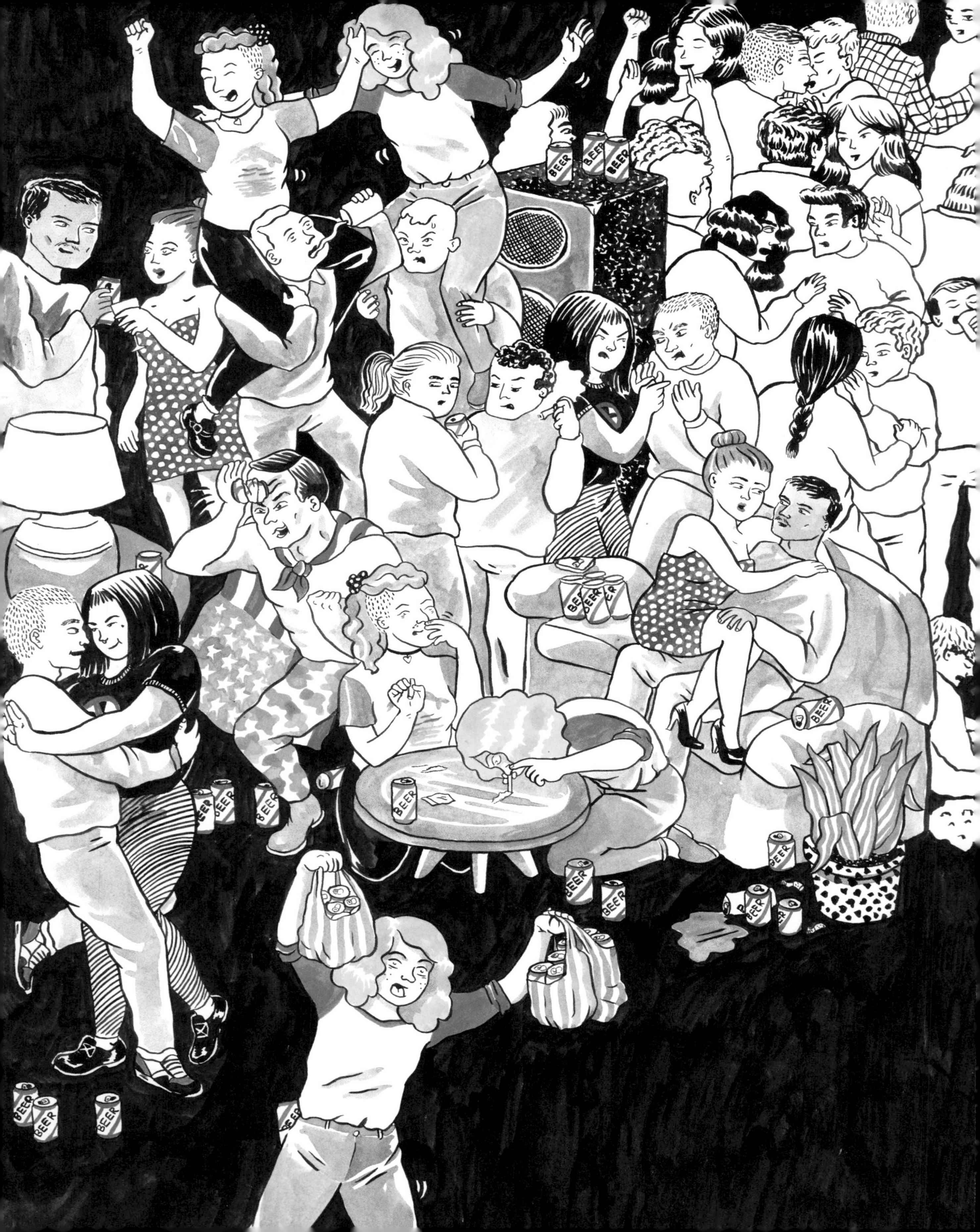
BEER

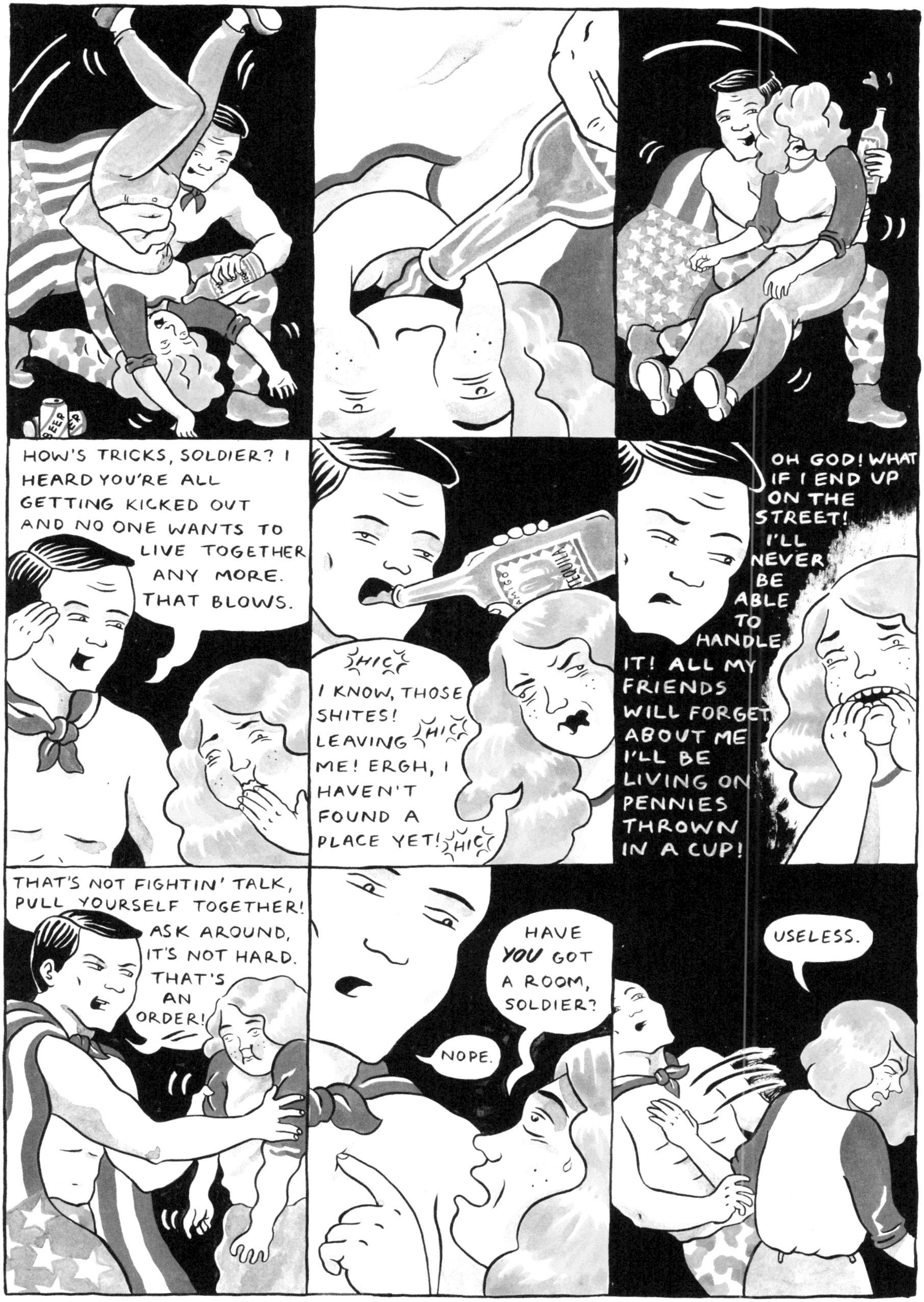
BEER
BEER
HOW'S TRICKS, SOLDIER? I HEARD YOU'RE ALL GETTING KICKED OUT AND NO ONE WANTS TO LIVE TOGETHER ANY MORE. THAT BLOWS.
AMIGO
TEQUILA
HIC
I KNOW, THOSE SHITES! LEAVING ME! ERGH, I HAVEN'T FOUND A PLACE YET!
HIC
HIC
OH GOD! WHAT IF I END UP ON THE STREET! I'LL NEVER BE ABLE TO HANDLE IT! ALL MY FRIENDS WILL FORGET ABOUT ME I'LL BE LIVING ON PENNIES THROWN IN A CUP!
THAT'S NOT FIGHTIN' TALK, PULL YOURSELF TOGETHER!
ASK AROUND, IT'S NOT HARD. THAT'S AN ORDER!
HAVE YOU GOT A ROOM, SOLDIER?
NOPE.
USELESS.

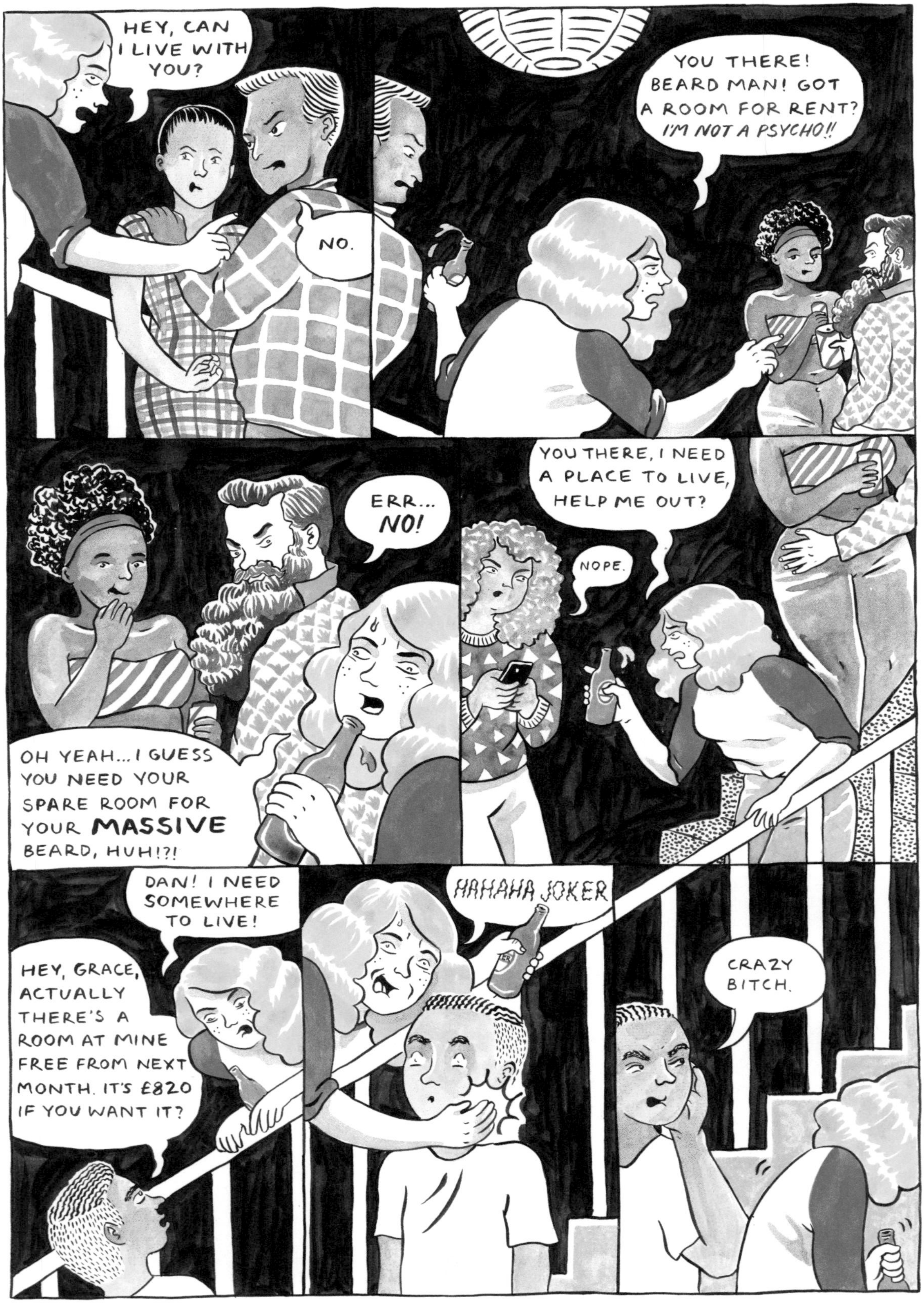
HEY, CAN I LIVE WITH YOU?
NO.
YOU THERE! BEARD MAN! GOT A ROOM FOR RENT? I'M NOT A PSYCHO!!
ERR... NO!
OH YEAH... I GUESS YOU NEED YOUR SPARE ROOM FOR YOUR MASSIVE BEARD, HUH!?!
YOU THERE, I NEED A PLACE TO LIVE, HELP ME OUT?
NOPE.
DAN! I NEED SOMEWHERE TO LIVE!
HEY, GRACE, ACTUALLY THERE'S A ROOM AT MINE FREE FROM NEXT MONTH. IT'S £820 IF YOU WANT IT?
HAHAHA JOKER
CRAZY BITCH.

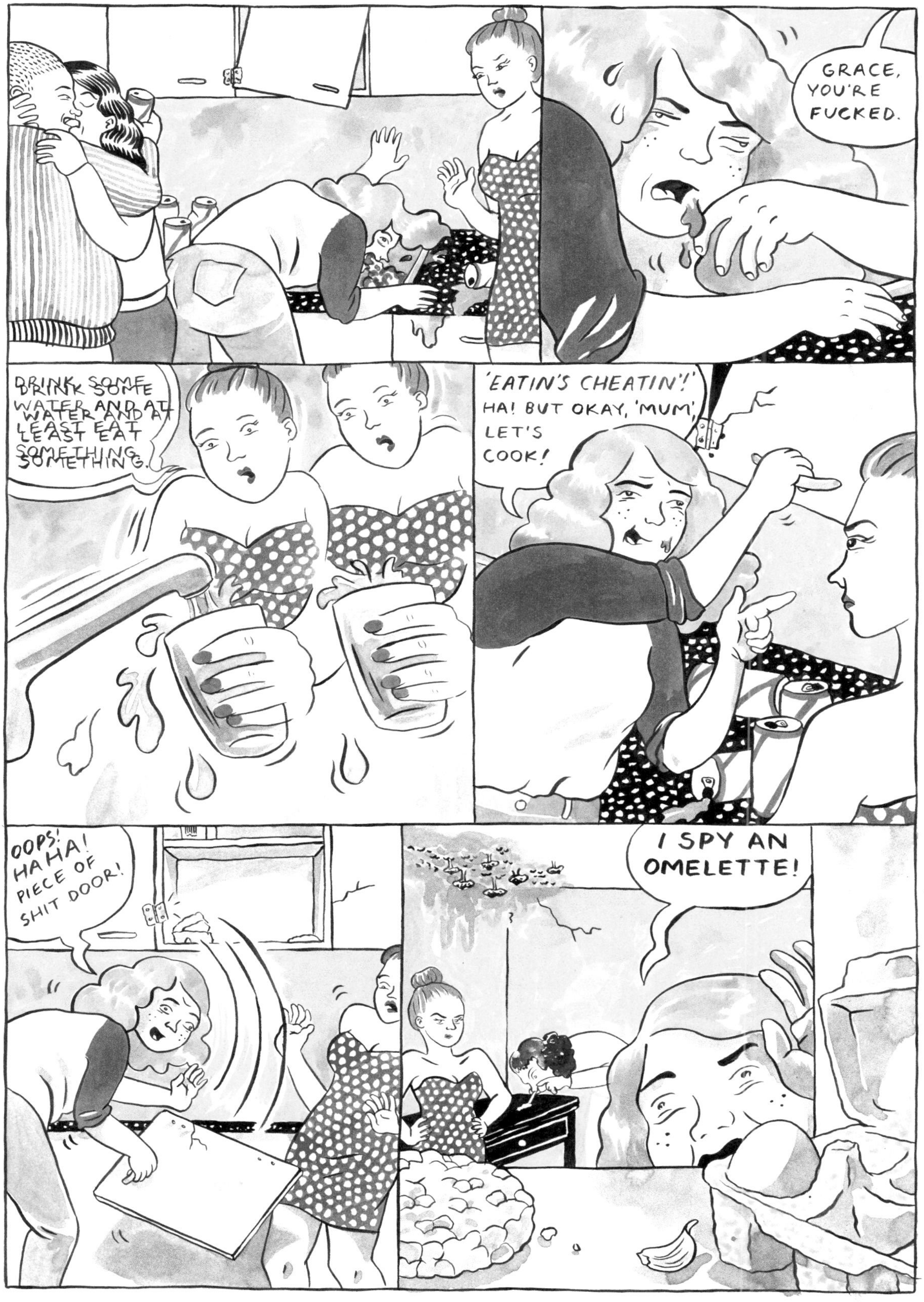
GRACE, YOU'RE FUCKED.
DRINK SOME WATER AND AT LEAST EAT SOMETHING.
'EATIN'S CHEATIN'!' HA! BUT OKAY, 'MUM', LET'S COOK!
OOPS! HAHA! PIECE OF SHIT DOOR!
I SPY AN OMELETTE!

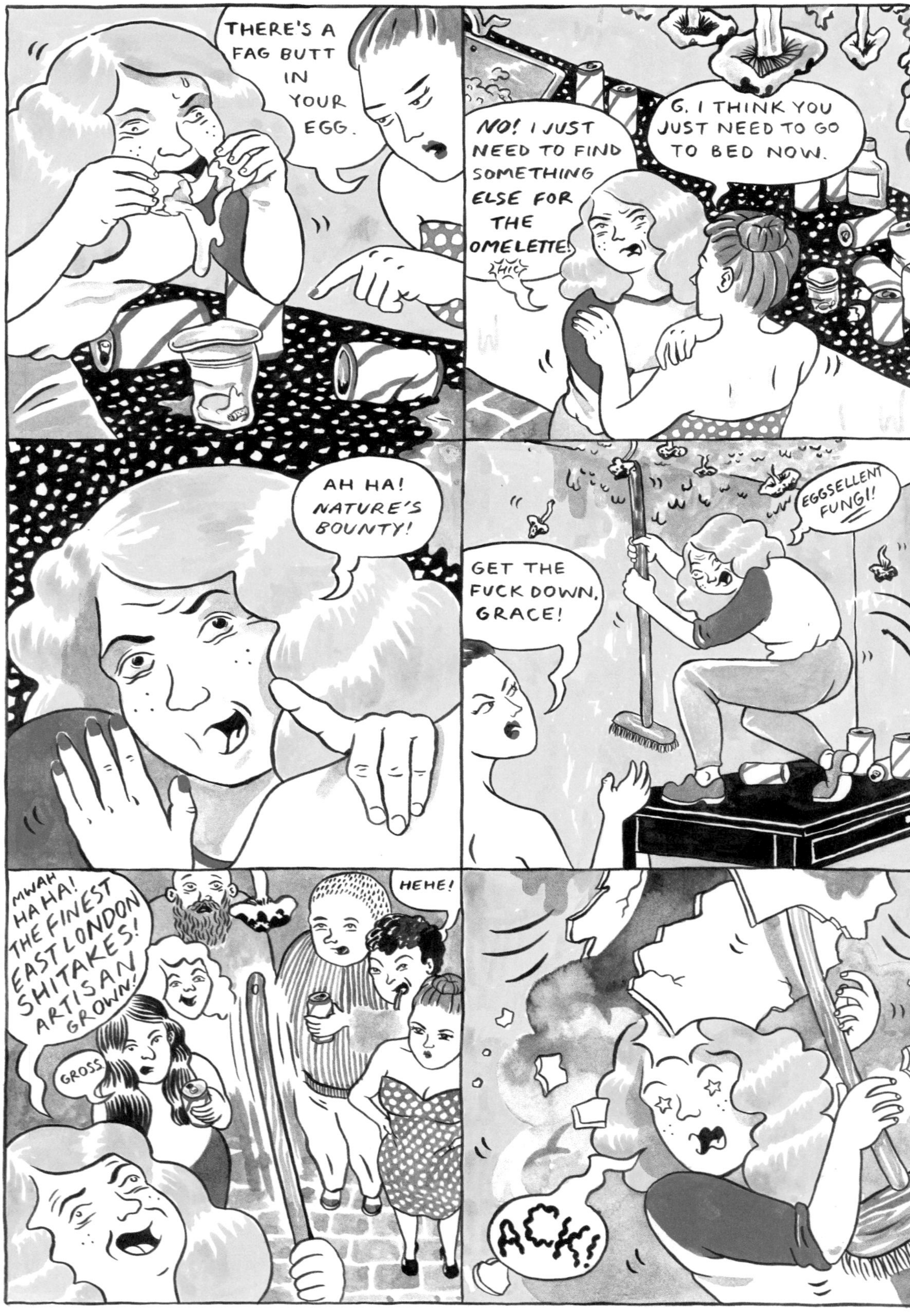
THERE'S A FAG BUTT IN YOUR EGG.
NO! I JUST NEED TO FIND SOMETHING ELSE FOR THE OMELETTE!
HIC
G. I THINK YOU JUST NEED TO GO TO BED NOW.
AH HA! NATURE'S BOUNTY!
EGGSELLENT FUNGI!
GET THE FUCK DOWN, GRACE!
MWAH HA HA! THE FINEST EAST LONDON SHITAKES! ARTISAN GROWN!
HEHE!
GROSS
ACK!

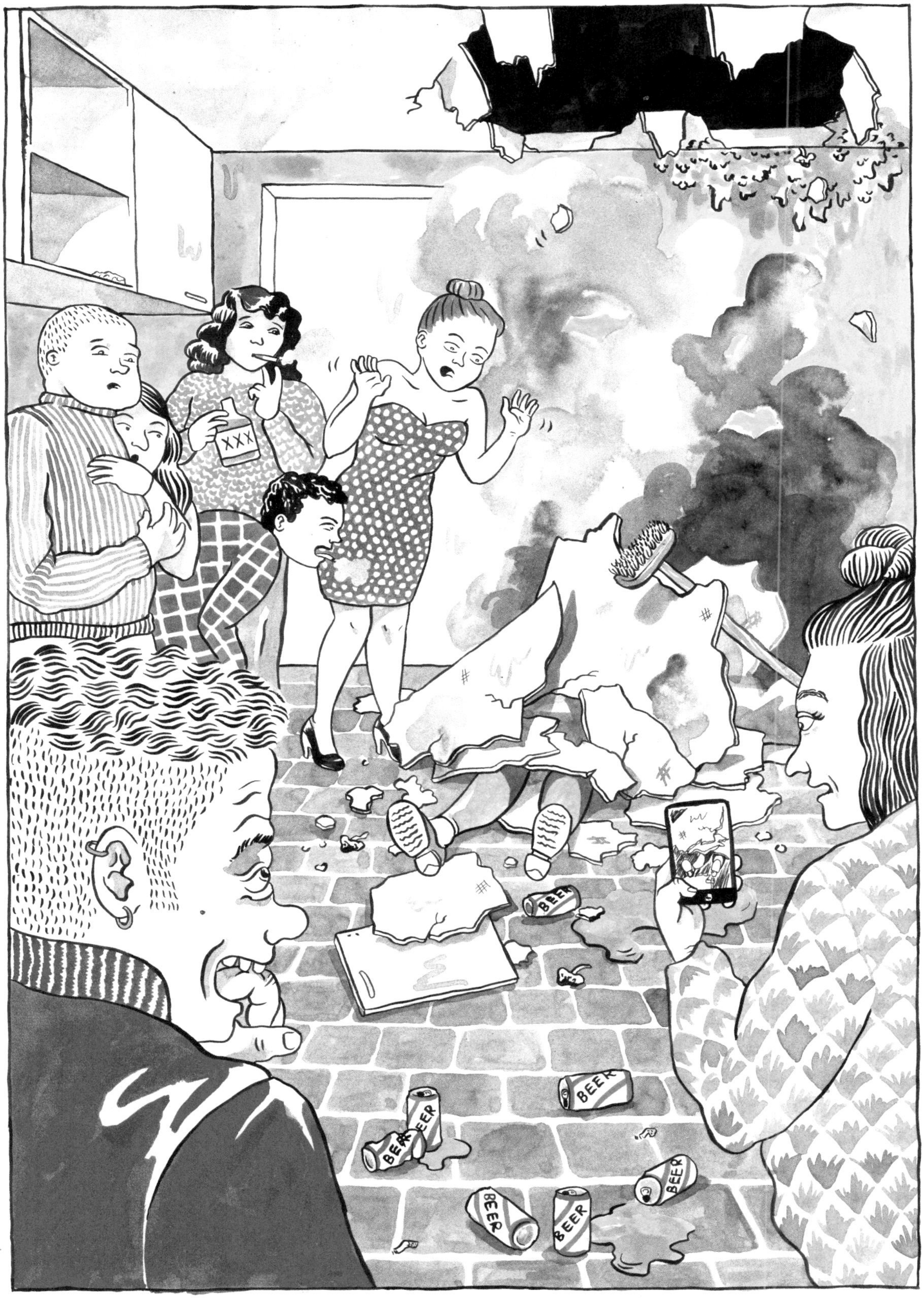
XXX
BEER
BEER
BEER
BEER
BEER
BEER

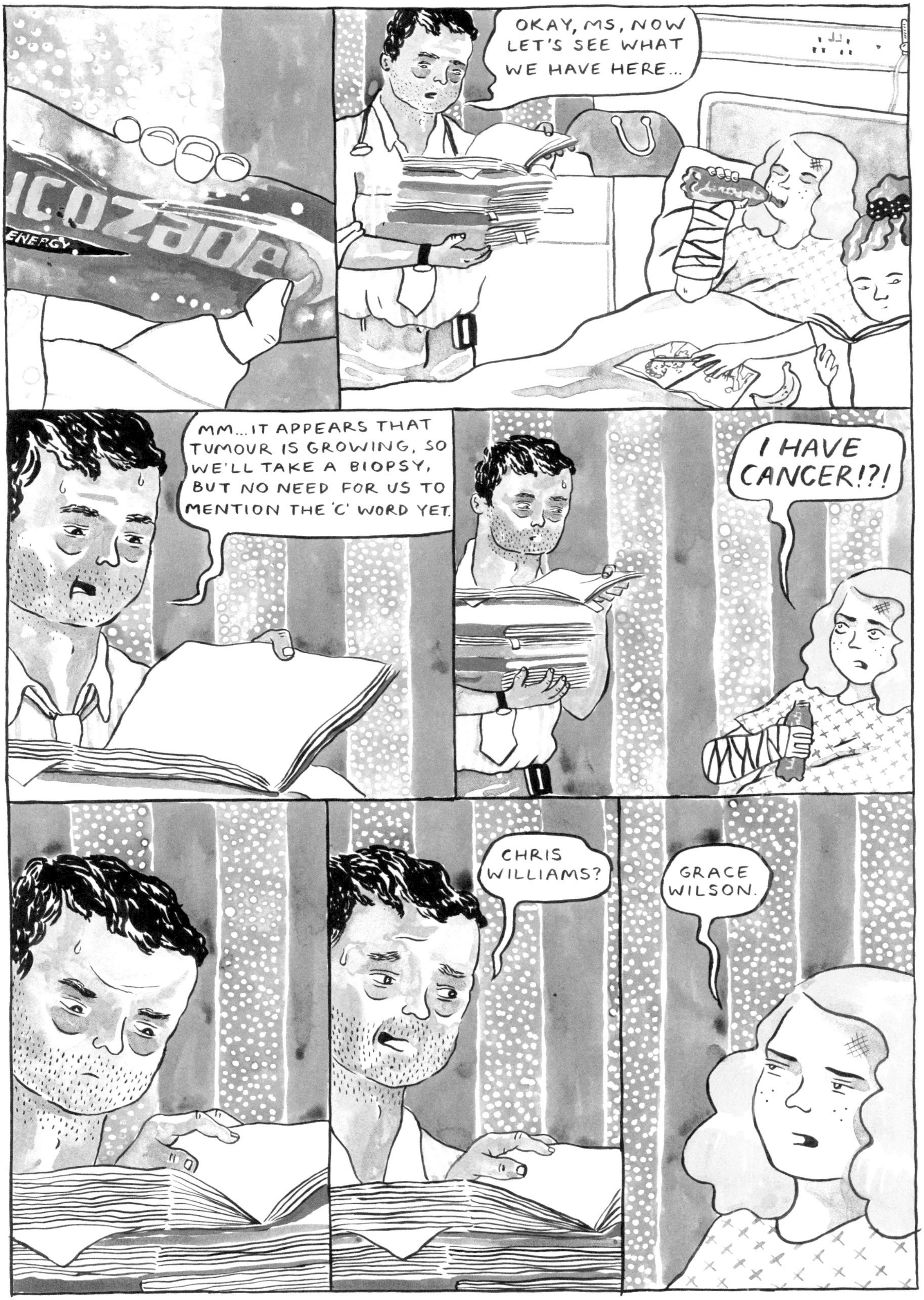
LUCOZADE
ENERGY
OKAY, MS, NOW LET'S SEE WHAT WE HAVE HERE...
MM... IT APPEARS THAT TUMOUR IS GROWING, SO WE'LL TAKE A BIOPSY, BUT NO NEED FOR US TO MENTION THE 'C' WORD YET.
I HAVE CANCER!?!
CHRIS WILLIAMS?
GRACE WILSON.

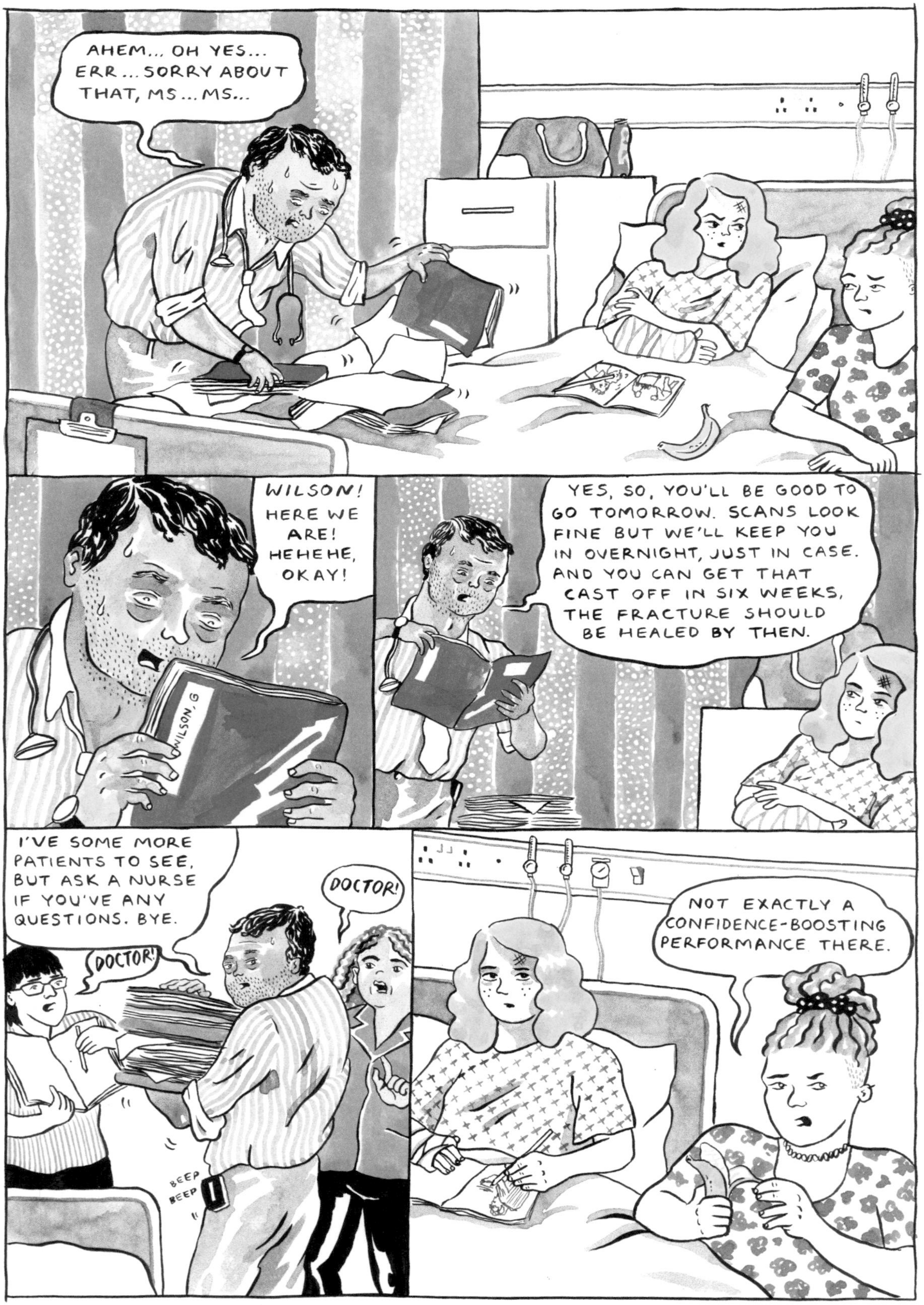
AHEM... OH YES... ERR... SORRY ABOUT THAT, MS... MS...
WILSON! HERE WE ARE! HEHEHE, OKAY!
WILSON, G
YES, SO, YOU'LL BE GOOD TO GO TOMORROW. SCANS LOOK FINE BUT WE'LL KEEP YOU IN OVERNIGHT, JUST IN CASE. AND YOU CAN GET THAT CAST OFF IN SIX WEEKS, THE FRACTURE SHOULD BE HEALED BY THEN.
I'VE SOME MORE PATIENTS TO SEE, BUT ASK A NURSE IF YOU'VE ANY QUESTIONS. BYE.
DOCTOR!
DOCTOR!
BEEP BEEP
NOT EXACTLY A CONFIDENCE-BOOSTING PERFORMANCE THERE.

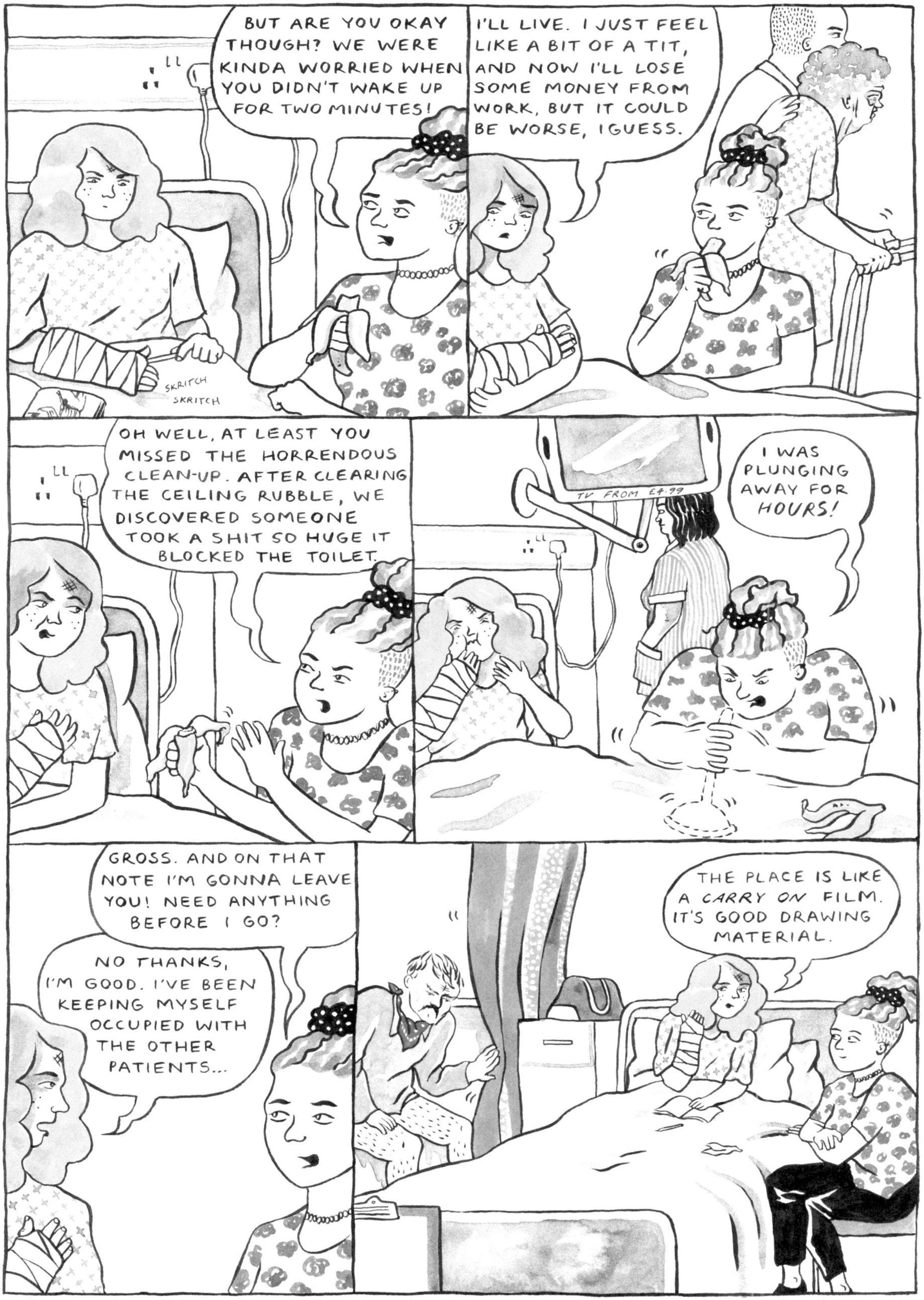
BUT ARE YOU OKAY THOUGH? WE WERE KINDA WORRIED WHEN YOU DIDN'T WAKE UP FOR TWO MINUTES!
SKRITCH SKRITCH
I'LL LIVE. I JUST FEEL LIKE A BIT OF A TIT, AND NOW I'LL LOSE SOME MONEY FROM WORK, BUT IT COULD BE WORSE, I GUESS.
OH WELL, AT LEAST YOU MISSED THE HORRENDOUS CLEAN-UP. AFTER CLEARING THE CEILING RUBBLE, WE DISCOVERED SOMEONE TOOK A SHIT SO HUGE IT BLOCKED THE TOILET.
TV FROM £4.99
I WAS PLUNGING AWAY FOR *HOURS!*
GROSS. AND ON THAT NOTE I'M GONNA LEAVE YOU! NEED ANYTHING BEFORE I GO?
NO THANKS, I'M GOOD. I'VE BEEN KEEPING MYSELF OCCUPIED WITH THE OTHER PATIENTS...
THE PLACE IS LIKE A *CARRY ON* FILM. IT'S GOOD DRAWING MATERIAL.

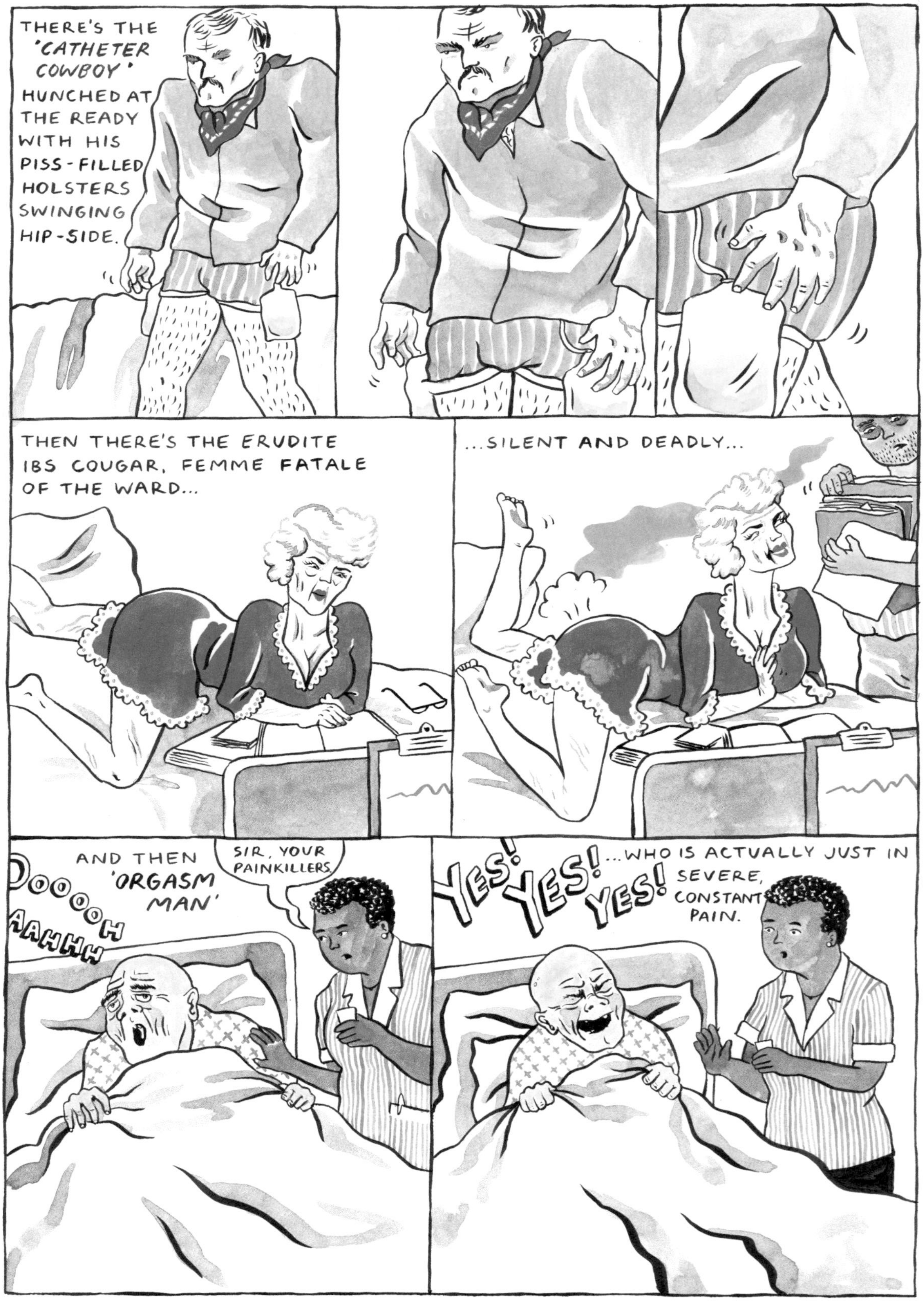
THERE'S THE 'CATHETER COWBOY' HUNCHED AT THE READY WITH HIS PISS-FILLED HOLSTERS SWINGING HIP-SIDE.
THEN THERE'S THE ERUDITE IBS COUGAR, FEMME FATALE OF THE WARD...
...SILENT AND DEADLY...
AND THEN 'ORGASM MAN'
OOOOOH AAHHHH
SIR, YOUR PAINKILLERS
YES! YES! YES!
...WHO IS ACTUALLY JUST IN SEVERE, CONSTANT PAIN.

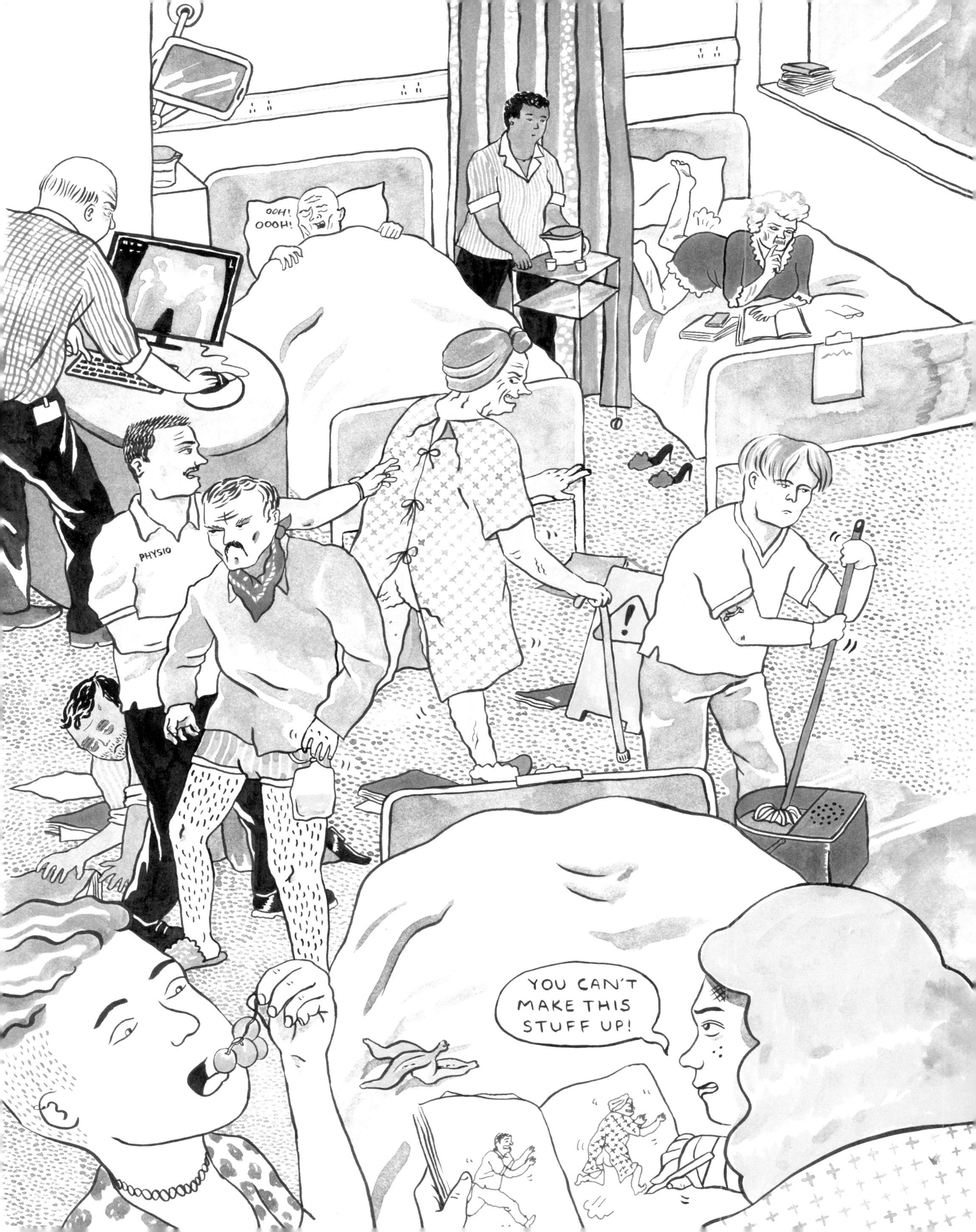
OOH! OOOH!
PHYSIO
YOU CAN'T MAKE THIS STUFF UP!

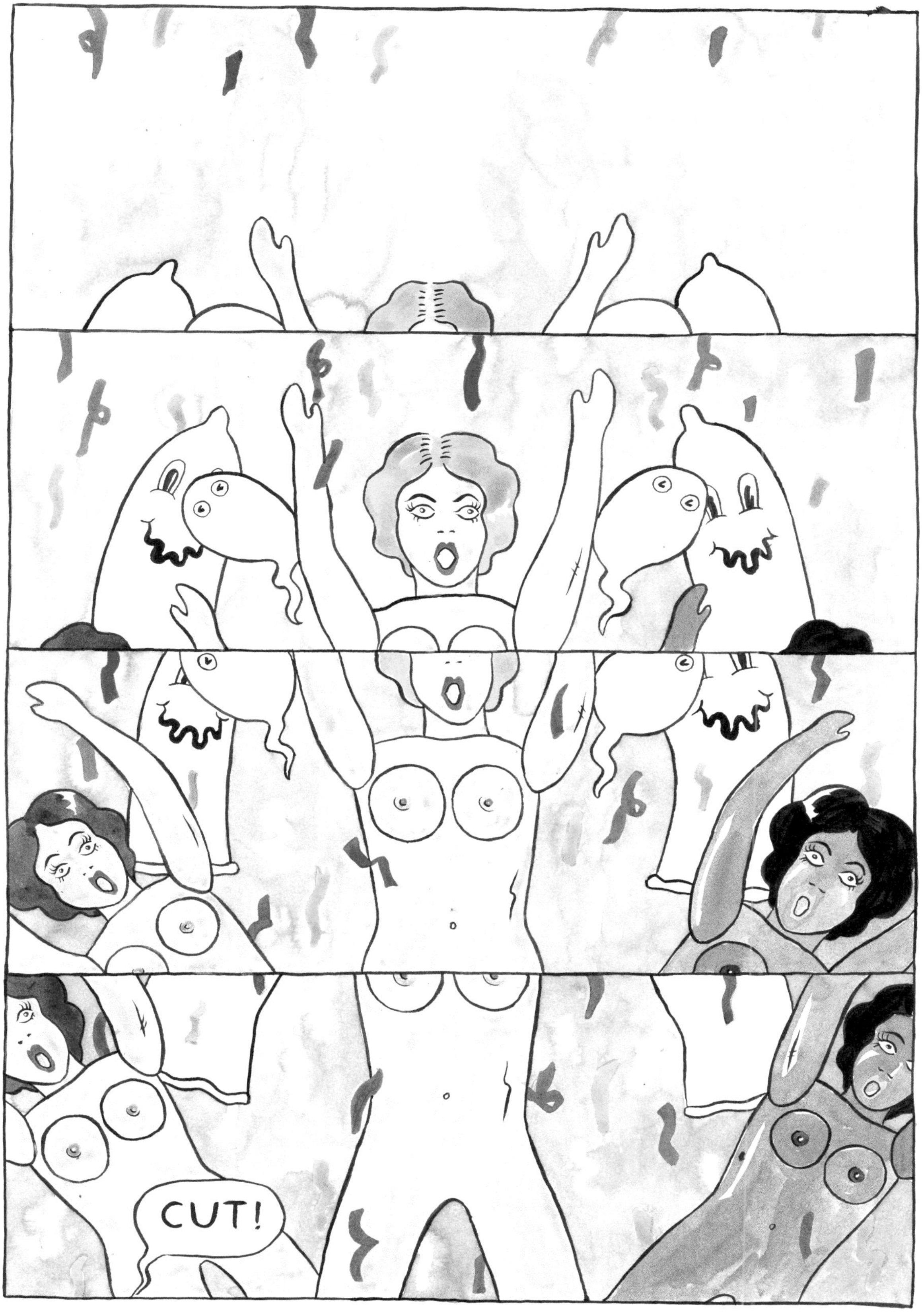
CUT!

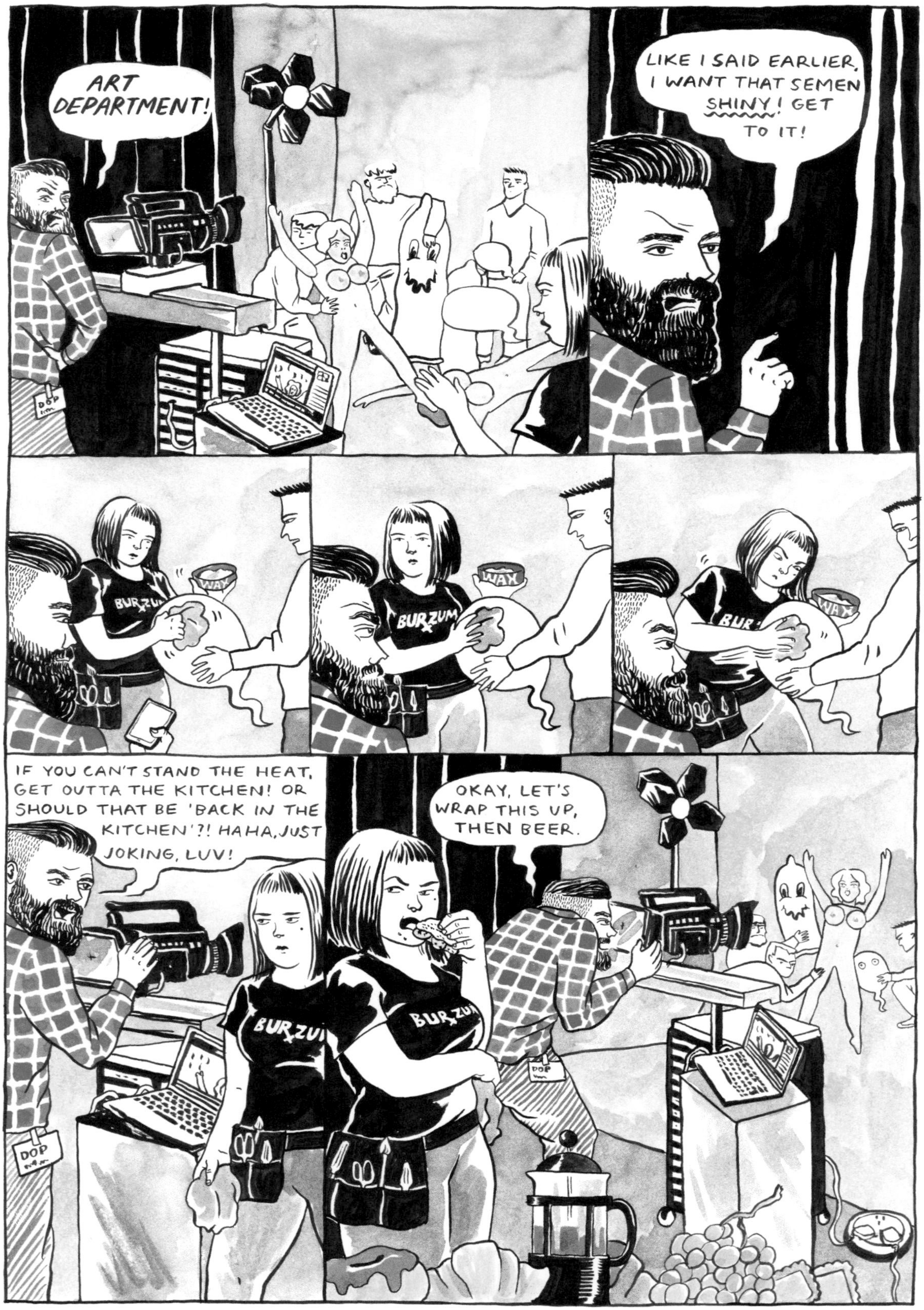
ART DEPARTMENT!
LIKE I SAID EARLIER, I WANT THAT SEMEN SHINY! GET TO IT!
IF YOU CAN'T STAND THE HEAT, GET OUTTA THE KITCHEN! OR SHOULD THAT BE 'BACK IN THE KITCHEN'?! HAHA, JUST JOKING, LUV!
OKAY, LET'S WRAP THIS UP, THEN BEER.

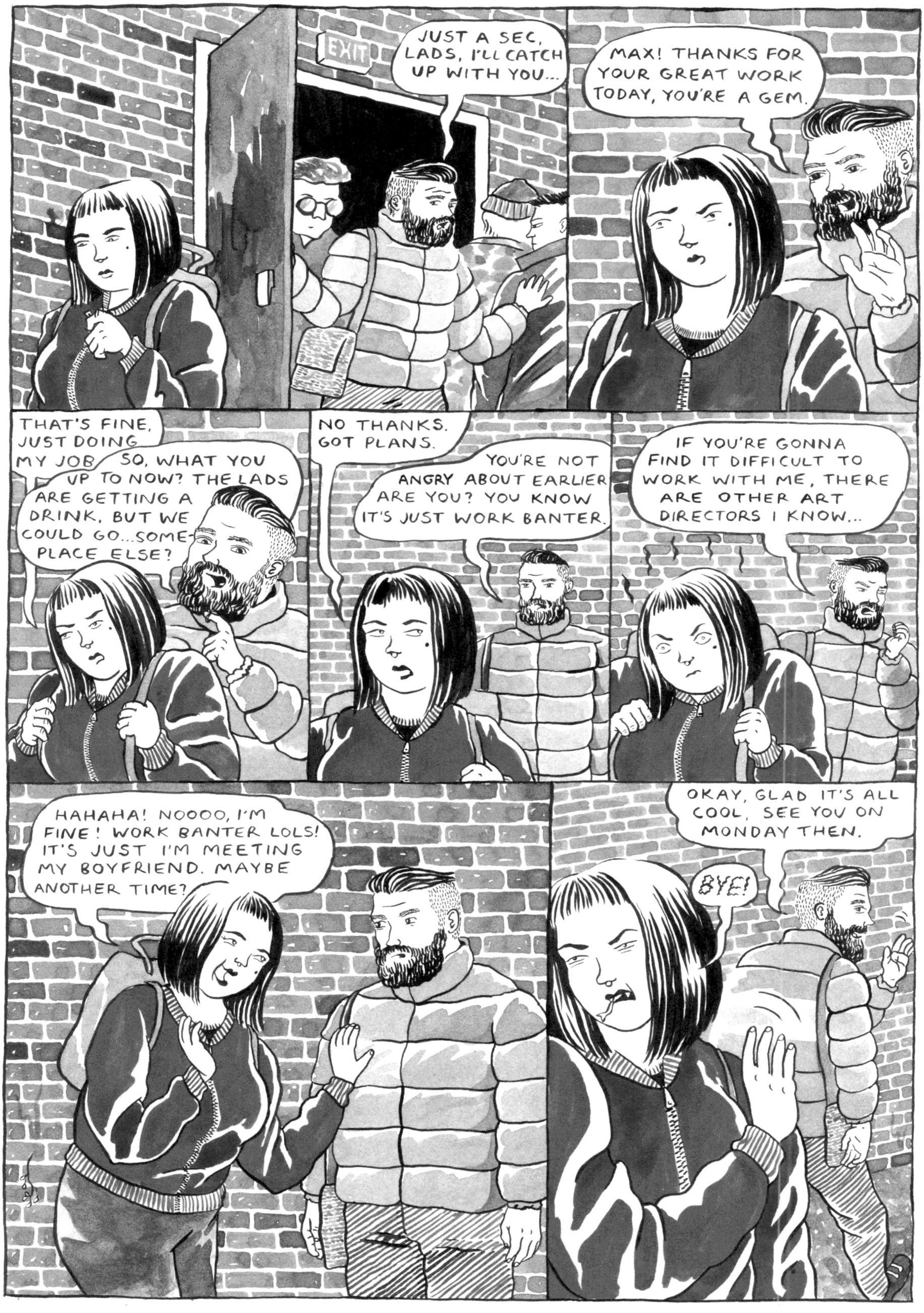
EXIT
JUST A SEC, LADS, I'LL CATCH UP WITH YOU...
MAX! THANKS FOR YOUR GREAT WORK TODAY, YOU'RE A GEM.
THAT'S FINE, JUST DOING MY JOB
SO, WHAT YOU UP TO NOW? THE LADS ARE GETTING A DRINK, BUT WE COULD GO...SOME-PLACE ELSE?
NO THANKS. GOT PLANS.
YOU'RE NOT ANGRY ABOUT EARLIER ARE YOU? YOU KNOW IT'S JUST WORK BANTER.
IF YOU'RE GONNA FIND IT DIFFICULT TO WORK WITH ME, THERE ARE OTHER ART DIRECTORS I KNOW...
HAHAHA! NOOOO, I'M FINE! WORK BANTER LOLS! IT'S JUST I'M MEETING MY BOYFRIEND. MAYBE ANOTHER TIME?
OKAY, GLAD IT'S ALL COOL, SEE YOU ON MONDAY THEN.
BYE!

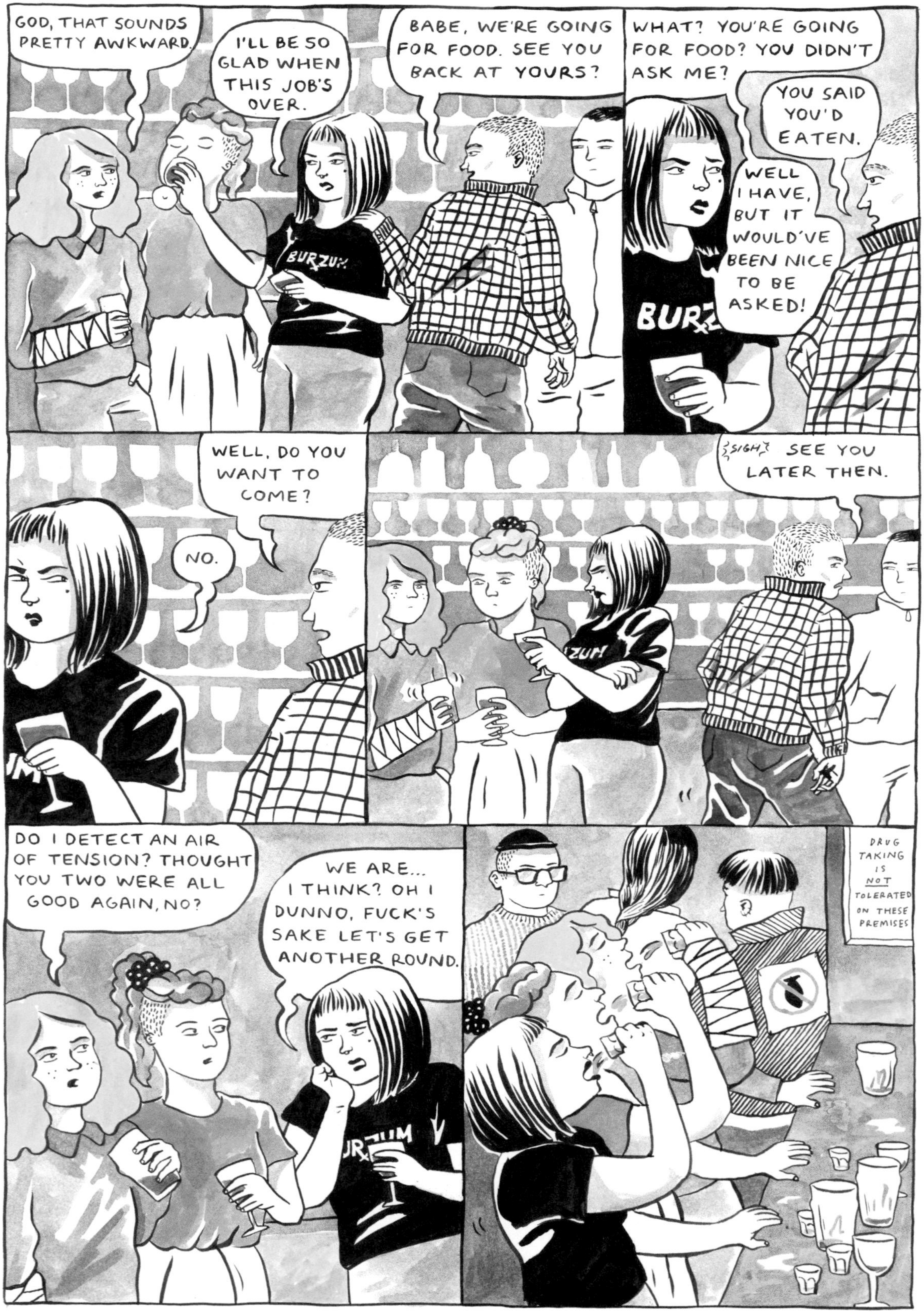
GOD, THAT SOUNDS PRETTY AWKWARD.
I'LL BE SO GLAD WHEN THIS JOB'S OVER.
BURZUM
BABE, WE'RE GOING FOR FOOD. SEE YOU BACK AT YOURS?
WHAT? YOU'RE GOING FOR FOOD? YOU DIDN'T ASK ME?
YOU SAID YOU'D EATEN.
WELL I HAVE, BUT IT WOULD'VE BEEN NICE TO BE ASKED!
WELL, DO YOU WANT TO COME?
NO.
SIGH SEE YOU LATER THEN.
DO I DETECT AN AIR OF TENSION? THOUGHT YOU TWO WERE ALL GOOD AGAIN, NO?
WE ARE... I THINK? OH I DUNNO, FUCK'S SAKE LET'S GET ANOTHER ROUND.
DRUG TAKING IS NOT TOLERATED ON THESE PREMISES

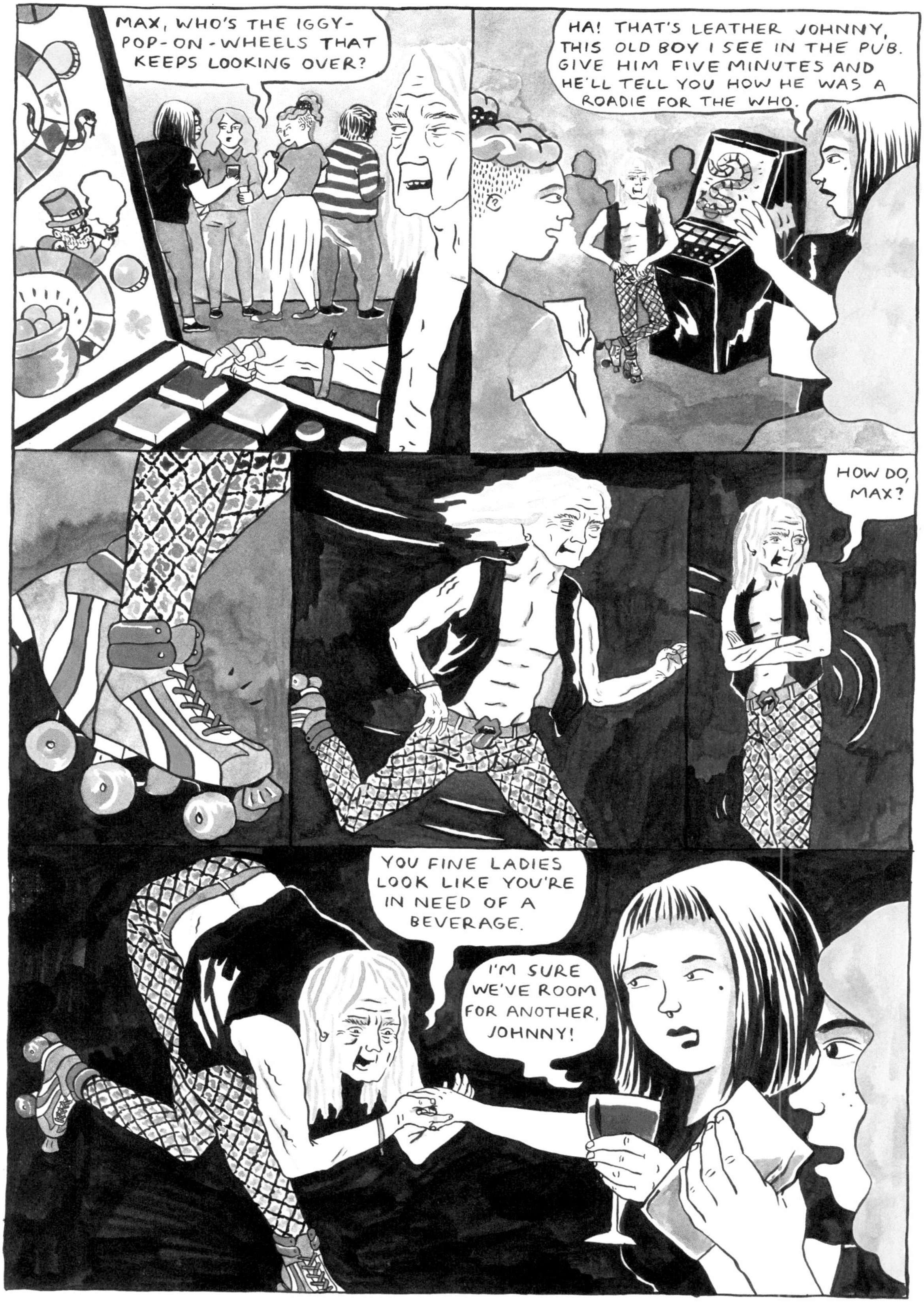
MAX, WHO'S THE IGGY-POP-ON-WHEELS THAT KEEPS LOOKING OVER?
HA! THAT'S LEATHER JOHNNY, THIS OLD BOY I SEE IN THE PUB. GIVE HIM FIVE MINUTES AND HE'LL TELL YOU HOW HE WAS A ROADIE FOR THE WHO.
HOW DO, MAX?
YOU FINE LADIES LOOK LIKE YOU'RE IN NEED OF A BEVERAGE.
I'M SURE WE'VE ROOM FOR ANOTHER, JOHNNY!

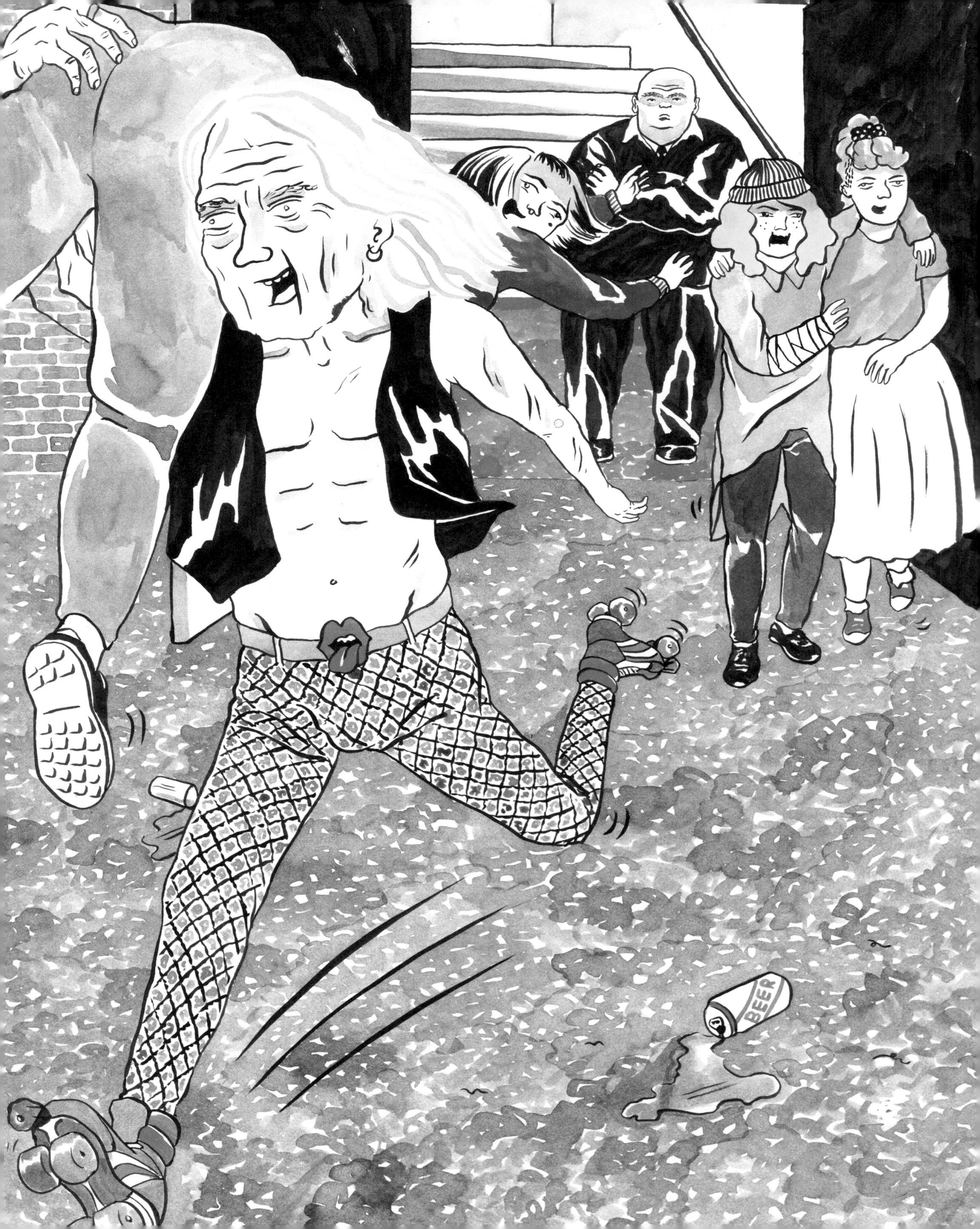
BEER

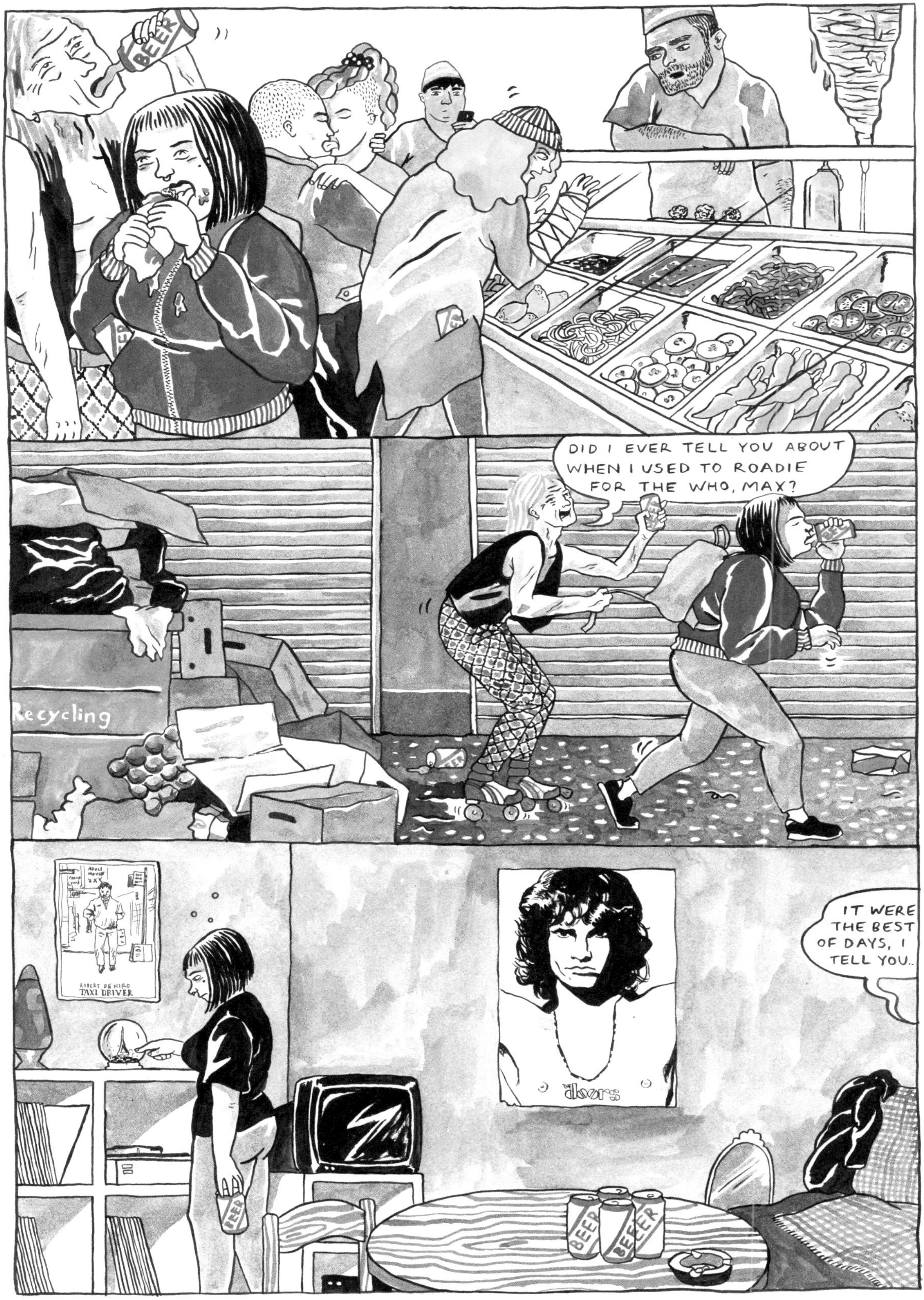
BEER
DID I EVER TELL YOU ABOUT WHEN I USED TO ROADIE FOR THE WHO, MAX?
Recycling
TAXI DRIVER
IT WERE THE BEST OF DAYS, I TELL YOU..
BEER
BEER
BEER

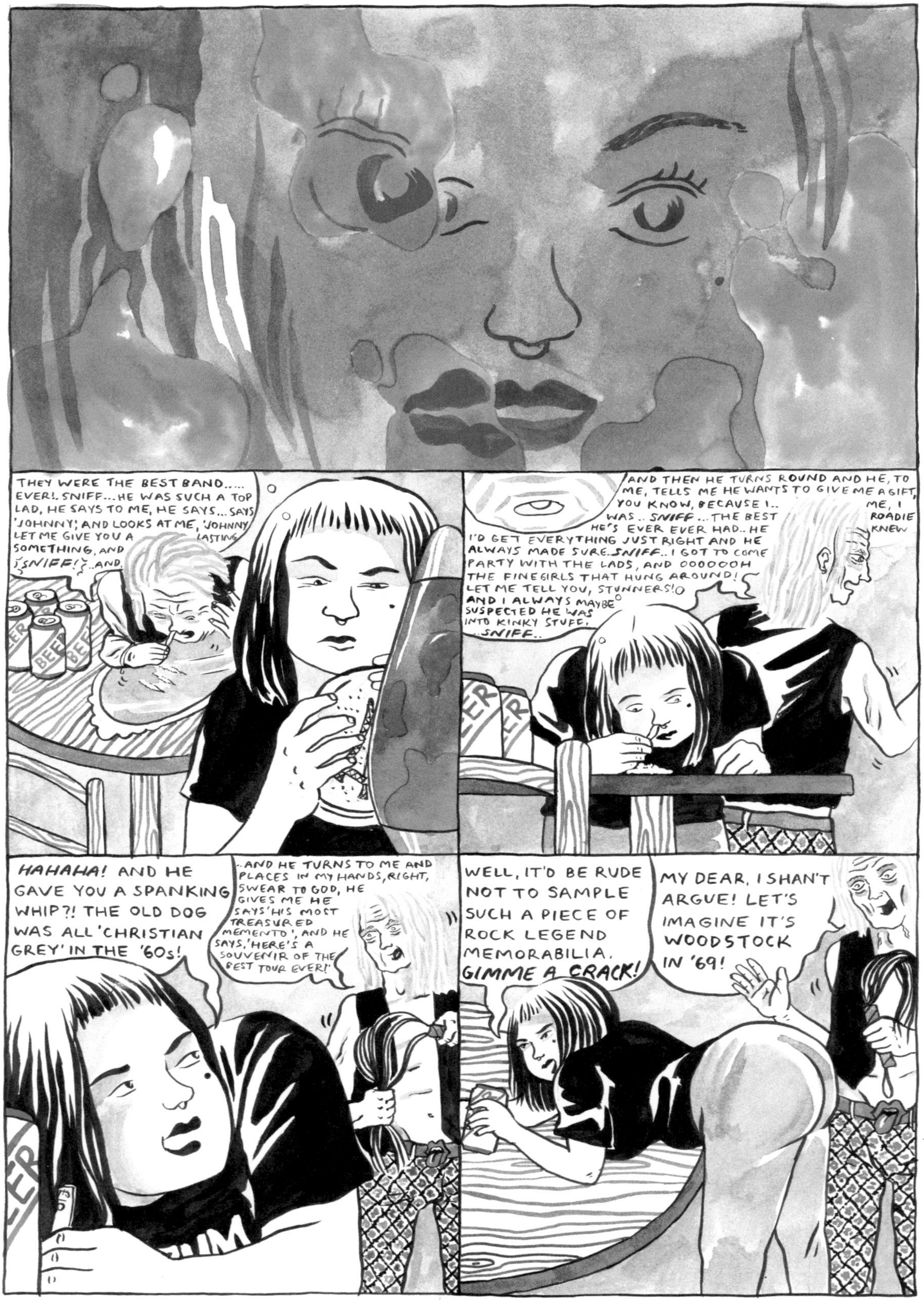
THEY WERE THE BEST BAND..... EVER!. SNIFF... HE WAS SUCH A TOP LAD, HE SAYS TO ME, HE SAYS... SAYS 'JOHNNY', AND LOOKS AT ME, 'JOHNNY LET ME GIVE YOU A LASTING SOMETHING, AND {SNIFF!} ..AND.
AND THEN HE TURNS ROUND AND HE, TO ME, TELLS ME HE WANTS TO GIVE ME A GIFT, YOU KNOW, BECAUSE I.. ME, I WAS.. SNIFF ... THE BEST ROADIE HE'S EVER EVER HAD.. HE KNEW I'D GET EVERYTHING JUST RIGHT AND HE ALWAYS MADE SURE.. SNIFF.. I GOT TO COME PARTY WITH THE LADS, AND OOOOOOH THE FINE GIRLS THAT HUNG AROUND! LET ME TELL YOU, STUNNERS!
AND I ALWAYS MAYBE SUSPECTED HE WAS INTO KINKY STUFF. ..SNIFF..
..AND HE TURNS TO ME AND PLACES IN MY HANDS, RIGHT, SWEAR TO GOD, HE GIVES ME HE SAYS 'HIS MOST TREASURED MEMENTO', AND HE SAYS, 'HERE'S A SOUVENIR OF THE BEST TOUR EVER!'
HAHAHA! AND HE GAVE YOU A SPANKING WHIP?! THE OLD DOG WAS ALL 'CHRISTIAN GREY' IN THE '60s!
WELL, IT'D BE RUDE NOT TO SAMPLE SUCH A PIECE OF ROCK LEGEND MEMORABILIA. GIMME A CRACK!
MY DEAR, I SHAN'T ARGUE! LET'S IMAGINE IT'S WOODSTOCK IN '69!

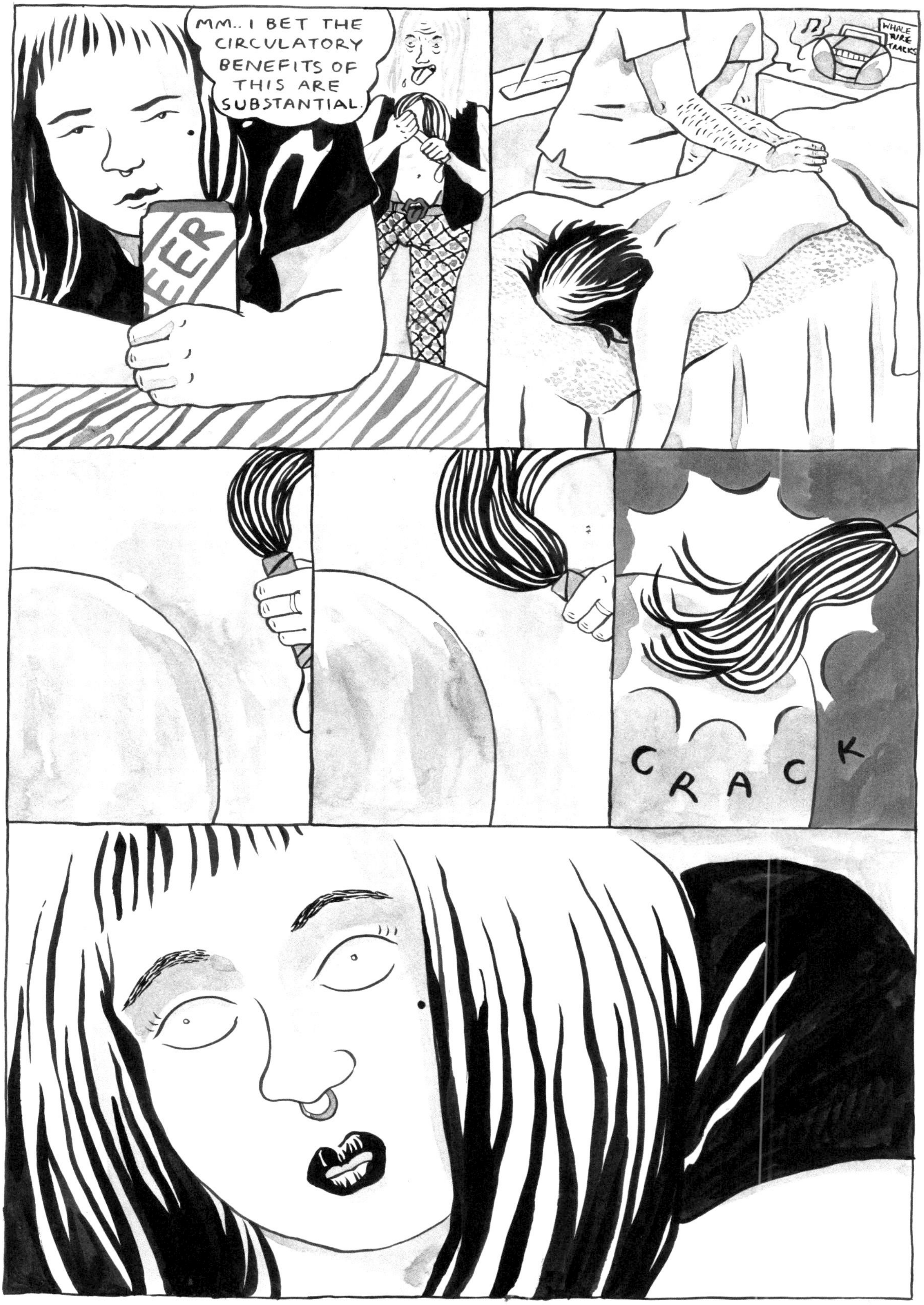
MM.. I BET THE CIRCULATORY BENEFITS OF THIS ARE SUBSTANTIAL.
WHALE
TRACKS
CRACK

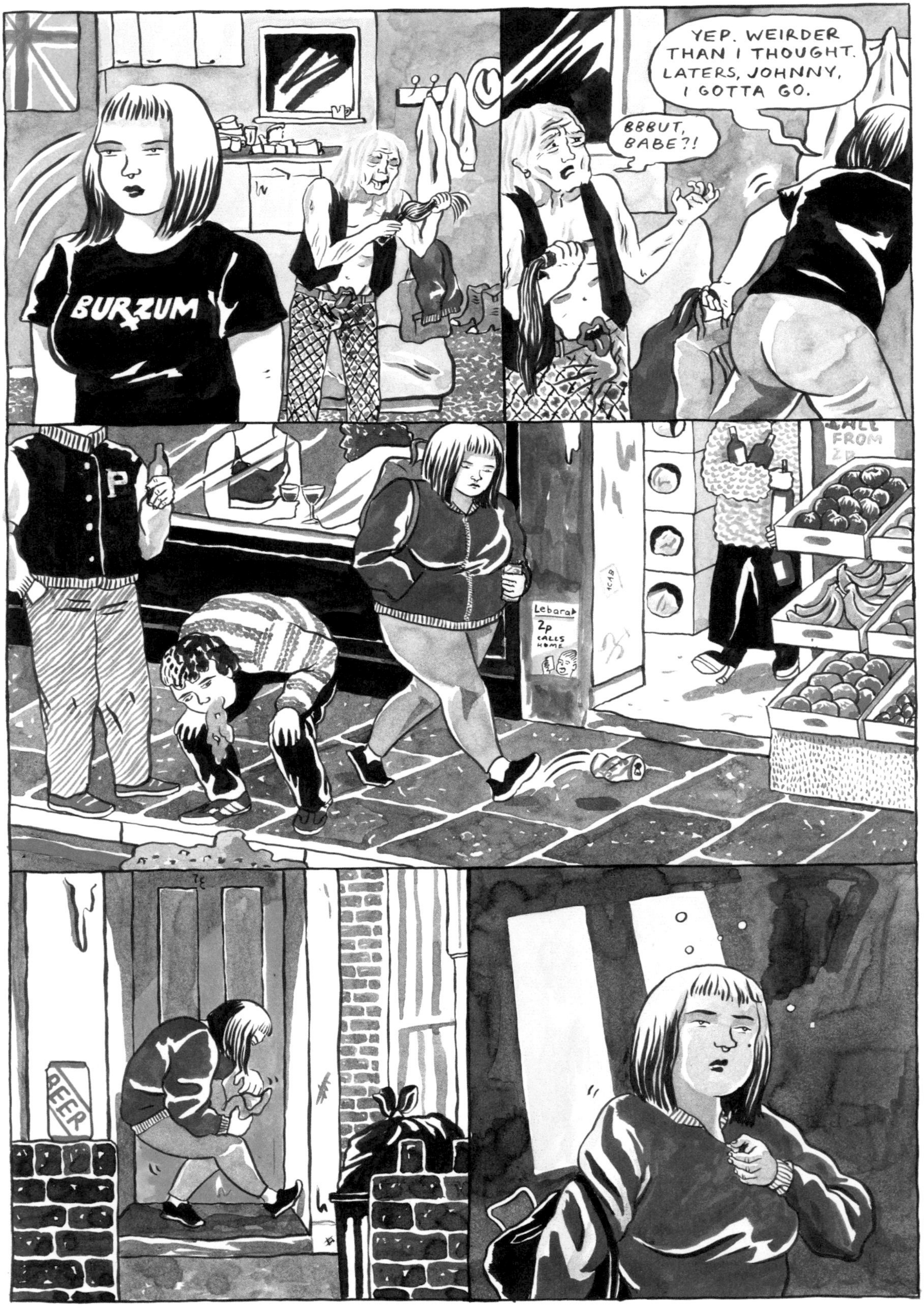
BURZUM
YEP. WEIRDER THAN I THOUGHT. LATERS, JOHNNY, I GOTTA GO.
BBBUT, BABE?!
Lebara
2p CALLS HOME
BEER

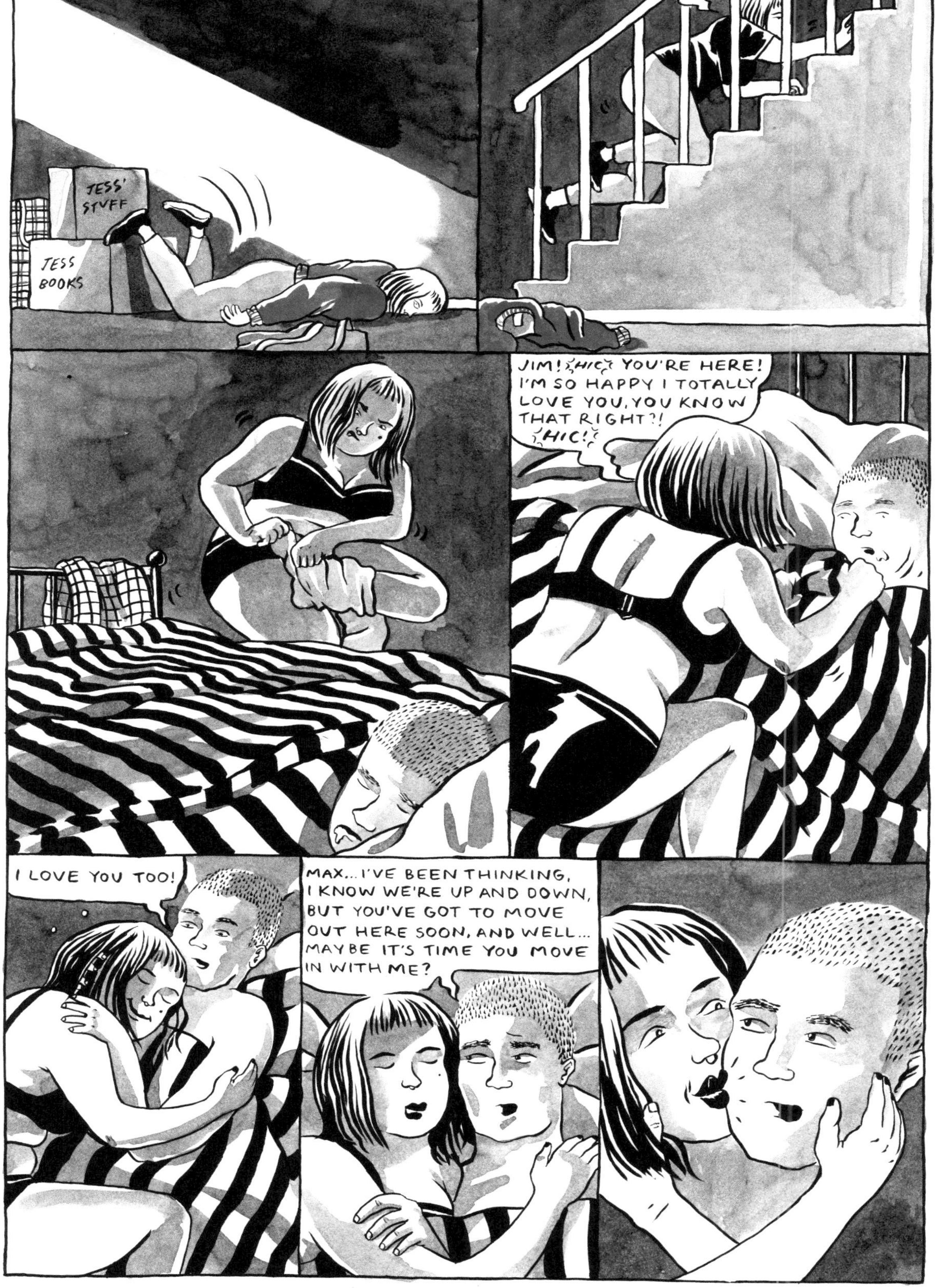
JESS' STUFF
JESS BOOKS
#!@¿!★
JIM! *HIC* YOU'RE HERE! I'M SO HAPPY I TOTALLY LOVE YOU, YOU KNOW THAT RIGHT?! *HIC!*
I LOVE YOU TOO!
MAX... I'VE BEEN THINKING, I KNOW WE'RE UP AND DOWN, BUT YOU'VE GOT TO MOVE OUT HERE SOON, AND WELL... MAYBE IT'S TIME YOU MOVE IN WITH ME?

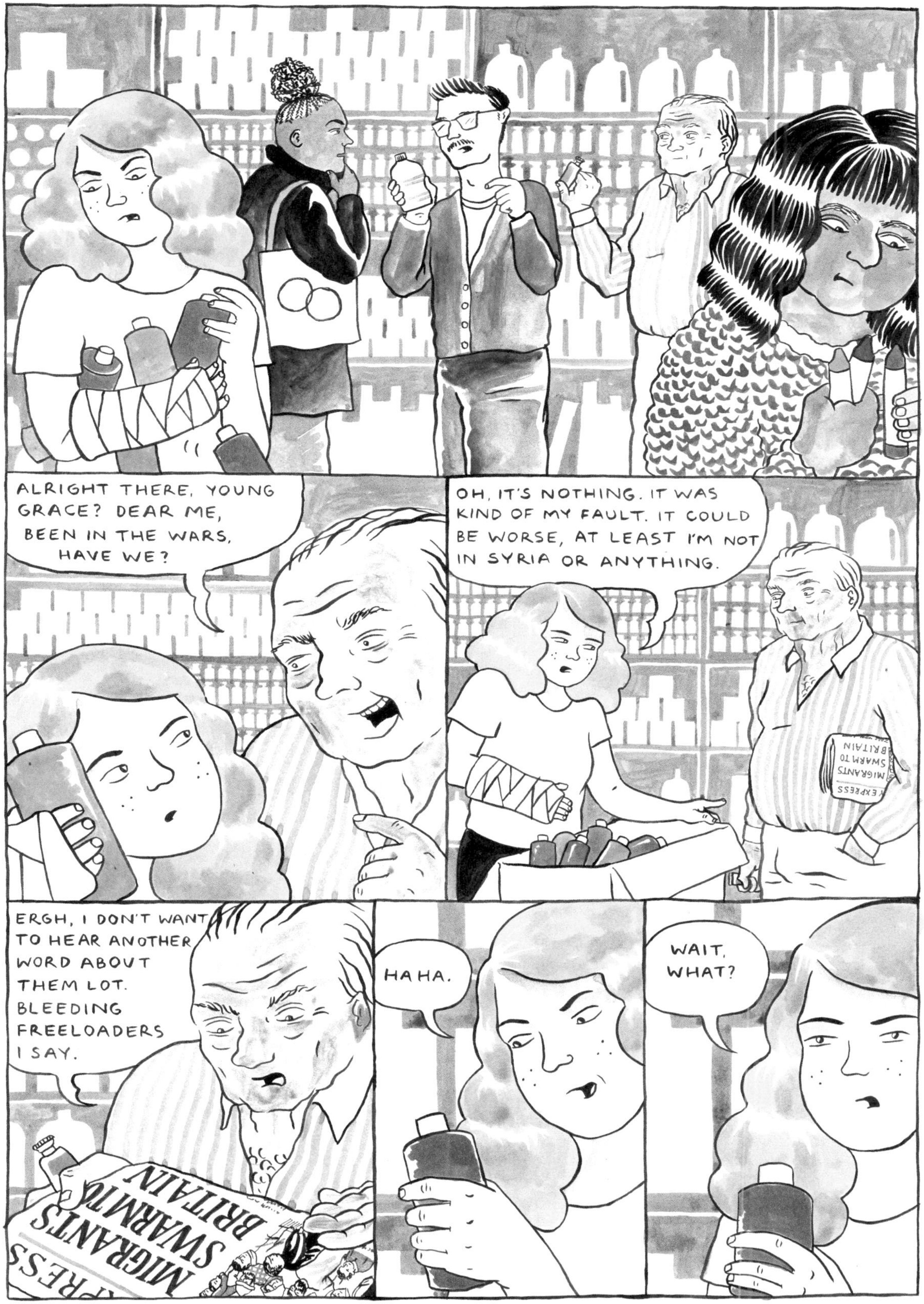
ALRIGHT THERE, YOUNG GRACE? DEAR ME, BEEN IN THE WARS, HAVE WE?
OH, IT'S NOTHING. IT WAS KIND OF MY FAULT. IT COULD BE WORSE, AT LEAST I'M NOT IN SYRIA OR ANYTHING.
EXPRESS MIGRANTS SWARM TO BRITAIN
ERGH, I DON'T WANT TO HEAR ANOTHER WORD ABOUT THEM LOT. BLEEDING FREELOADERS I SAY.
MIGRANTS SWARM TO BRITAIN
HA HA.
WAIT, WHAT?

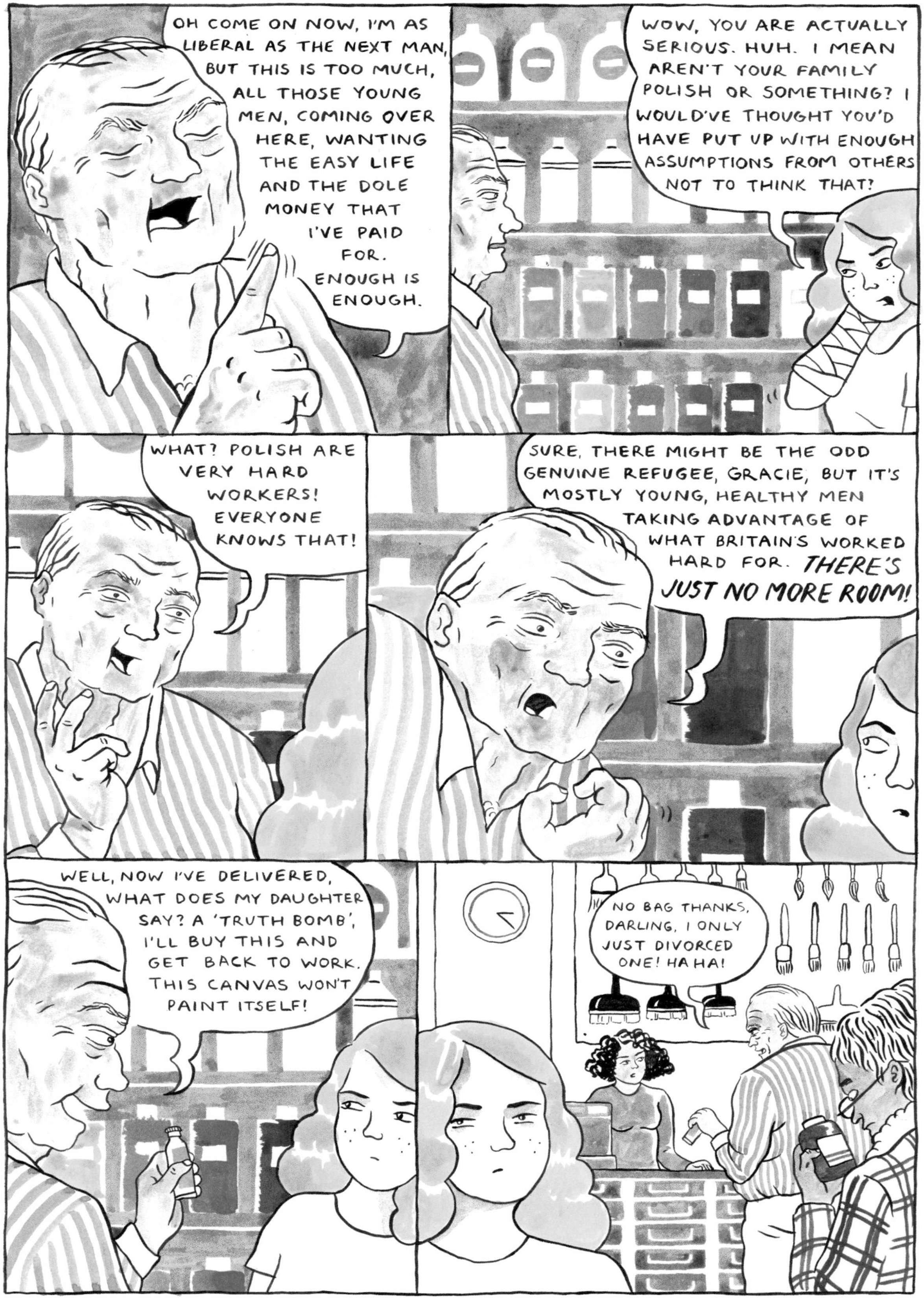
OH COME ON NOW, I'M AS LIBERAL AS THE NEXT MAN, BUT THIS IS TOO MUCH, ALL THOSE YOUNG MEN, COMING OVER HERE, WANTING THE EASY LIFE AND THE DOLE MONEY THAT I'VE PAID FOR. ENOUGH IS ENOUGH.
WOW, YOU ARE ACTUALLY SERIOUS. HUH. I MEAN AREN'T YOUR FAMILY POLISH OR SOMETHING? I WOULD'VE THOUGHT YOU'D HAVE PUT UP WITH ENOUGH ASSUMPTIONS FROM OTHERS NOT TO THINK THAT?
WHAT? POLISH ARE VERY HARD WORKERS! EVERYONE KNOWS THAT!
SURE, THERE MIGHT BE THE ODD GENUINE REFUGEE, GRACIE, BUT IT'S MOSTLY YOUNG, HEALTHY MEN TAKING ADVANTAGE OF WHAT BRITAIN'S WORKED HARD FOR. THERE'S JUST NO MORE ROOM!
WELL, NOW I'VE DELIVERED, WHAT DOES MY DAUGHTER SAY? A 'TRUTH BOMB', I'LL BUY THIS AND GET BACK TO WORK. THIS CANVAS WON'T PAINT ITSELF!
NO BAG THANKS, DARLING, I ONLY JUST DIVORCED ONE! HA HA!

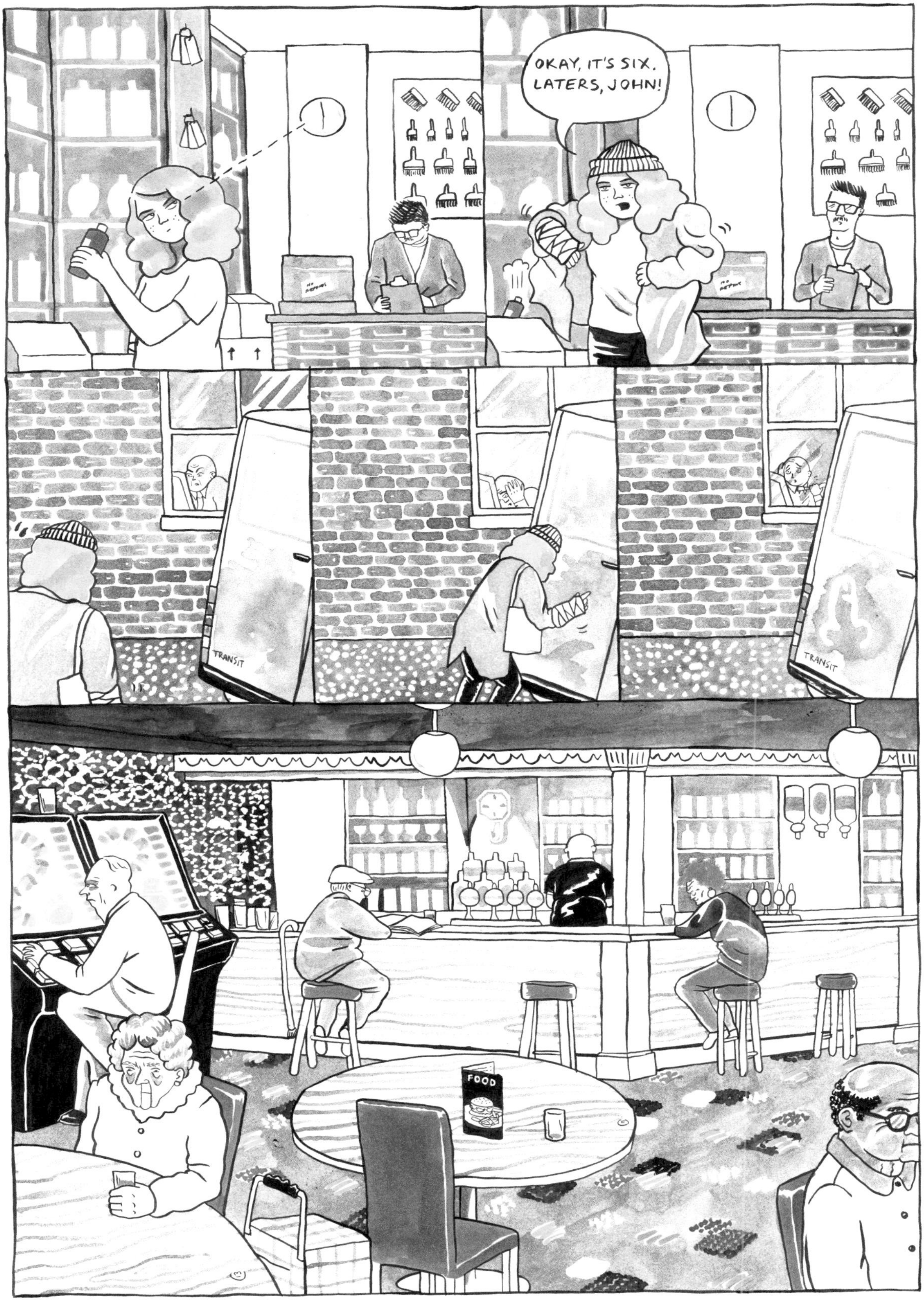
OKAY, IT'S SIX.
LATERS, JOHN!
TRANSIT
TRANSIT
FOOD

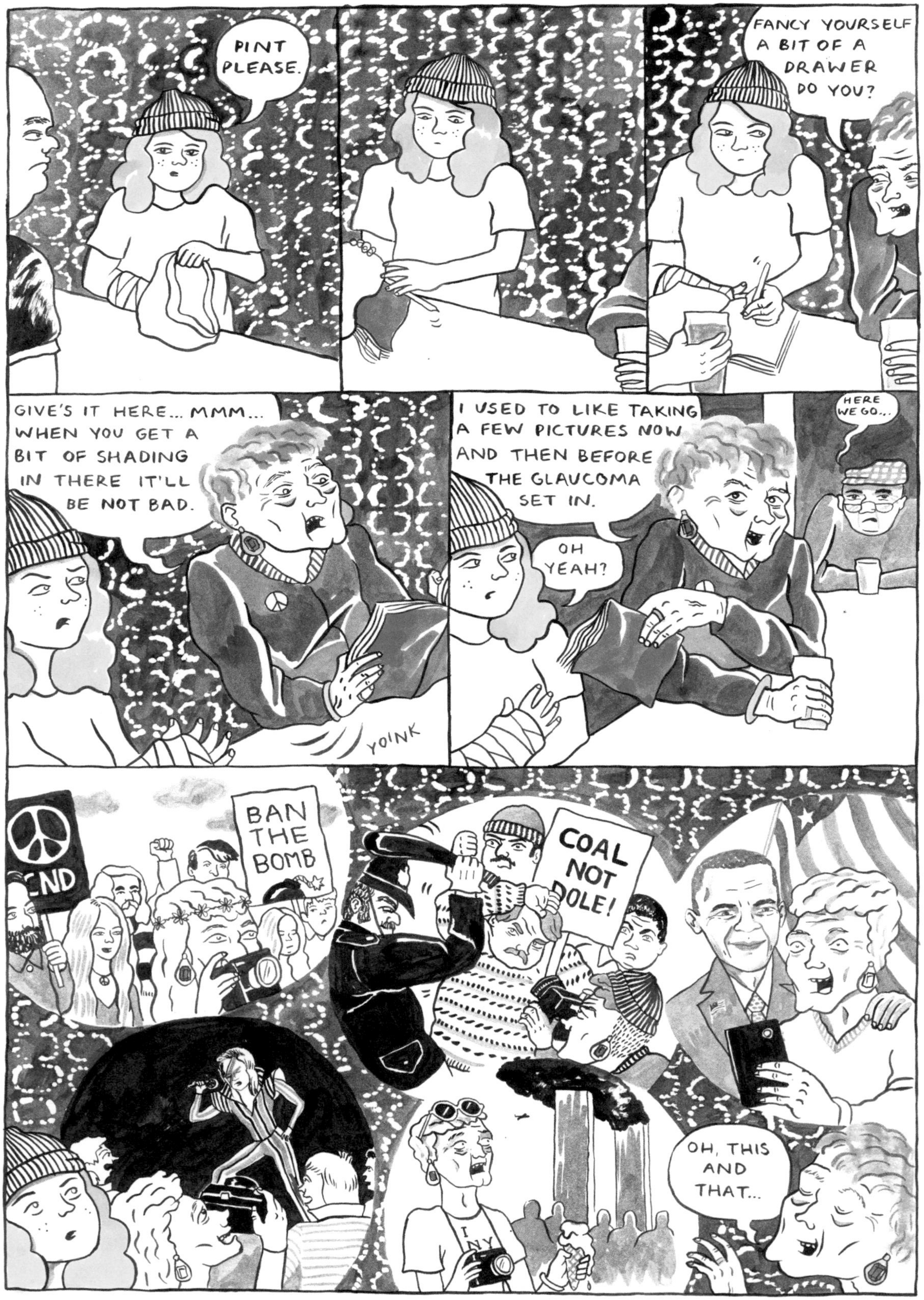
PINT PLEASE.
FANCY YOURSELF A BIT OF A DRAWER DO YOU?
GIVE'S IT HERE... MMM... WHEN YOU GET A BIT OF SHADING IN THERE IT'LL BE NOT BAD.
YOINK
I USED TO LIKE TAKING A FEW PICTURES NOW AND THEN BEFORE THE GLAUCOMA SET IN.
HERE WE GO...
OH YEAH?
CND
BAN THE BOMB
COAL NOT DOLE!
I NY
OH, THIS AND THAT...

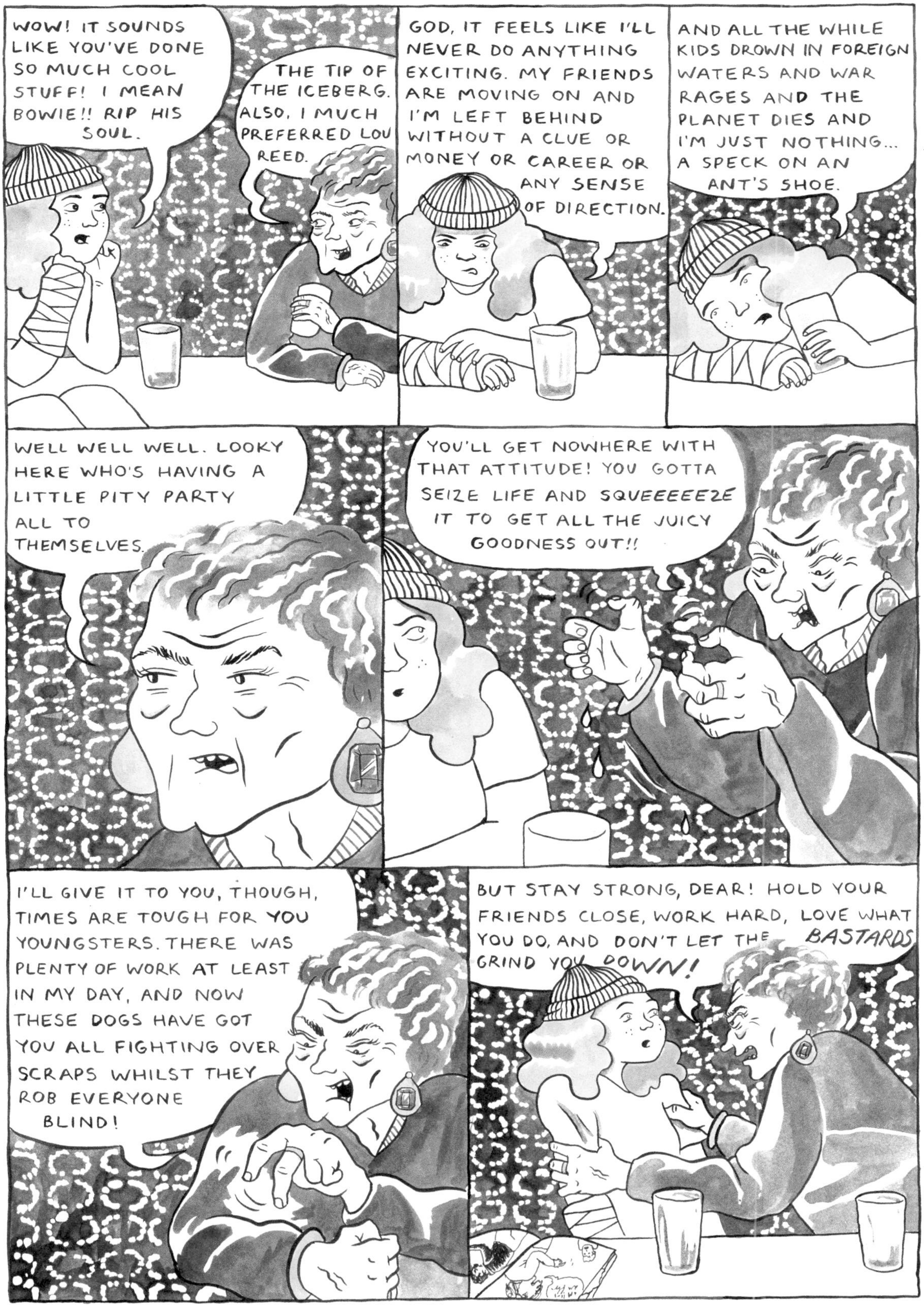
WOW! IT SOUNDS LIKE YOU'VE DONE SO MUCH COOL STUFF! I MEAN BOWIE!! RIP HIS SOUL.
THE TIP OF THE ICEBERG. ALSO, I MUCH PREFERRED LOU REED.
GOD, IT FEELS LIKE I'LL NEVER DO ANYTHING EXCITING. MY FRIENDS ARE MOVING ON AND I'M LEFT BEHIND WITHOUT A CLUE OR MONEY OR CAREER OR ANY SENSE OF DIRECTION.
AND ALL THE WHILE KIDS DROWN IN FOREIGN WATERS AND WAR RAGES AND THE PLANET DIES AND I'M JUST NOTHING... A SPECK ON AN ANT'S SHOE.
WELL WELL WELL. LOOKY HERE WHO'S HAVING A LITTLE PITY PARTY ALL TO THEMSELVES.
YOU'LL GET NOWHERE WITH THAT ATTITUDE! YOU GOTTA SEIZE LIFE AND SQUEEEEEZE IT TO GET ALL THE JUICY GOODNESS OUT!!
I'LL GIVE IT TO YOU, THOUGH, TIMES ARE TOUGH FOR YOU YOUNGSTERS. THERE WAS PLENTY OF WORK AT LEAST IN MY DAY, AND NOW THESE DOGS HAVE GOT YOU ALL FIGHTING OVER SCRAPS WHILST THEY ROB EVERYONE BLIND!
BUT STAY STRONG, DEAR! HOLD YOUR FRIENDS CLOSE, WORK HARD, LOVE WHAT YOU DO, AND DON'T LET THE BASTARDS GRIND YOU DOWN!

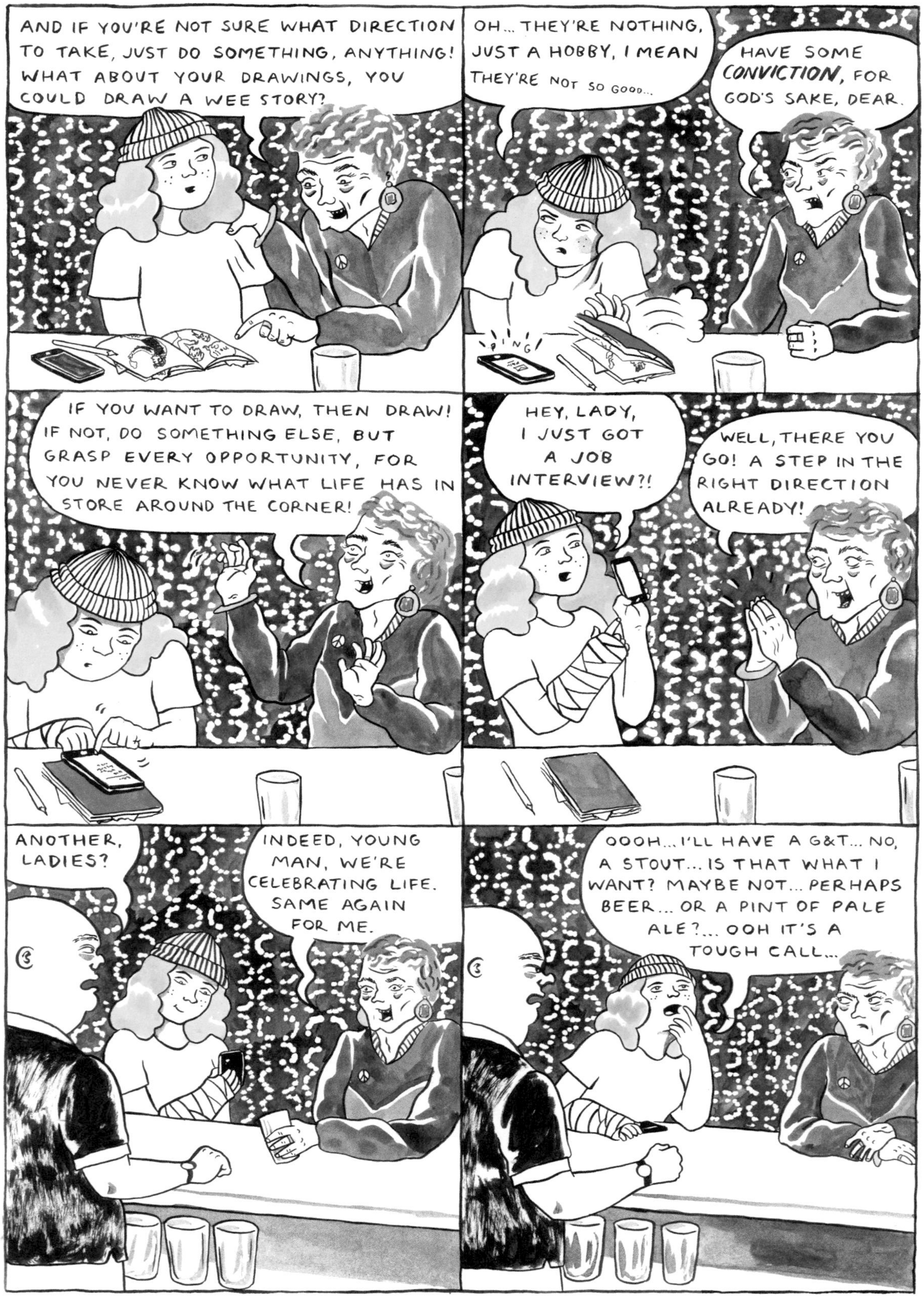
AND IF YOU'RE NOT SURE WHAT DIRECTION TO TAKE, JUST DO SOMETHING, ANYTHING! WHAT ABOUT YOUR DRAWINGS, YOU COULD DRAW A WEE STORY?
OH... THEY'RE NOTHING, JUST A HOBBY, I MEAN THEY'RE NOT SO GOOD...
HAVE SOME CONVICTION, FOR GOD'S SAKE, DEAR.
PING!
IF YOU WANT TO DRAW, THEN DRAW! IF NOT, DO SOMETHING ELSE, BUT GRASP EVERY OPPORTUNITY, FOR YOU NEVER KNOW WHAT LIFE HAS IN STORE AROUND THE CORNER!
HEY, LADY, I JUST GOT A JOB INTERVIEW?!
WELL, THERE YOU GO! A STEP IN THE RIGHT DIRECTION ALREADY!
ANOTHER, LADIES?
INDEED, YOUNG MAN, WE'RE CELEBRATING LIFE. SAME AGAIN FOR ME.
OOOH... I'LL HAVE A G&T... NO, A STOUT... IS THAT WHAT I WANT? MAYBE NOT... PERHAPS BEER... OR A PINT OF PALE ALE?... OOH IT'S A TOUGH CALL...

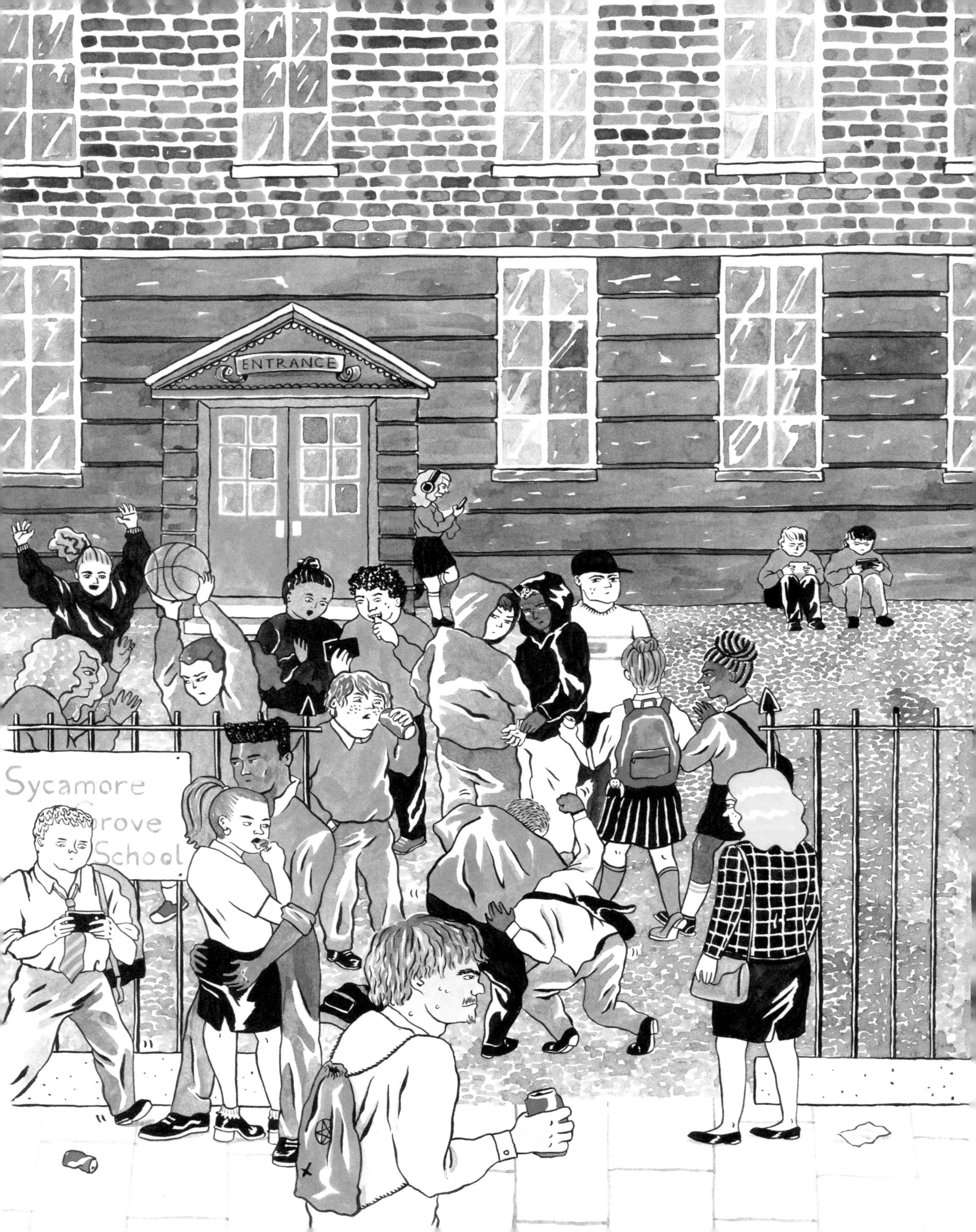
ENTRANCE
Sycamore
Grove
School

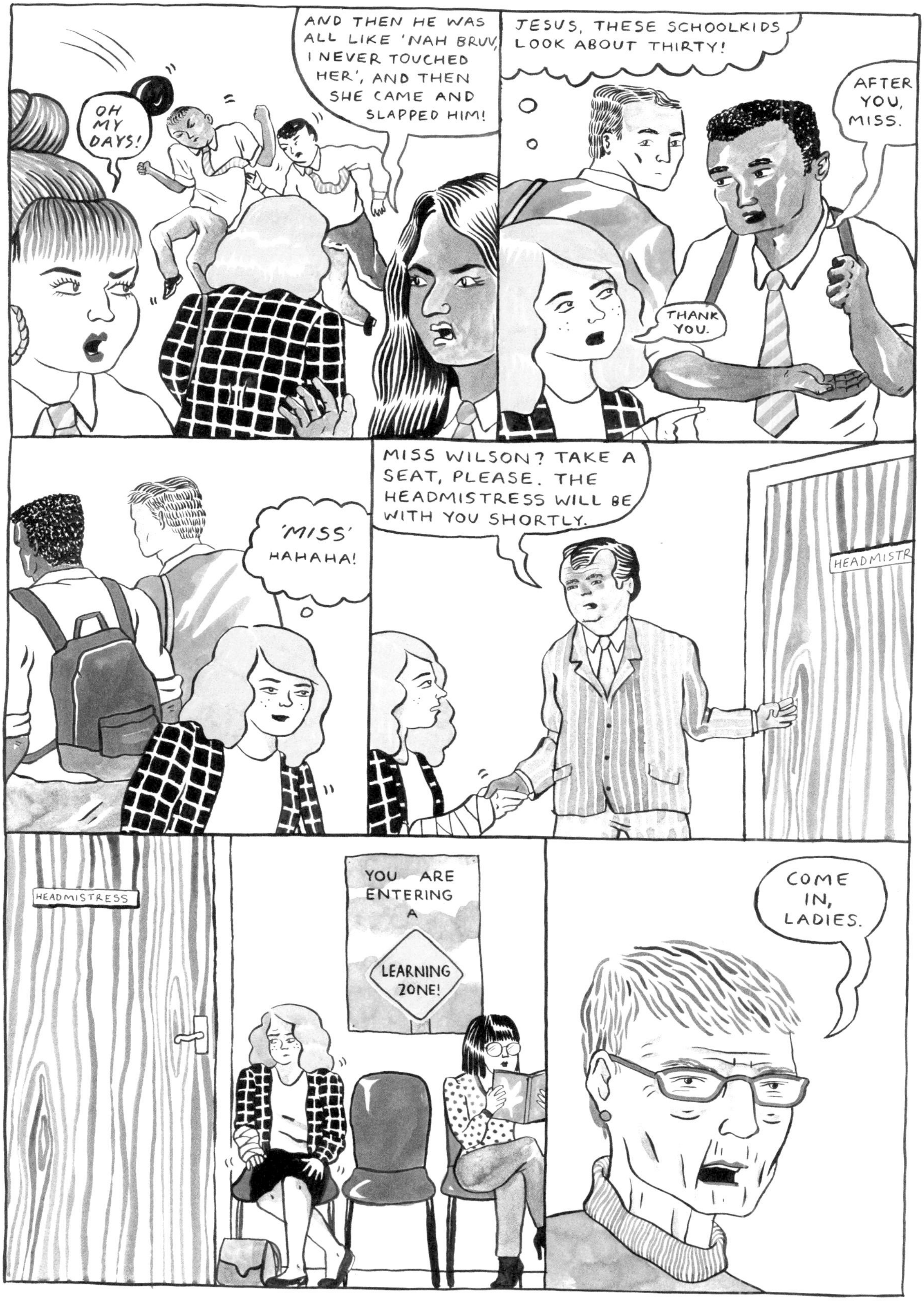
OH MY DAYS!
AND THEN HE WAS ALL LIKE 'NAH BRUV, I NEVER TOUCHED HER', AND THEN SHE CAME AND SLAPPED HIM!
JESUS, THESE SCHOOLKIDS LOOK ABOUT THIRTY!
AFTER YOU, MISS.
THANK YOU.
'MISS' HAHAHA!
MISS WILSON? TAKE A SEAT, PLEASE. THE HEADMISTRESS WILL BE WITH YOU SHORTLY.
HEADMISTR
HEADMISTRESS
YOU ARE ENTERING A
LEARNING ZONE!
COME IN, LADIES.

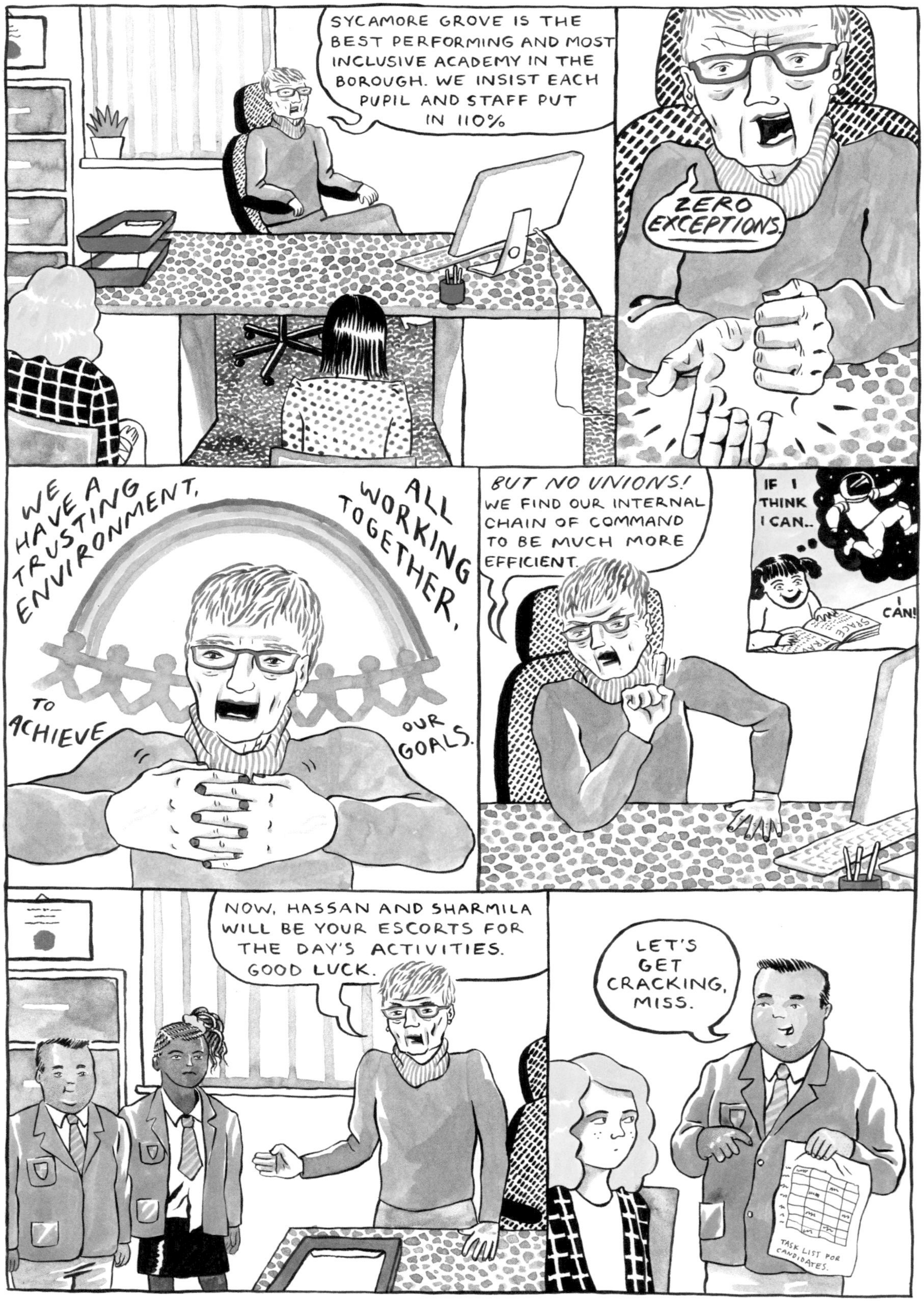
SYCAMORE GROVE IS THE BEST PERFORMING AND MOST INCLUSIVE ACADEMY IN THE BOROUGH. WE INSIST EACH PUPIL AND STAFF PUT IN 110%
ZERO EXCEPTIONS.
WE HAVE A TRUSTING ENVIRONMENT,
ALL WORKING TOGETHER,
TO ACHIEVE
OUR GOALS.
BUT NO UNIONS!
WE FIND OUR INTERNAL CHAIN OF COMMAND TO BE MUCH MORE EFFICIENT.
IF I THINK I CAN..
I CAN!
NOW, HASSAN AND SHARMILA WILL BE YOUR ESCORTS FOR THE DAY'S ACTIVITIES. GOOD LUCK.
LET'S GET CRACKING, MISS.
TASK LIST FOR CANDIDATES.

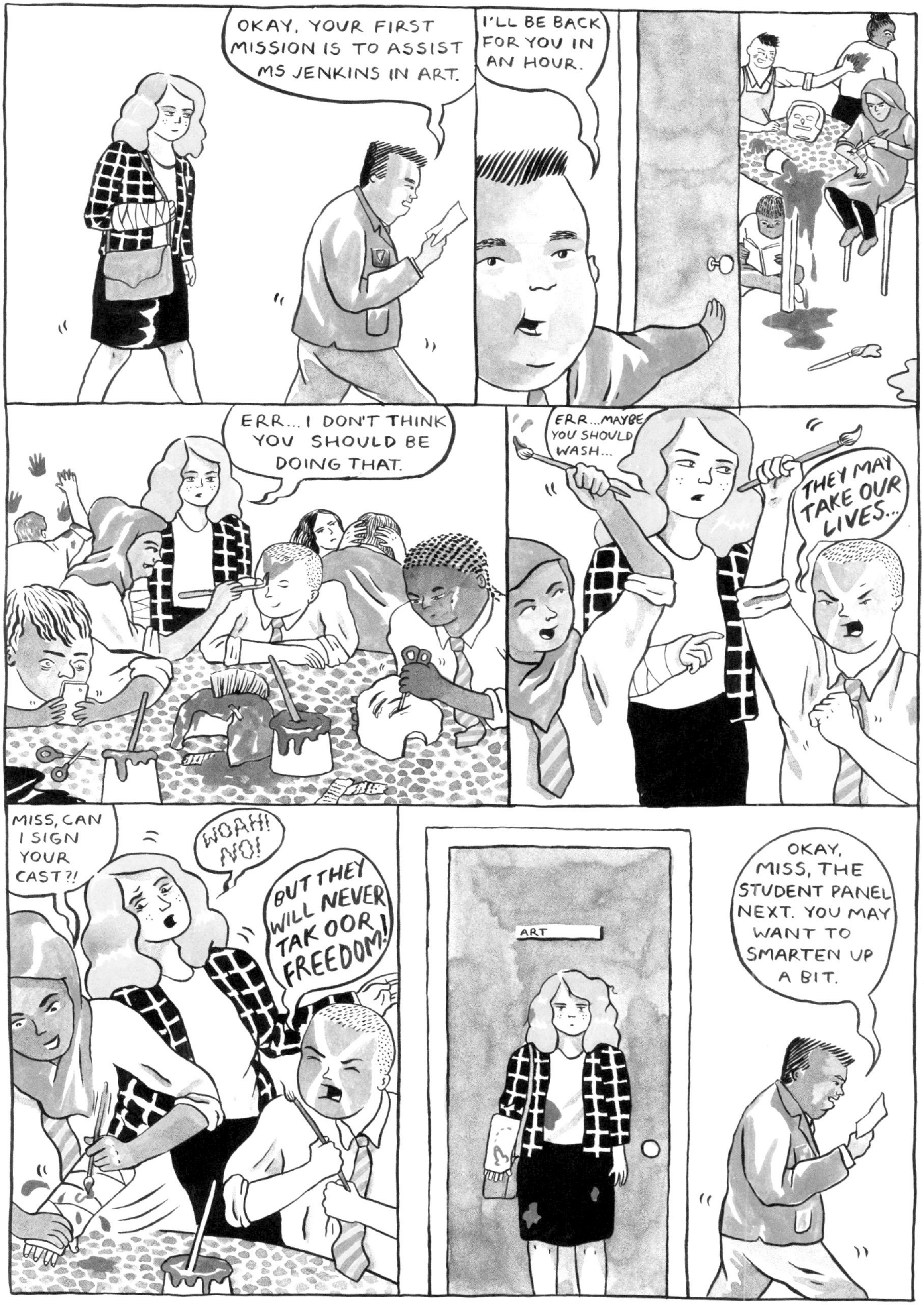
OKAY, YOUR FIRST MISSION IS TO ASSIST MS JENKINS IN ART.
I'LL BE BACK FOR YOU IN AN HOUR.
ERR... I DON'T THINK YOU SHOULD BE DOING THAT.
ERR...MAYBE YOU SHOULD WASH...
THEY MAY TAKE OUR LIVES...
MISS, CAN I SIGN YOUR CAST?!
WOAH! NO!
BUT THEY WILL NEVER TAK OOR FREEDOM!
ART
OKAY, MISS, THE STUDENT PANEL NEXT. YOU MAY WANT TO SMARTEN UP A BIT.

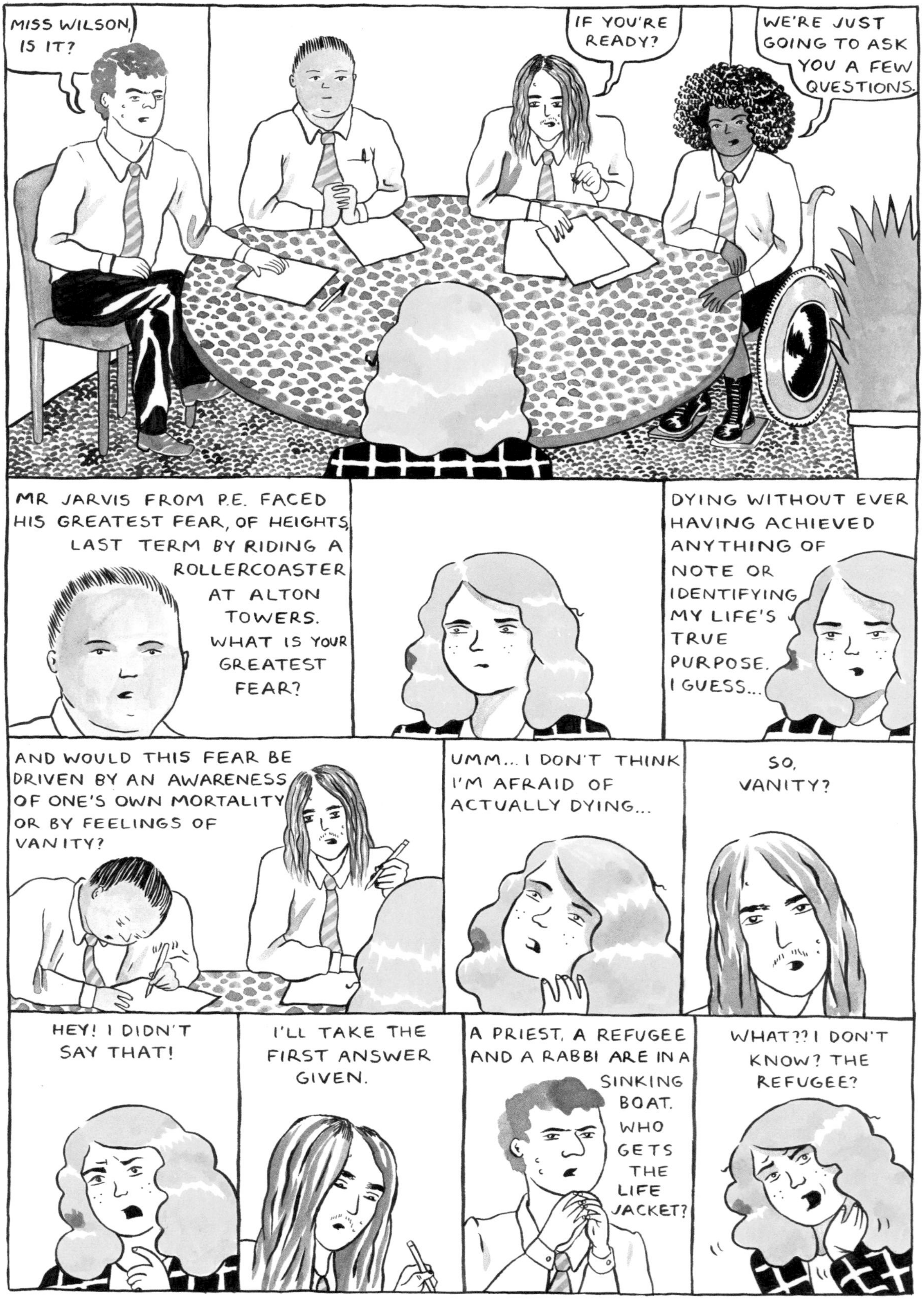
MISS WILSON, IS IT?
IF YOU'RE READY?
WE'RE JUST GOING TO ASK YOU A FEW QUESTIONS.
MR JARVIS FROM P.E. FACED HIS GREATEST FEAR, OF HEIGHTS, LAST TERM BY RIDING A ROLLERCOASTER AT ALTON TOWERS. WHAT IS YOUR GREATEST FEAR?
DYING WITHOUT EVER HAVING ACHIEVED ANYTHING OF NOTE OR IDENTIFYING MY LIFE'S TRUE PURPOSE. I GUESS...
AND WOULD THIS FEAR BE DRIVEN BY AN AWARENESS OF ONE'S OWN MORTALITY OR BY FEELINGS OF VANITY?
UMM... I DON'T THINK I'M AFRAID OF ACTUALLY DYING...
SO, VANITY?
HEY! I DIDN'T SAY THAT!
I'LL TAKE THE FIRST ANSWER GIVEN.
A PRIEST, A REFUGEE AND A RABBI ARE IN A SINKING BOAT. WHO GETS THE LIFE JACKET?
WHAT?? I DON'T KNOW? THE REFUGEE?

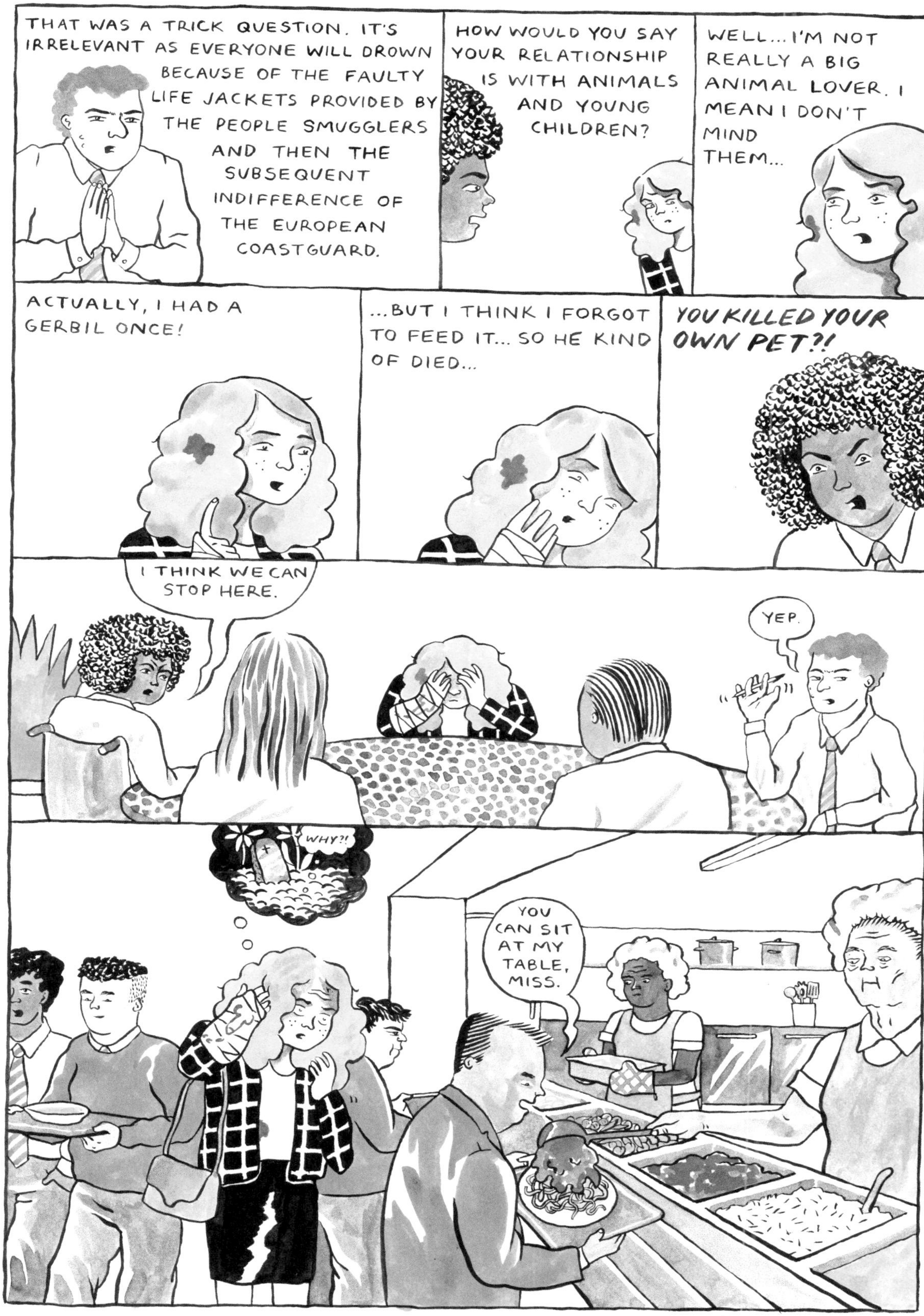
THAT WAS A TRICK QUESTION. IT'S IRRELEVANT AS EVERYONE WILL DROWN BECAUSE OF THE FAULTY LIFE JACKETS PROVIDED BY THE PEOPLE SMUGGLERS AND THEN THE SUBSEQUENT INDIFFERENCE OF THE EUROPEAN COASTGUARD.
HOW WOULD YOU SAY YOUR RELATIONSHIP IS WITH ANIMALS AND YOUNG CHILDREN?
WELL... I'M NOT REALLY A BIG ANIMAL LOVER. I MEAN I DON'T MIND THEM...
ACTUALLY, I HAD A GERBIL ONCE!
...BUT I THINK I FORGOT TO FEED IT... SO HE KIND OF DIED...
YOU KILLED YOUR OWN PET?!
I THINK WE CAN STOP HERE.
YEP.
WHY?!
YOU CAN SIT AT MY TABLE, MISS.

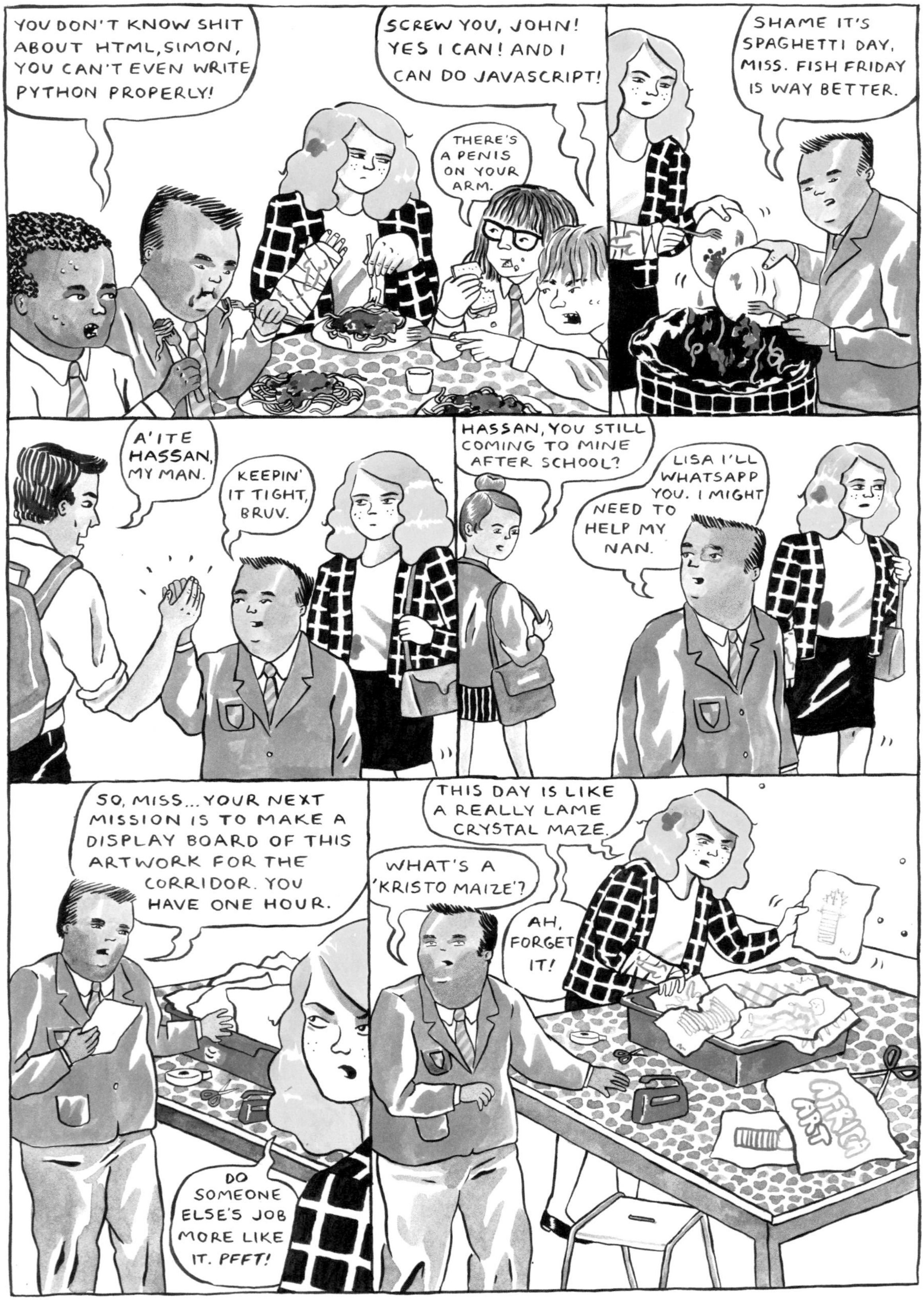
YOU DON'T KNOW SHIT ABOUT HTML, SIMON, YOU CAN'T EVEN WRITE PYTHON PROPERLY!
SCREW YOU, JOHN! YES I CAN! AND I CAN DO JAVASCRIPT!
THERE'S A PENIS ON YOUR ARM.
SHAME IT'S SPAGHETTI DAY, MISS. FISH FRIDAY IS WAY BETTER.
A'ITE HASSAN, MY MAN.
KEEPIN' IT TIGHT, BRUV.
HASSAN, YOU STILL COMING TO MINE AFTER SCHOOL?
LISA I'LL WHATSAPP YOU. I MIGHT NEED TO HELP MY NAN.
SO, MISS... YOUR NEXT MISSION IS TO MAKE A DISPLAY BOARD OF THIS ARTWORK FOR THE CORRIDOR. YOU HAVE ONE HOUR.
DO SOMEONE ELSE'S JOB MORE LIKE IT. PFFT!
THIS DAY IS LIKE A REALLY LAME CRYSTAL MAZE.
WHAT'S A 'KRISTO MAIZE'?
AH, FORGET IT!
AFRICA ART

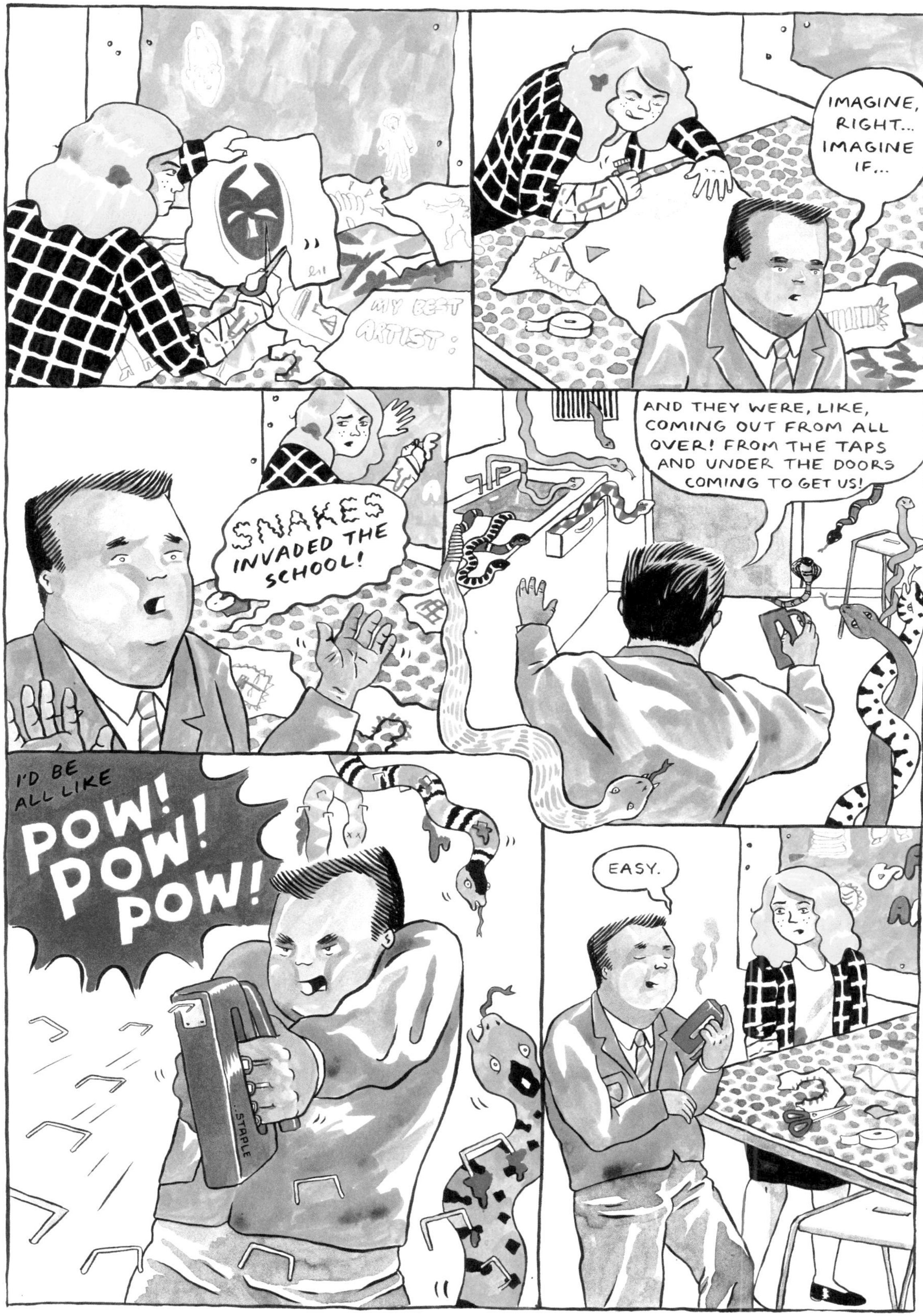
MY BEST ARTIST:
IMAGINE, RIGHT... IMAGINE IF...
SNAKES INVADED THE SCHOOL!
AND THEY WERE, LIKE, COMING OUT FROM ALL OVER! FROM THE TAPS AND UNDER THE DOORS COMING TO GET US!
I'D BE ALL LIKE
POW! POW! POW!
STAPLE
EASY.

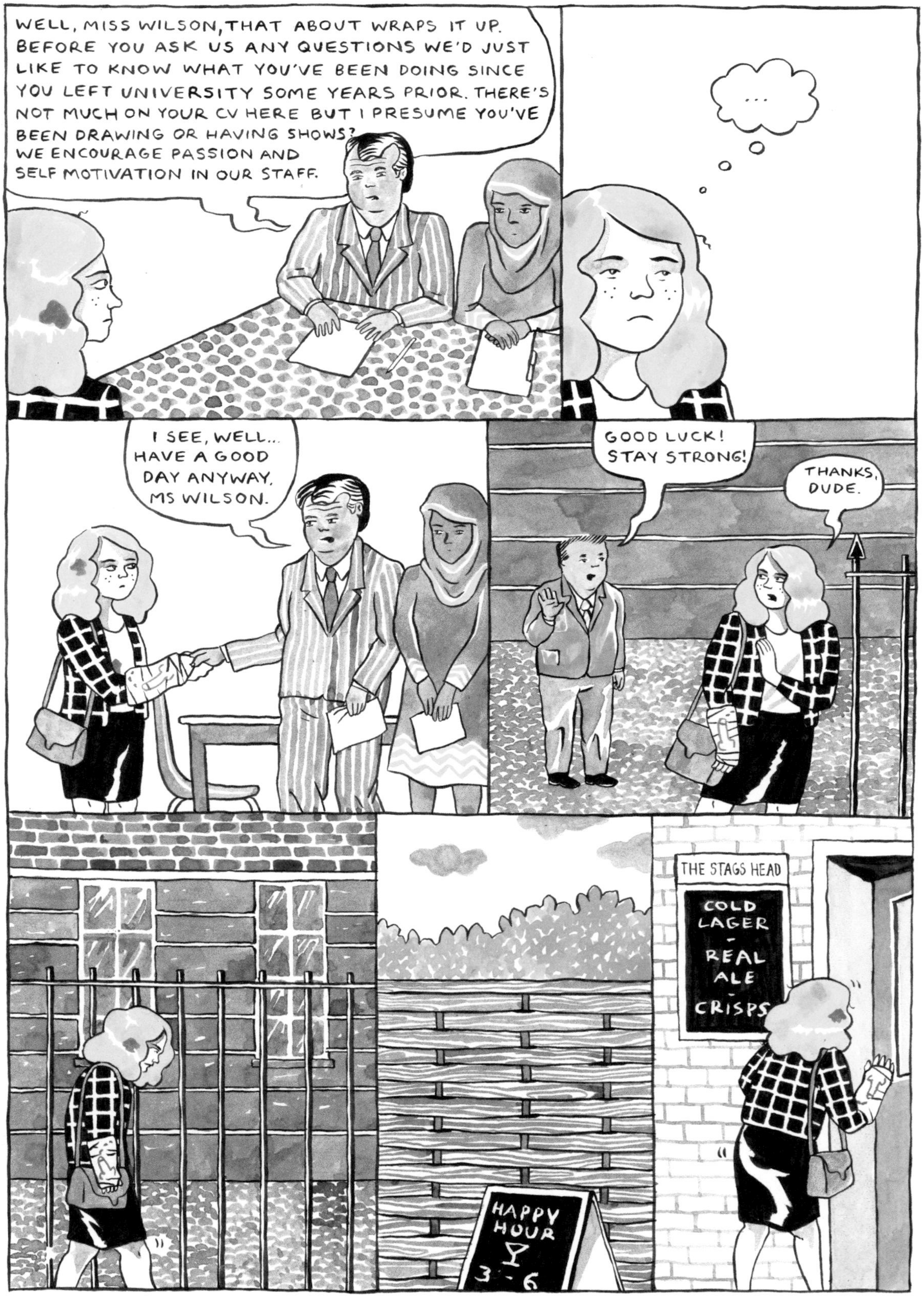
WELL, MISS WILSON, THAT ABOUT WRAPS IT UP. BEFORE YOU ASK US ANY QUESTIONS WE'D JUST LIKE TO KNOW WHAT YOU'VE BEEN DOING SINCE YOU LEFT UNIVERSITY SOME YEARS PRIOR. THERE'S NOT MUCH ON YOUR CV HERE BUT I PRESUME YOU'VE BEEN DRAWING OR HAVING SHOWS? WE ENCOURAGE PASSION AND SELF MOTIVATION IN OUR STAFF.
...
I SEE, WELL... HAVE A GOOD DAY ANYWAY, MS WILSON.
GOOD LUCK! STAY STRONG!
THANKS, DUDE.
HAPPY HOUR 3 - 6
THE STAGS HEAD
COLD LAGER - REAL ALE - CRISPS

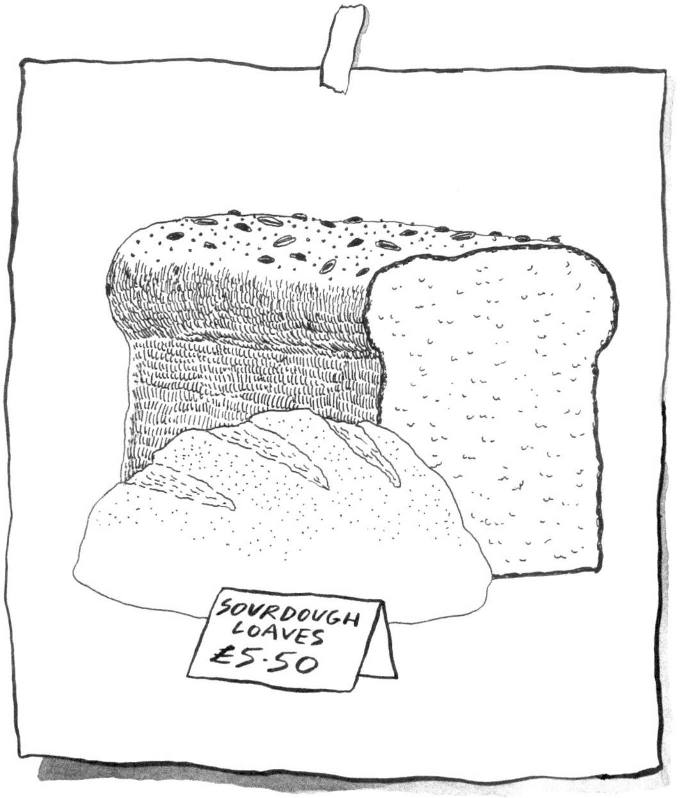
SOURDOUGH
LOAVES
£5·50

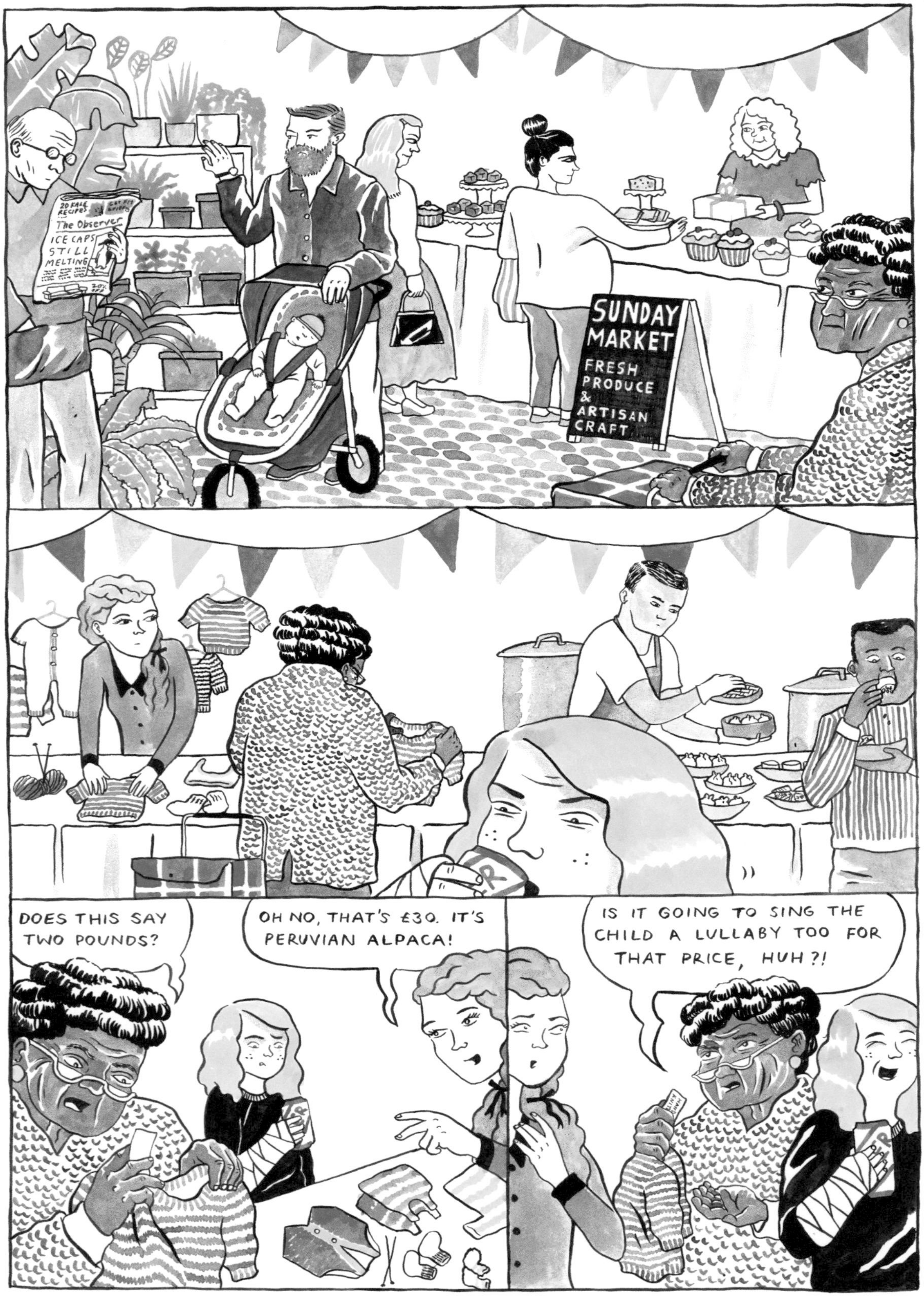
The Observer
ICE CAPS STILL MELTING
SUNDAY MARKET
FRESH PRODUCE & ARTISAN CRAFT
DOES THIS SAY TWO POUNDS?
OH NO, THAT'S £30. IT'S PERUVIAN ALPACA!
IS IT GOING TO SING THE CHILD A LULLABY TOO FOR THAT PRICE, HUH?!

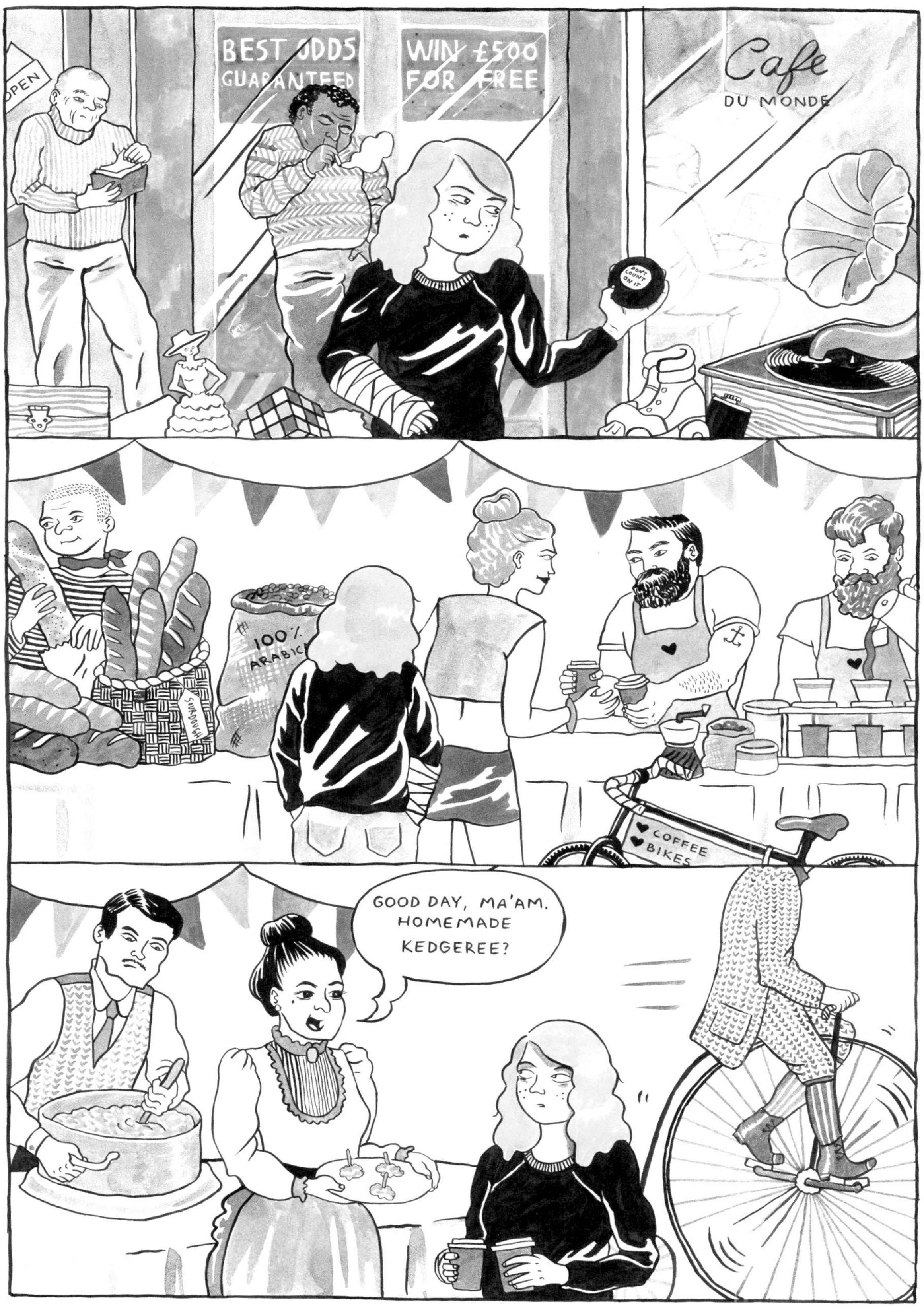

OPEN
BEST ODDS GUARANTEED
WIN £500 FOR FREE
Cafe DU MONDE
DON'T COUNT ON IT
100% ARABICA
SOURDOUGH
COFFEE BIKES
GOOD DAY, MA'AM. HOMEMADE KEDGEREE?

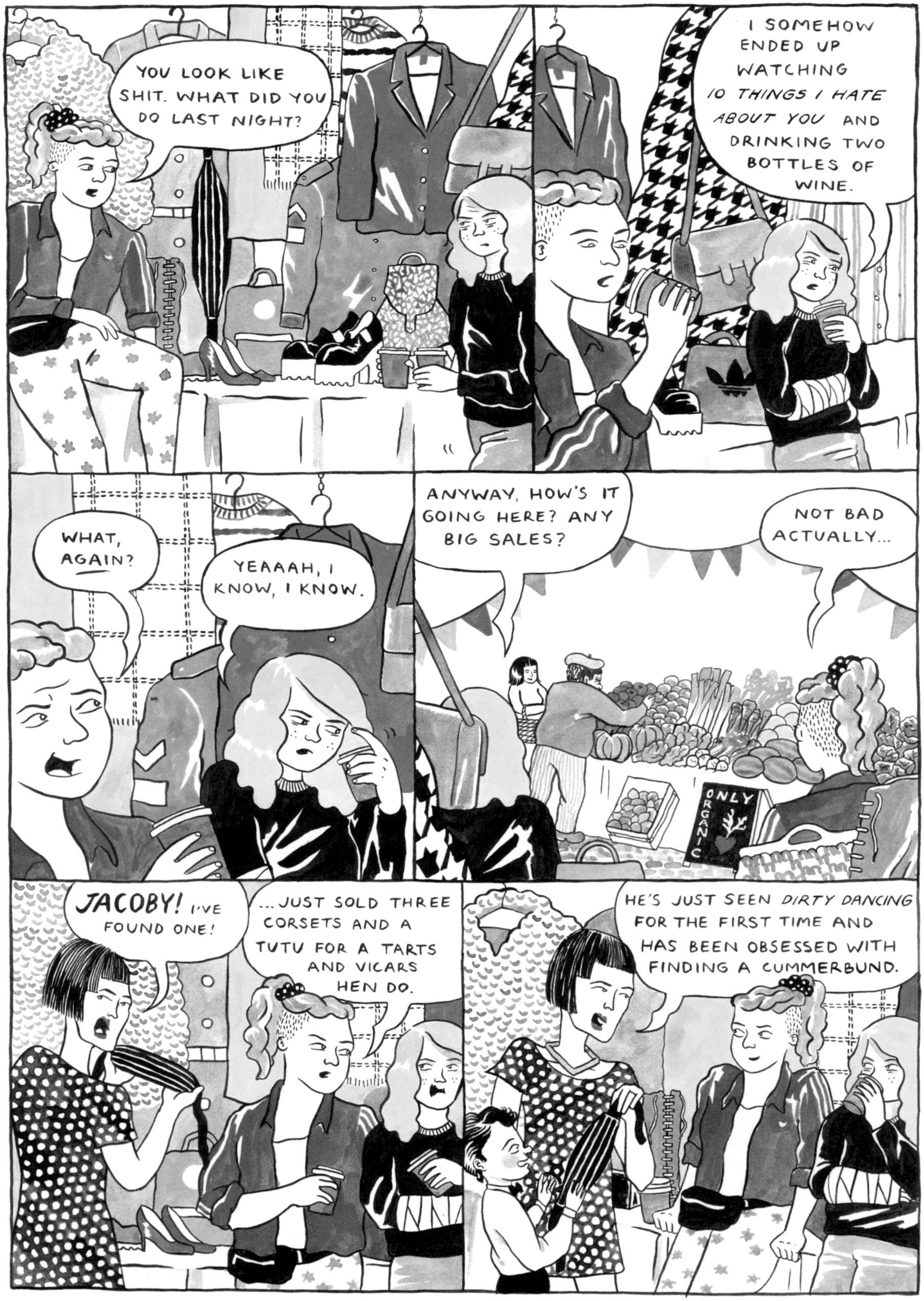
YOU LOOK LIKE SHIT. WHAT DID YOU DO LAST NIGHT?
I SOMEHOW ENDED UP WATCHING *10 THINGS I HATE ABOUT YOU* AND DRINKING TWO BOTTLES OF WINE.
WHAT, AGAIN?
YEAAAH, I KNOW, I KNOW.
ANYWAY, HOW'S IT GOING HERE? ANY BIG SALES?
NOT BAD ACTUALLY...
ONLY ORGANIC
JACOBY! I'VE FOUND ONE!
...JUST SOLD THREE CORSETS AND A TUTU FOR A TARTS AND VICARS HEN DO.
HE'S JUST SEEN *DIRTY DANCING* FOR THE FIRST TIME AND HAS BEEN OBSESSED WITH FINDING A CUMMERBUND.

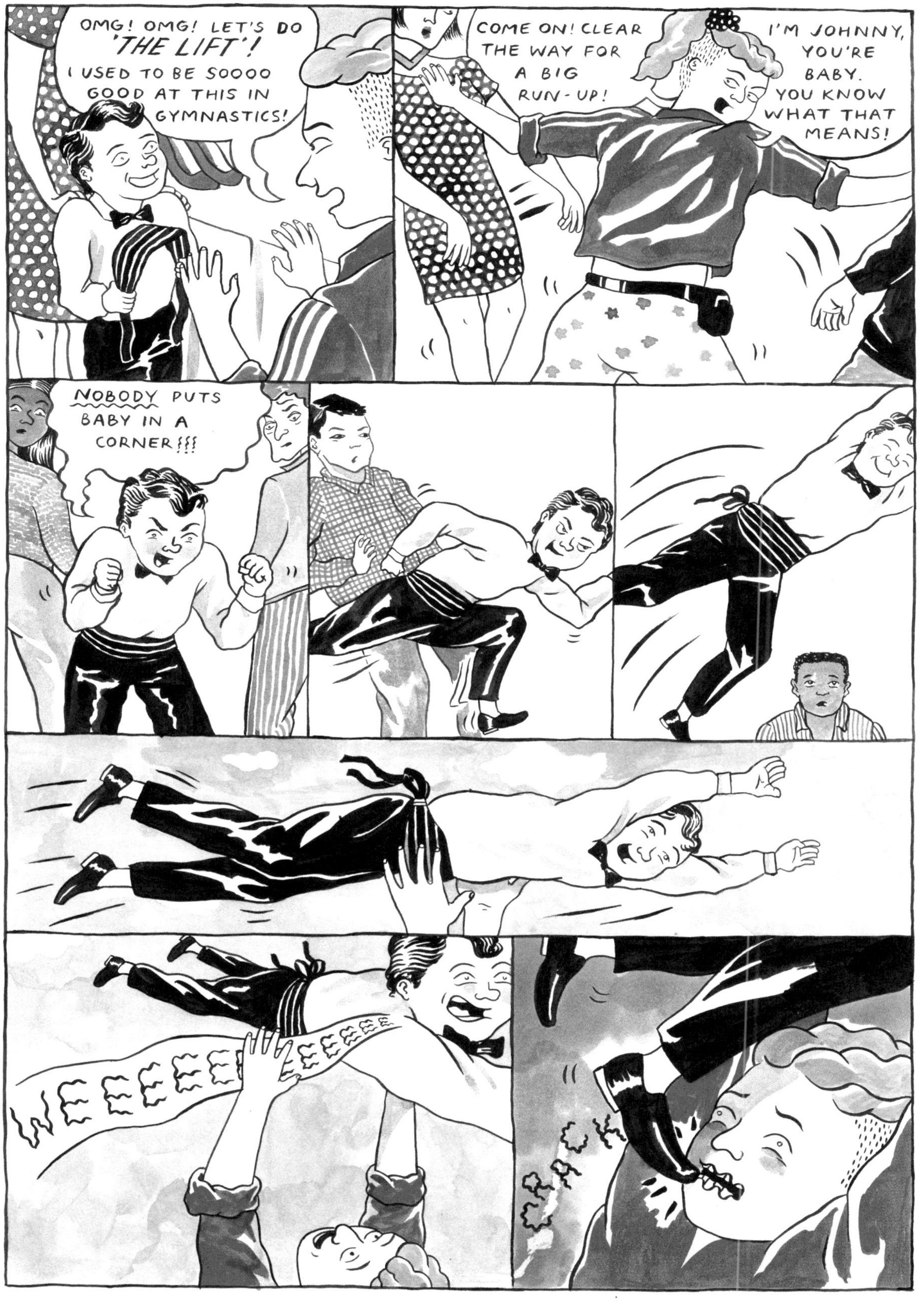
OMG! OMG! LET'S DO 'THE LIFT'! I USED TO BE SOOOO GOOD AT THIS IN GYMNASTICS!
COME ON! CLEAR THE WAY FOR A BIG RUN-UP!
I'M JOHNNY, YOU'RE BABY. YOU KNOW WHAT THAT MEANS!
NOBODY PUTS BABY IN A CORNER!!!
CRACK

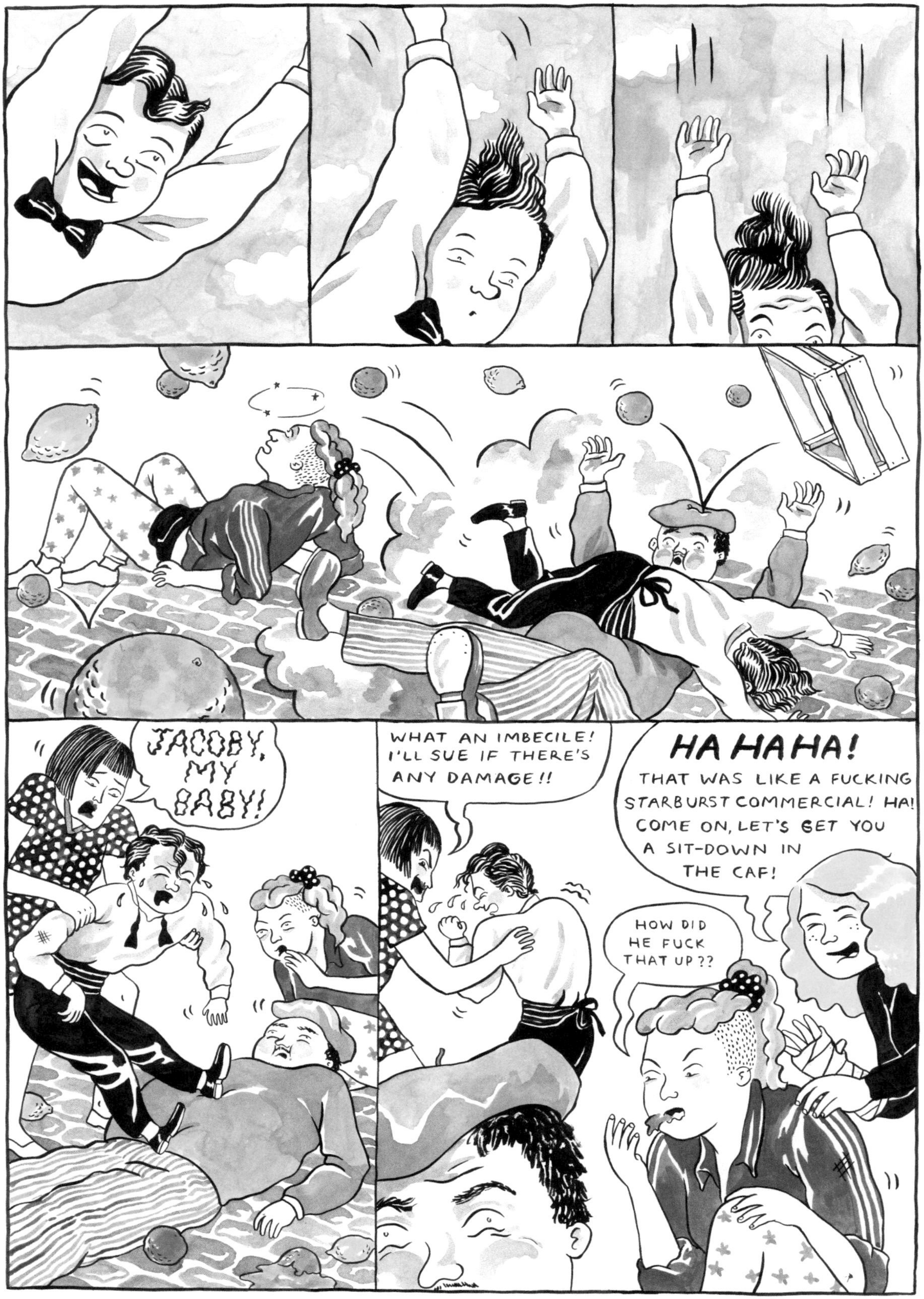
JACOBY, MY BABY!
WHAT AN IMBECILE! I'LL SUE IF THERE'S ANY DAMAGE!!
HA HAHA! THAT WAS LIKE A FUCKING STARBURST COMMERCIAL! HA! COME ON, LET'S GET YOU A SIT-DOWN IN THE CAF!
HOW DID HE FUCK THAT UP??

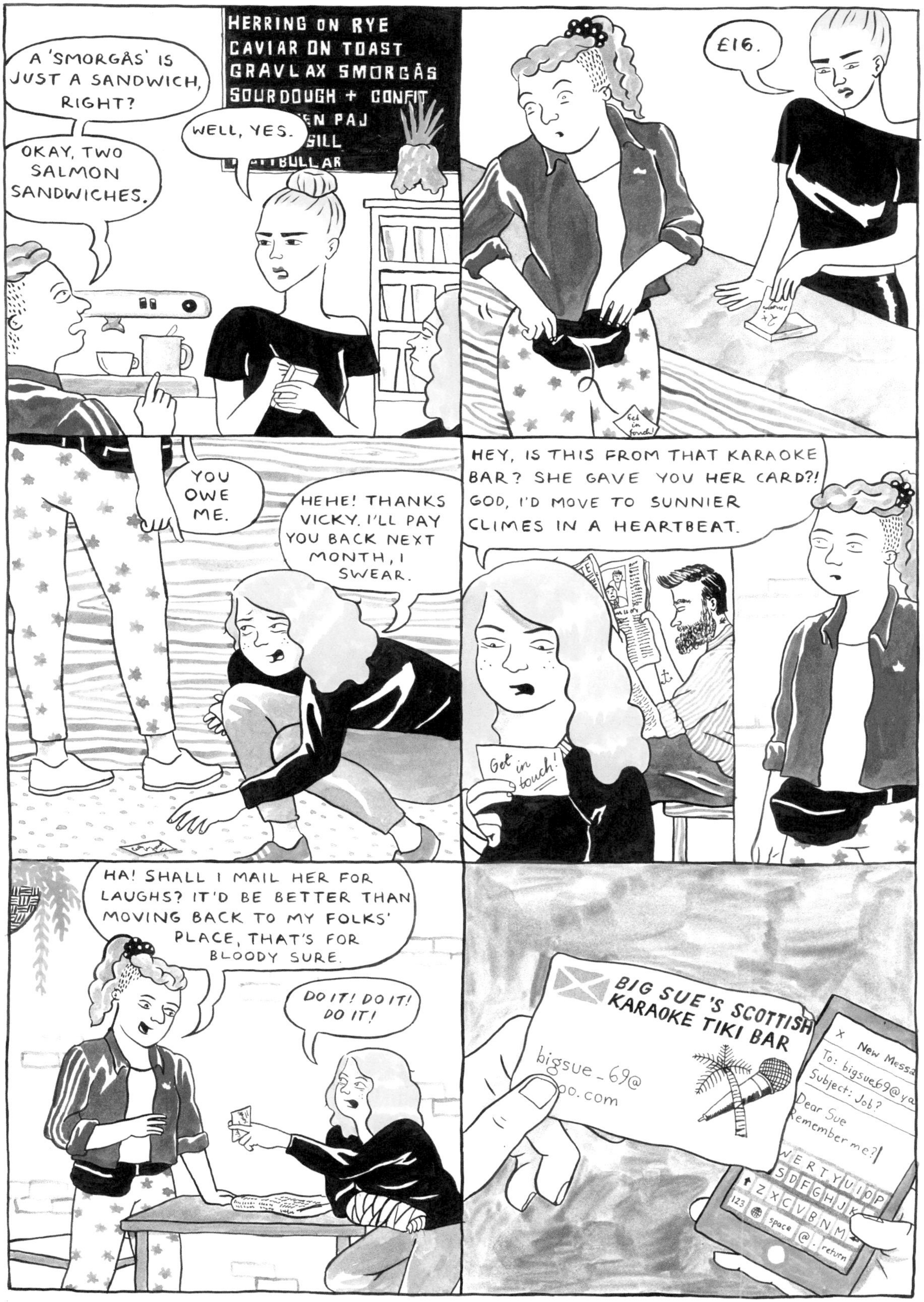
HERRING ON RYE
CAVIAR ON TOAST
GRAVLAX SMÖRGÅS
SOURDOUGH + CONFIT
A 'SMÖRGÅS' IS JUST A SANDWICH, RIGHT?
WELL, YES.
OKAY, TWO SALMON SANDWICHES.
£16.
Get in touch!
YOU OWE ME.
HEHE! THANKS VICKY. I'LL PAY YOU BACK NEXT MONTH, I SWEAR.
HEY, IS THIS FROM THAT KARAOKE BAR? SHE GAVE YOU HER CARD?! GOD, I'D MOVE TO SUNNIER CLIMES IN A HEARTBEAT.
Get in touch!
HA! SHALL I MAIL HER FOR LAUGHS? IT'D BE BETTER THAN MOVING BACK TO MY FOLKS' PLACE, THAT'S FOR BLOODY SURE.
DO IT! DO IT! DO IT!
BIG SUE'S SCOTTISH KARAOKE TIKI BAR
Subject: Job?
Dear Sue
Remember me?

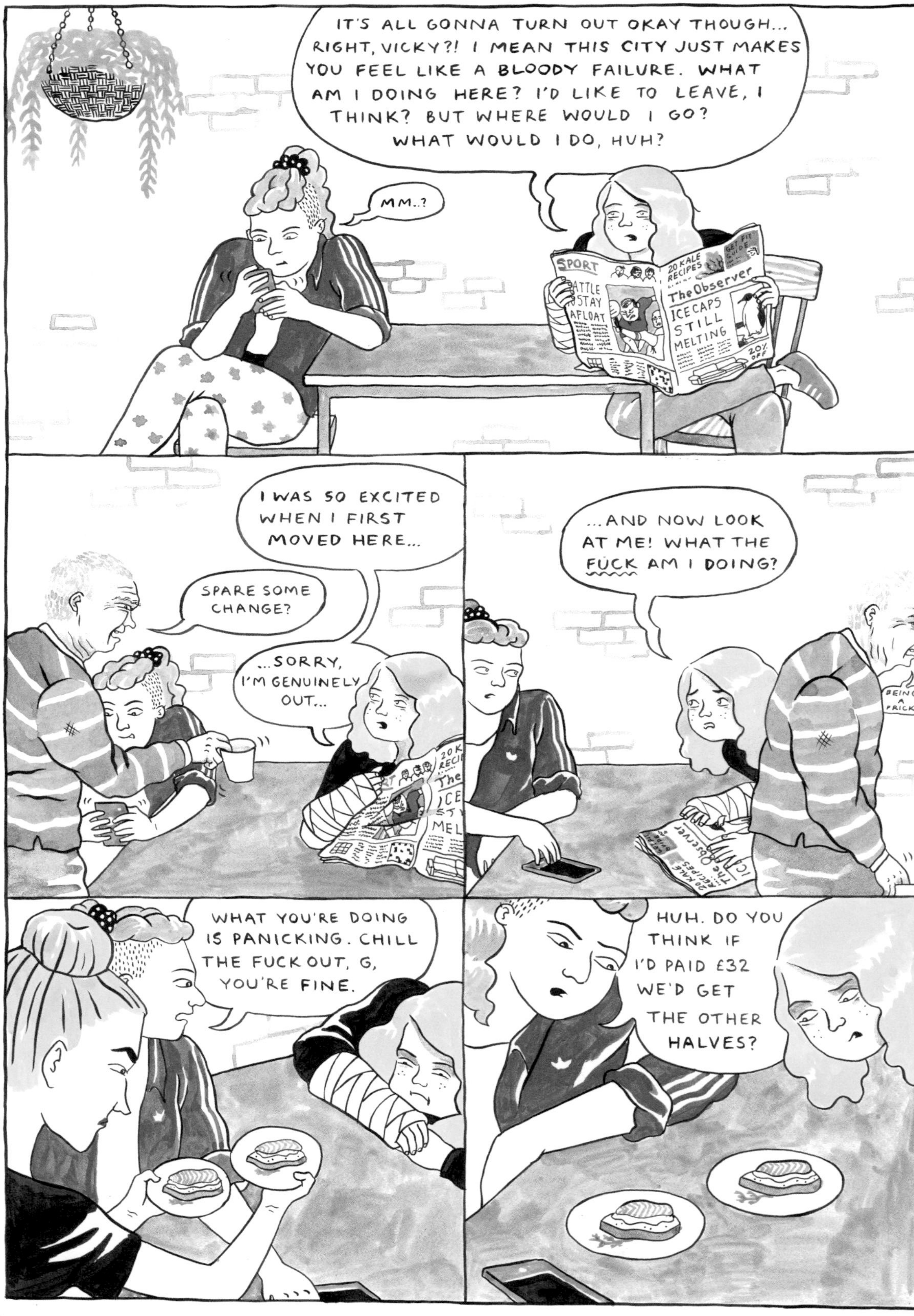
IT'S ALL GONNA TURN OUT OKAY THOUGH... RIGHT, VICKY?! I MEAN THIS CITY JUST MAKES YOU FEEL LIKE A BLOODY FAILURE. WHAT AM I DOING HERE? I'D LIKE TO LEAVE, I THINK? BUT WHERE WOULD I GO? WHAT WOULD I DO, HUH?
MM..?
SPORT
20 KALE RECIPES
The Observer
ICE CAPS STILL MELTING
20% OFF
I WAS SO EXCITED WHEN I FIRST MOVED HERE...
SPARE SOME CHANGE?
...SORRY, I'M GENUINELY OUT...
...AND NOW LOOK AT ME! WHAT THE FUCK AM I DOING?
BEING A FRICK..
WHAT YOU'RE DOING IS PANICKING. CHILL THE FUCK OUT, G, YOU'RE FINE.
HUH. DO YOU THINK IF I'D PAID £32 WE'D GET THE OTHER HALVES?

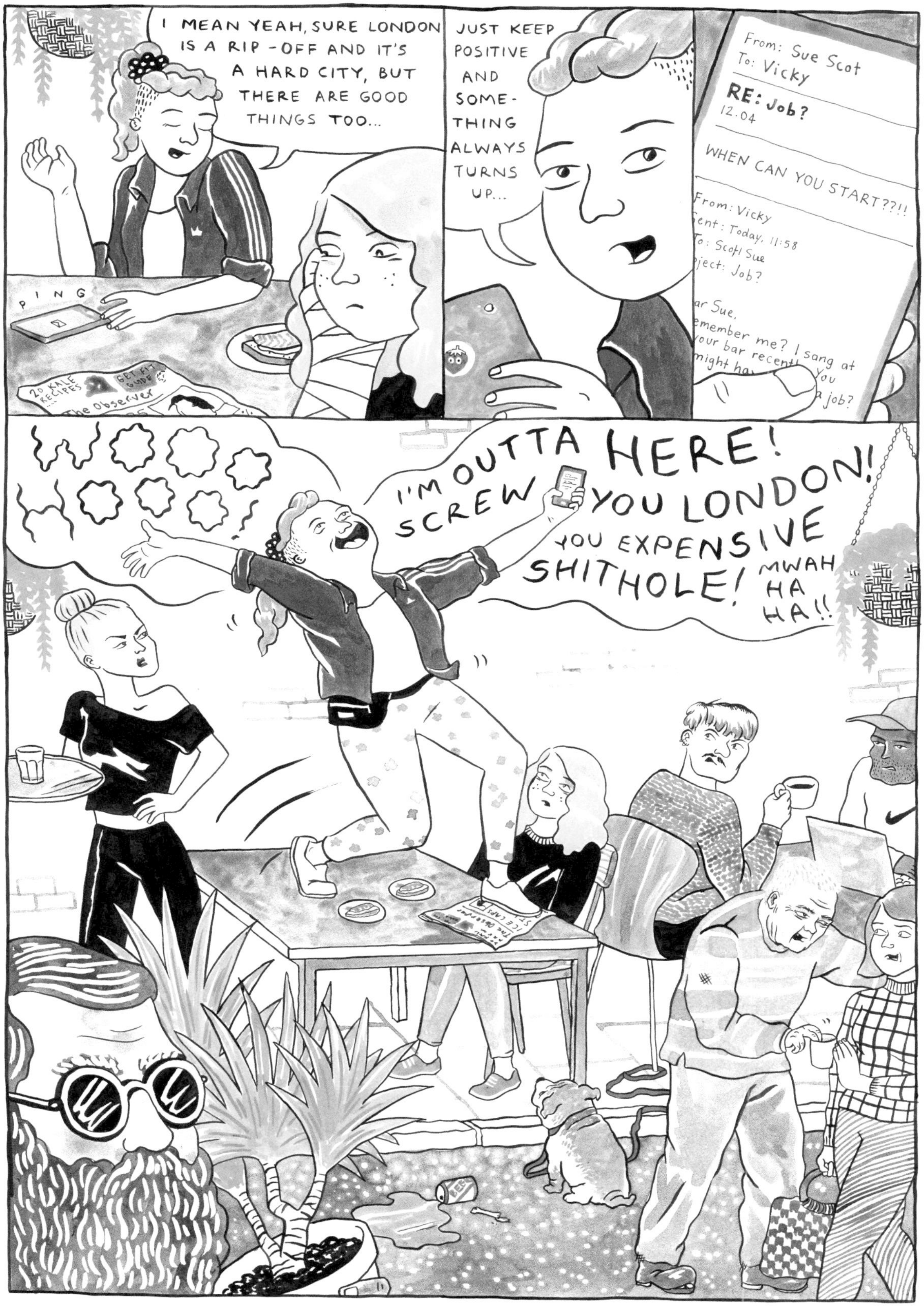
I MEAN YEAH, SURE LONDON IS A RIP-OFF AND IT'S A HARD CITY, BUT THERE ARE GOOD THINGS TOO...
PING
20 KALE RECIPES
GET FIT GUIDE
The Observer
JUST KEEP POSITIVE AND SOME-THING ALWAYS TURNS UP...
From: Sue Scot
To: Vicky
RE: Job?
12.04
WHEN CAN YOU START??!!
From: Vicky
WOOO HOOOO!
I'M OUTTA HERE!
SCREW YOU LONDON!
YOU EXPENSIVE SHITHOLE!
MWAH HA HA!!

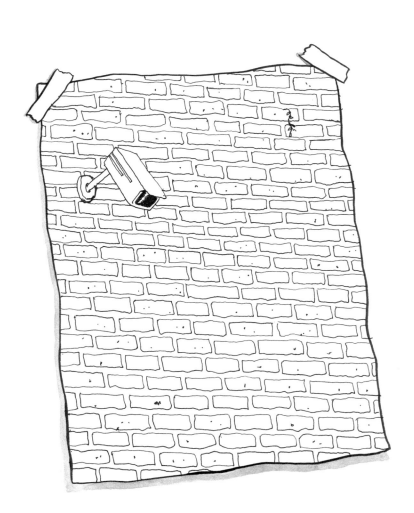

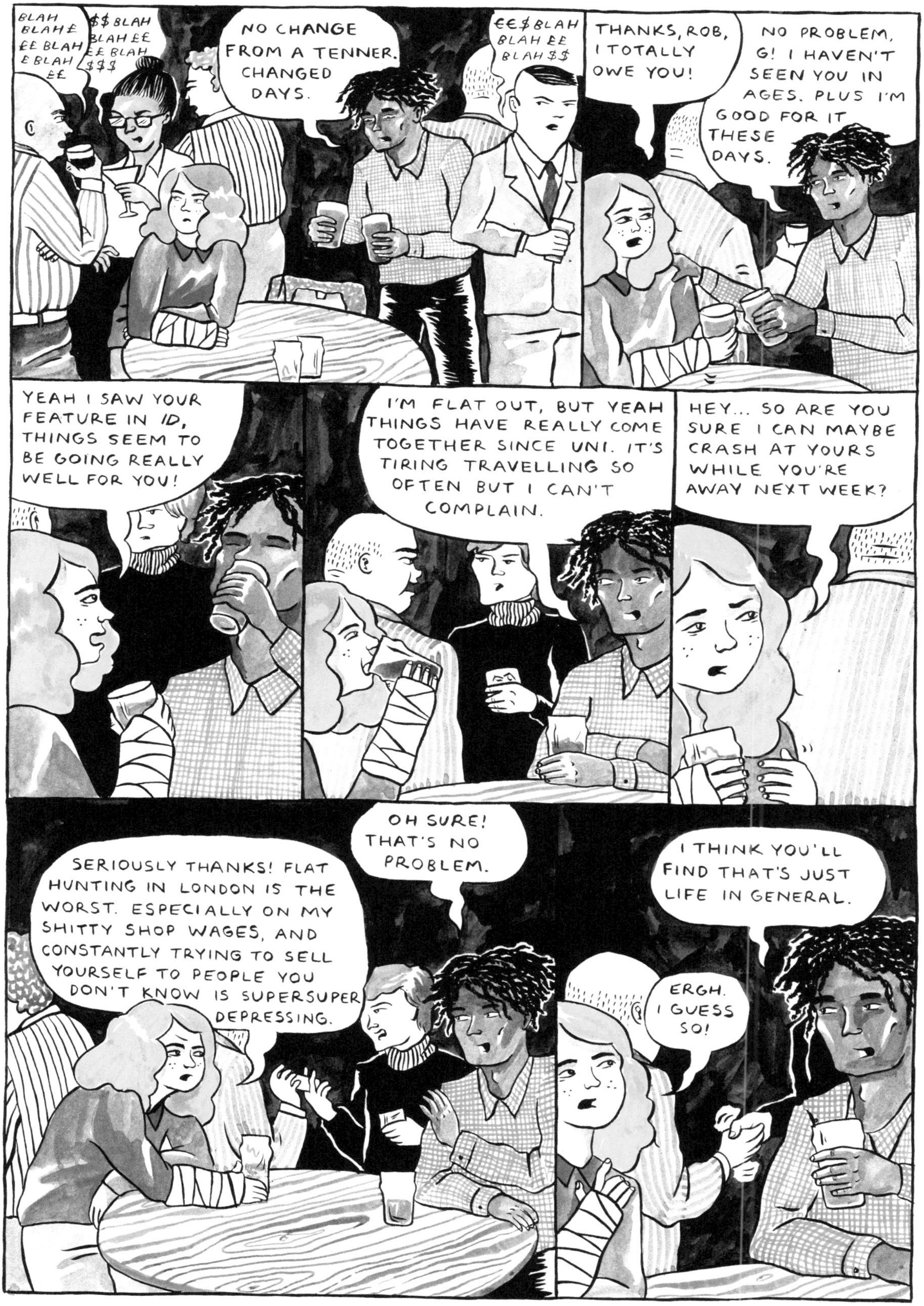
BLAH BLAH£ ££ BLAH £ BLAH ££
$$ BLAH BLAH ££ ££ BLAH $$$
NO CHANGE FROM A TENNER. CHANGED DAYS.
€€$ BLAH BLAH ££ BLAH $$
THANKS, ROB, I TOTALLY OWE YOU!
NO PROBLEM, G! I HAVEN'T SEEN YOU IN AGES. PLUS I'M GOOD FOR IT THESE DAYS.
YEAH I SAW YOUR FEATURE IN ID, THINGS SEEM TO BE GOING REALLY WELL FOR YOU!
I'M FLAT OUT, BUT YEAH THINGS HAVE REALLY COME TOGETHER SINCE UNI. IT'S TIRING TRAVELLING SO OFTEN BUT I CAN'T COMPLAIN.
HEY... SO ARE YOU SURE I CAN MAYBE CRASH AT YOURS WHILE YOU'RE AWAY NEXT WEEK?
OH SURE! THAT'S NO PROBLEM.
SERIOUSLY THANKS! FLAT HUNTING IN LONDON IS THE WORST. ESPECIALLY ON MY SHITTY SHOP WAGES, AND CONSTANTLY TRYING TO SELL YOURSELF TO PEOPLE YOU DON'T KNOW IS SUPERSUPER DEPRESSING.
I THINK YOU'LL FIND THAT'S JUST LIFE IN GENERAL.
ERGH. I GUESS SO!

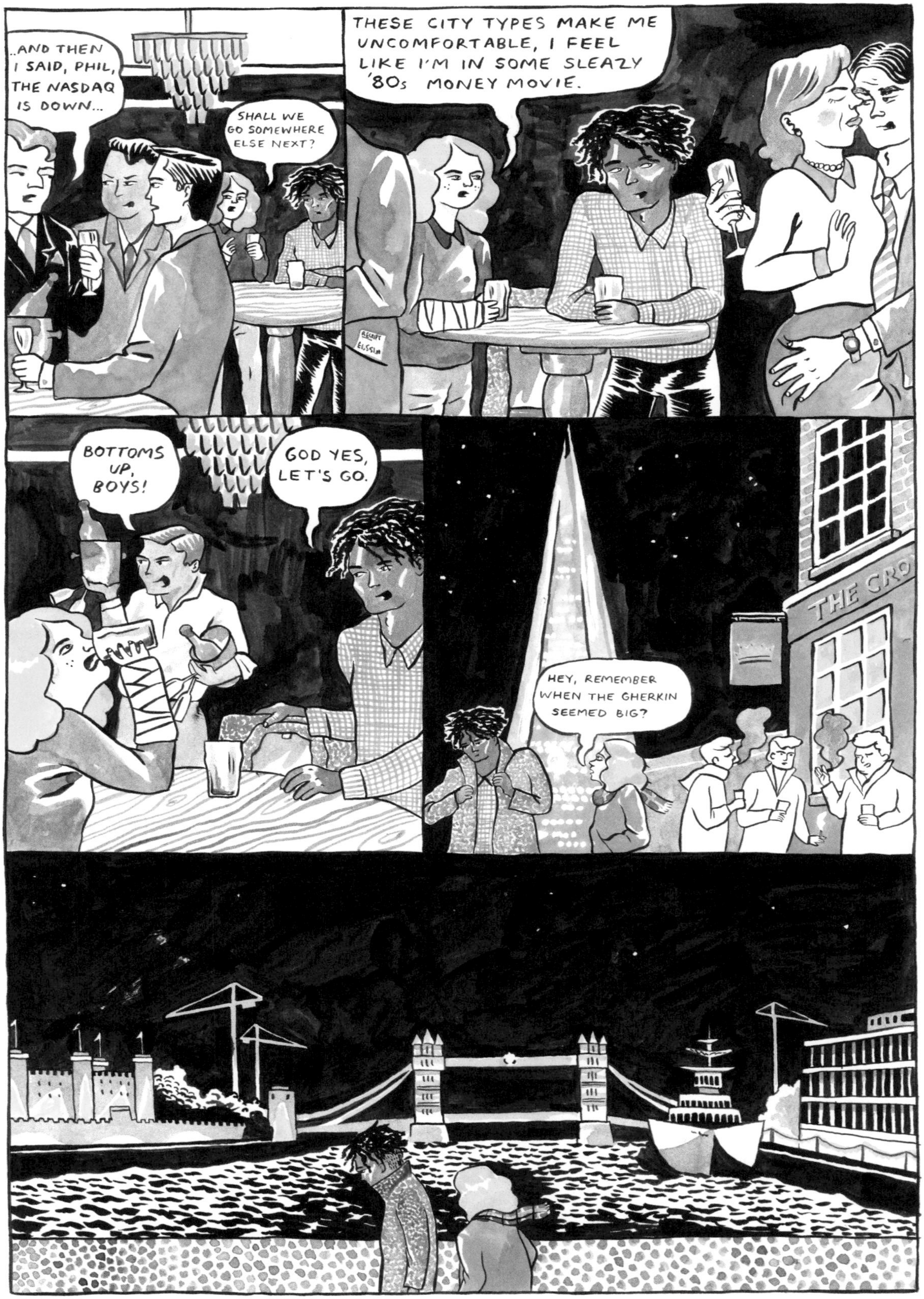
..AND THEN I SAID, PHIL, THE NASDAQ IS DOWN...
SHALL WE GO SOMEWHERE ELSE NEXT?
THESE CITY TYPES MAKE ME UNCOMFORTABLE, I FEEL LIKE I'M IN SOME SLEAZY '80s MONEY MOVIE.
BOTTOMS UP, BOYS!
GOD YES, LET'S GO.
THE CRO
HEY, REMEMBER WHEN THE GHERKIN SEEMED BIG?

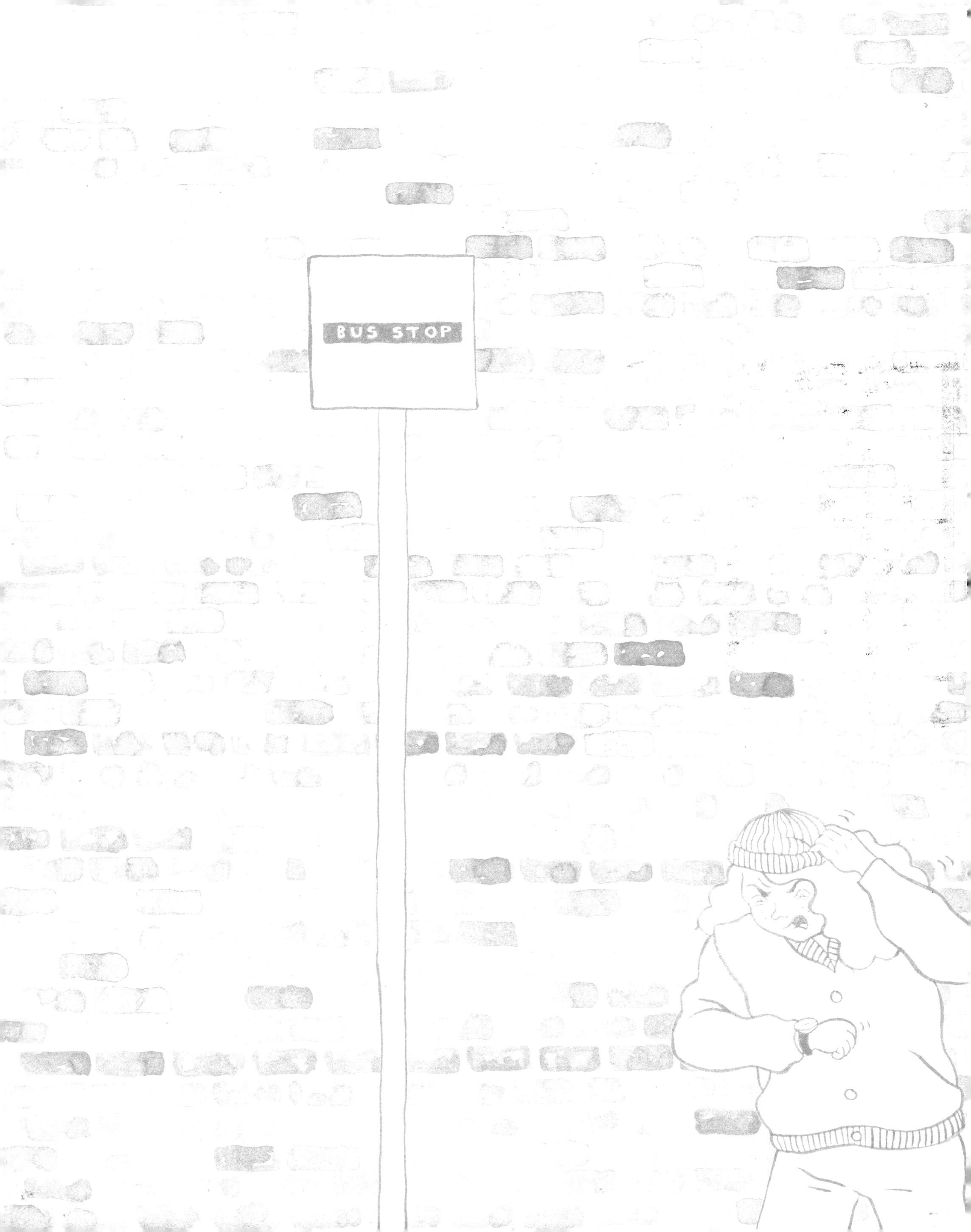
BUS STOP

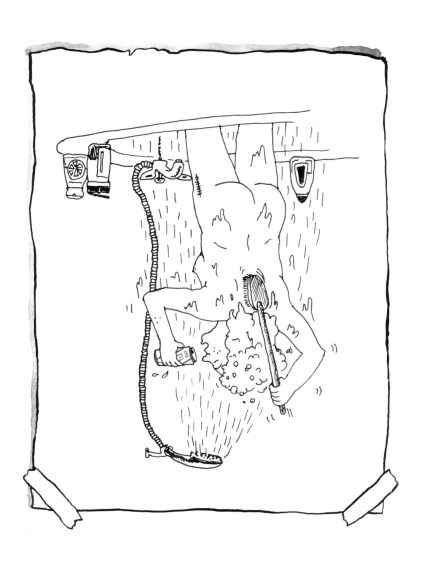

THE IDIOT

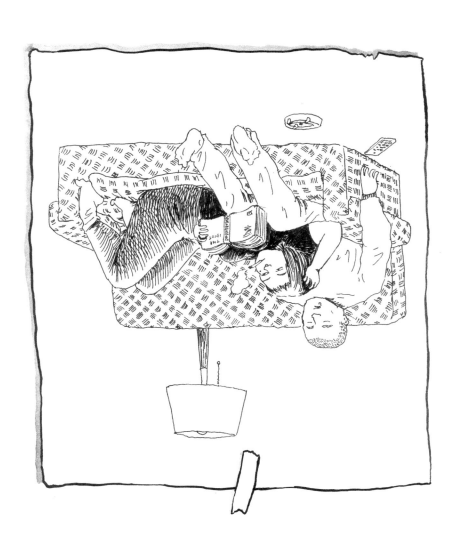

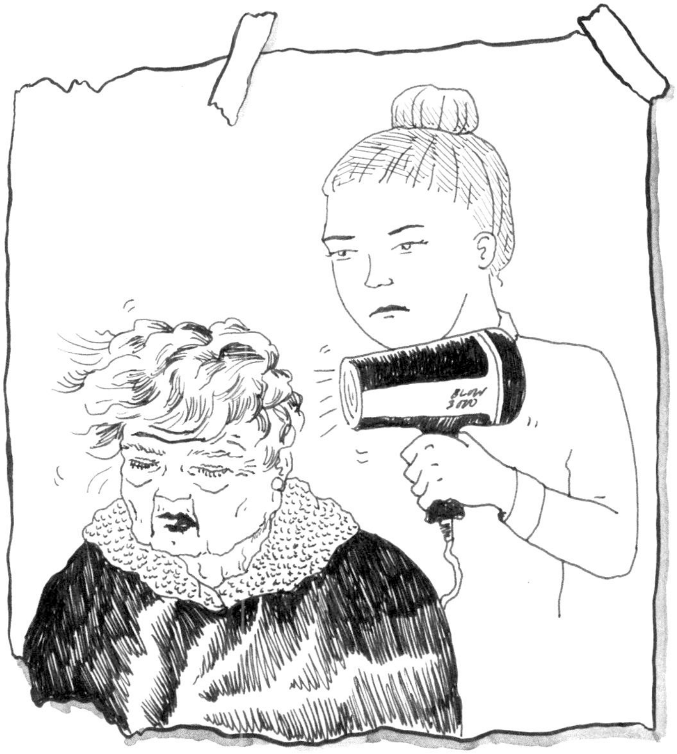
BLOW 3000

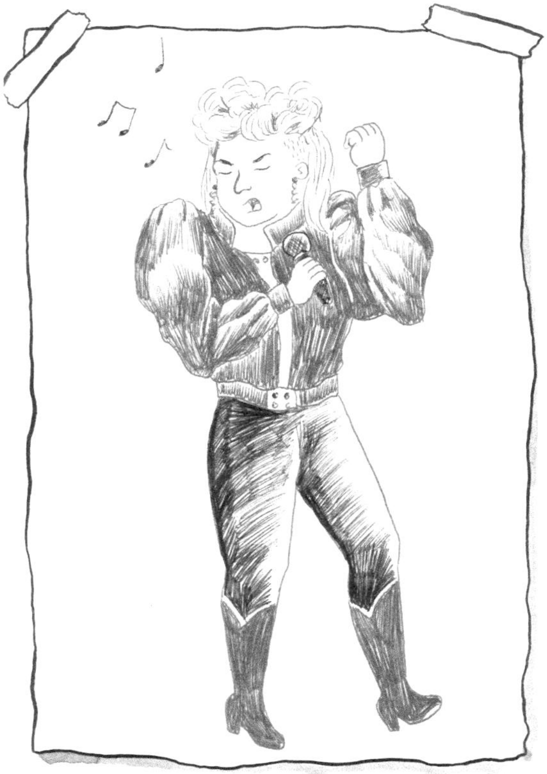

THANK YOU!

DAN FRANKLIN AND ALL AT JONATHAN CAPE
FOR THE WONDERFUL OPPORTUNITY, EMMA RENDEL
FOR THE SPARK TO START THIS, JOANNA
RUBIN DRANGER FOR ALL THE PEP TALKS AND
EARLY ENCOURAGEMENT, ROSANNA & TOM AND
KATIE & ELLIE FOR WARM BEDS AND HOT
DINNERS, K.P. & ADAM FOR SO MUCH, ALL
MY PROOF READERS AND GENERAL HELPERS,
ESPECIALLY BELLA, LINA, BRIGID, HUGH,
PEDRO, RIC, RUDY, BEN, GOULVEN, JOSH, AND
KRISTIAN MÖLLER'S TYPE SKILLS.
SPECIAL THANKS TO LA MAISON DES AUTEURS
AND ALL THE GREAT COMICS PEOPLE I GOT
TO HANG WITH AND LEARN FROM.
BEST OF ALL, ETERNAL LOVE
AND THANKS TO MA, PA & G XXX

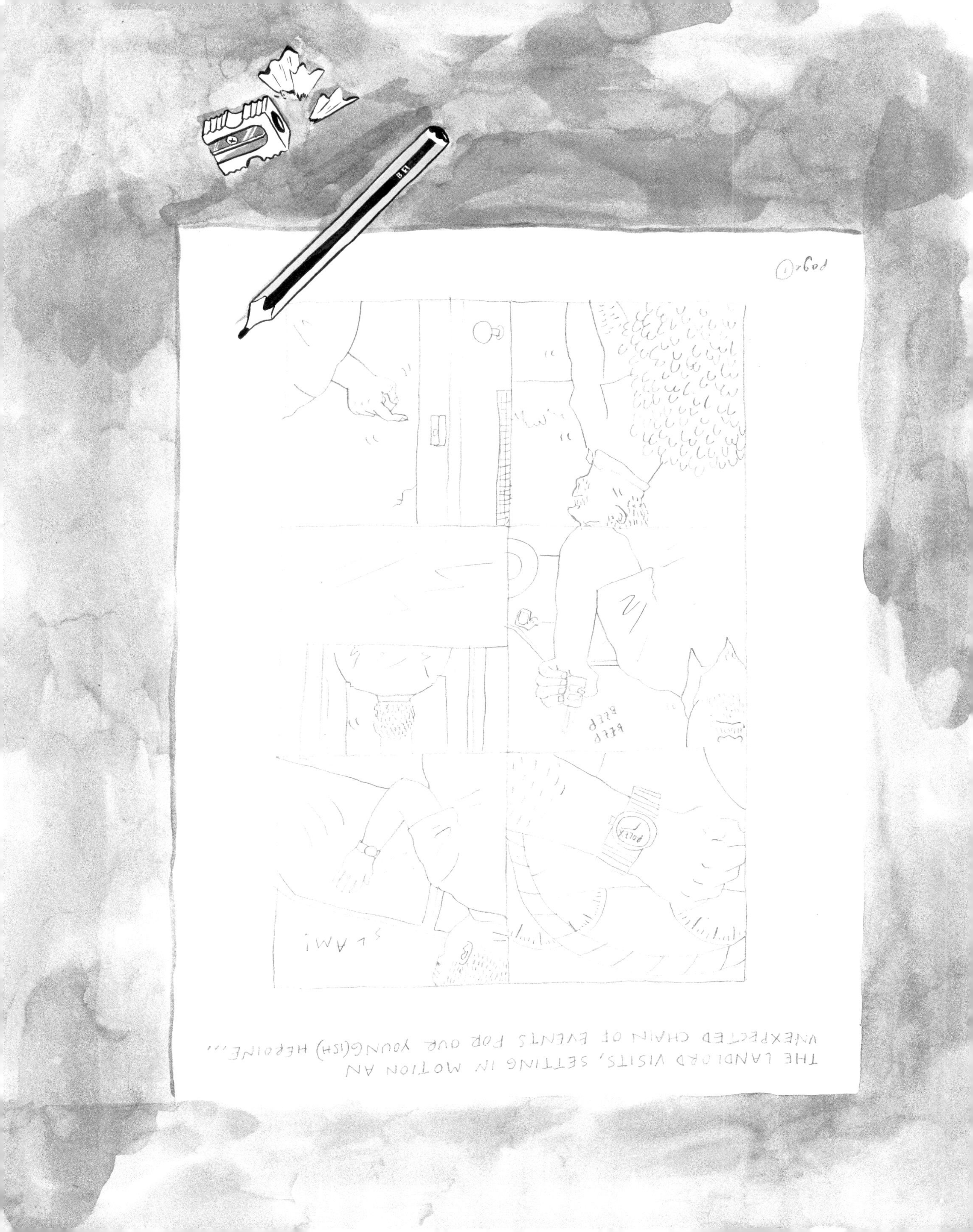
page 1
SLAM!
BEEP BEEP
ROLEX
THE LANDLORD VISITS, SETTING IN MOTION AN
UNEXPECTED CHAIN OF EVENTS FOR OUR YOUNG(ISH) HEROINE....

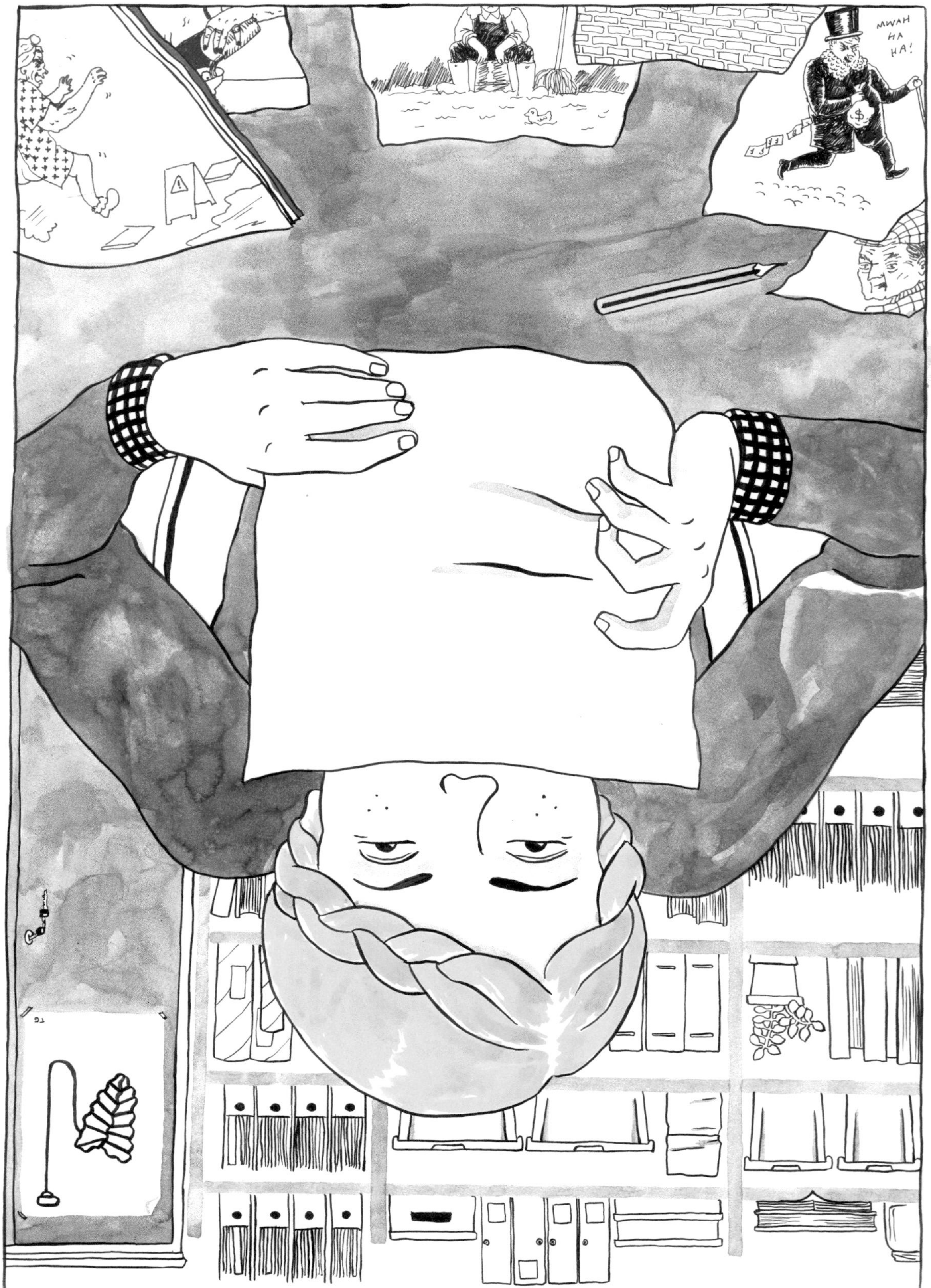
MWAH HA HA!

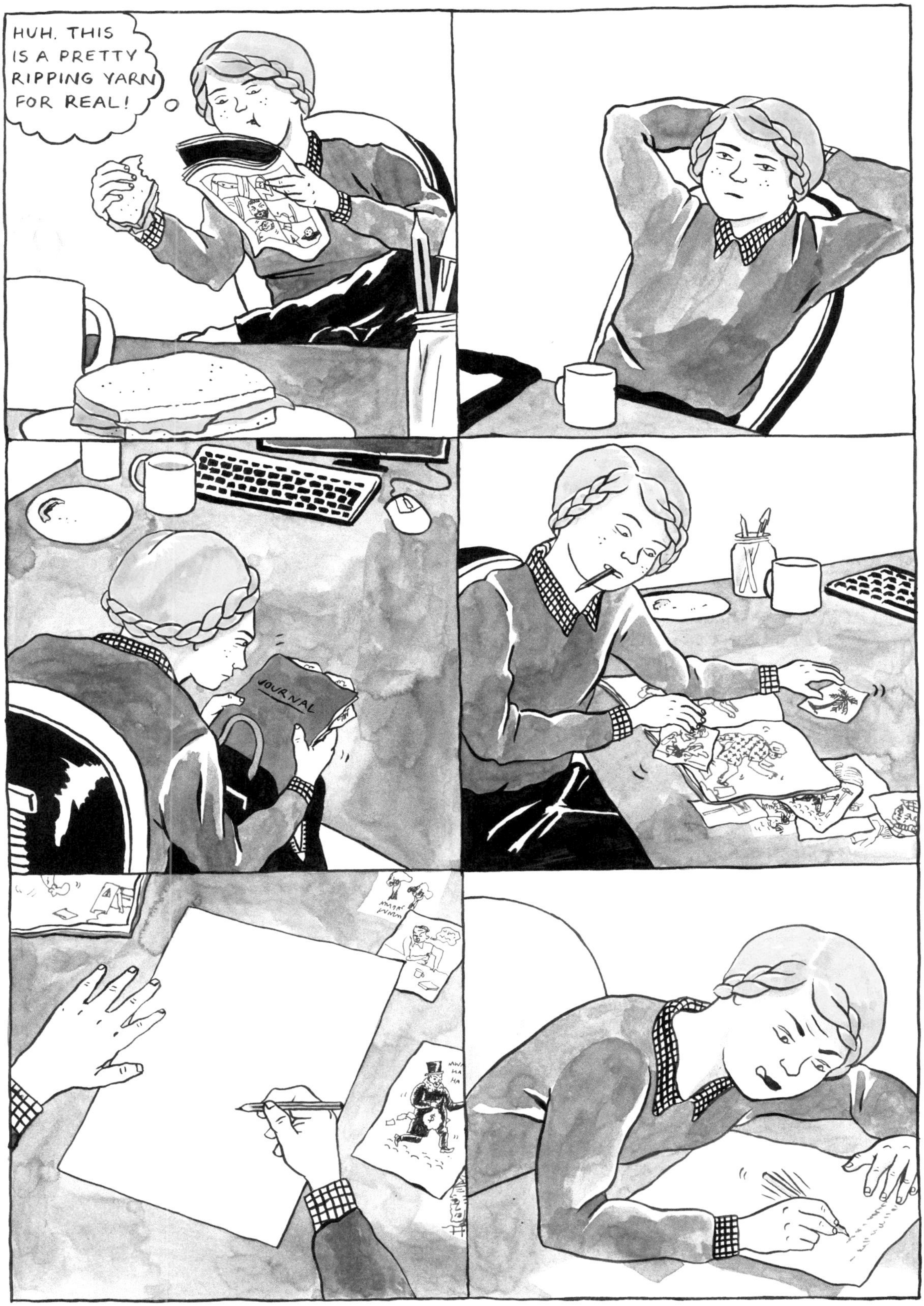
HUH. THIS IS A PRETTY RIPPING YARN FOR REAL!
JOURNAL

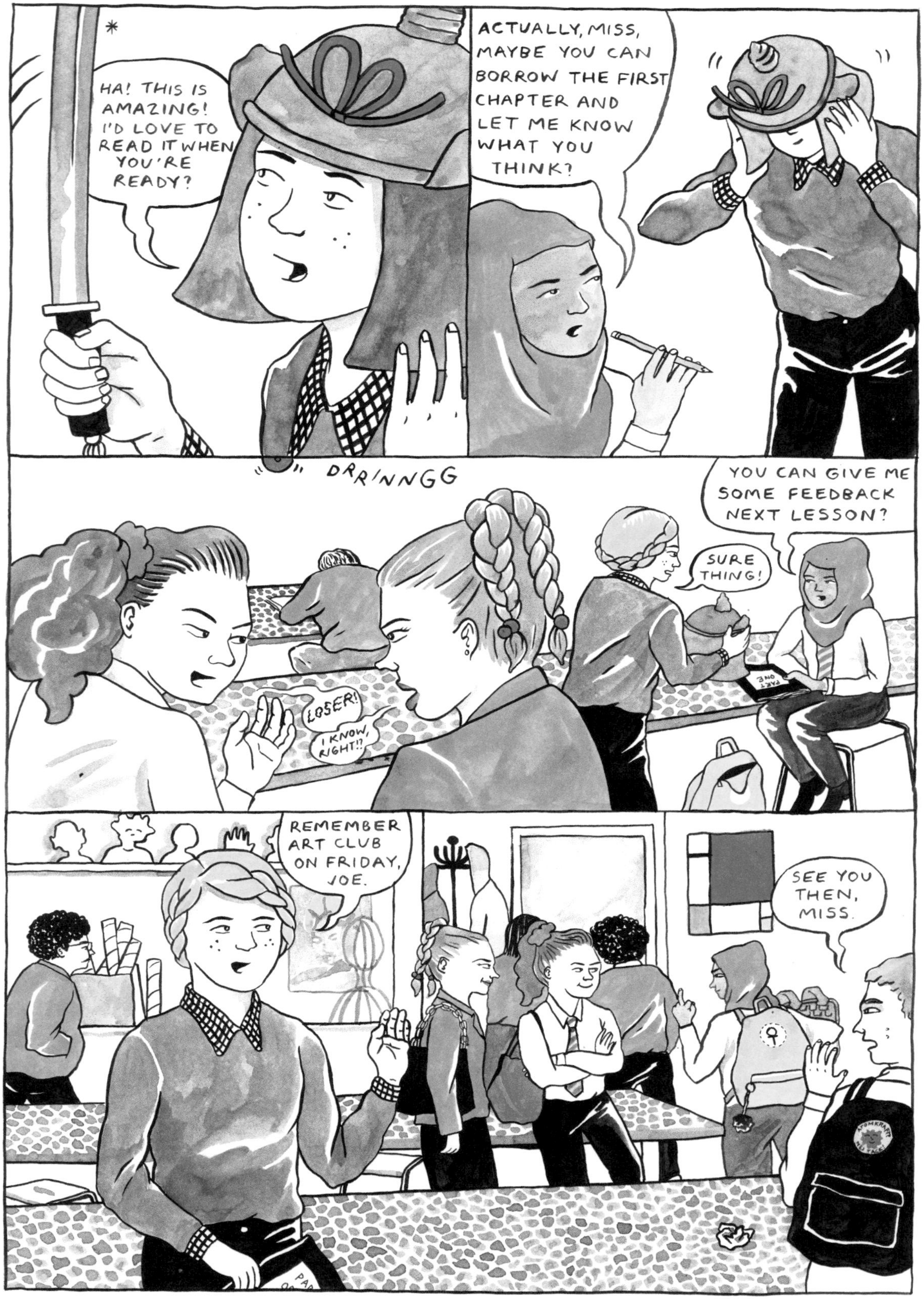
*
HA! THIS IS AMAZING! I'D LOVE TO READ IT WHEN YOU'RE READY?
ACTUALLY, MISS, MAYBE YOU CAN BORROW THE FIRST CHAPTER AND LET ME KNOW WHAT YOU THINK?
DRRINNGG
YOU CAN GIVE ME SOME FEEDBACK NEXT LESSON?
SURE THING!
LOSER!
I KNOW, RIGHT!?
PART ONE
REMEMBER ART CLUB ON FRIDAY, JOE.
SEE YOU THEN, MISS.

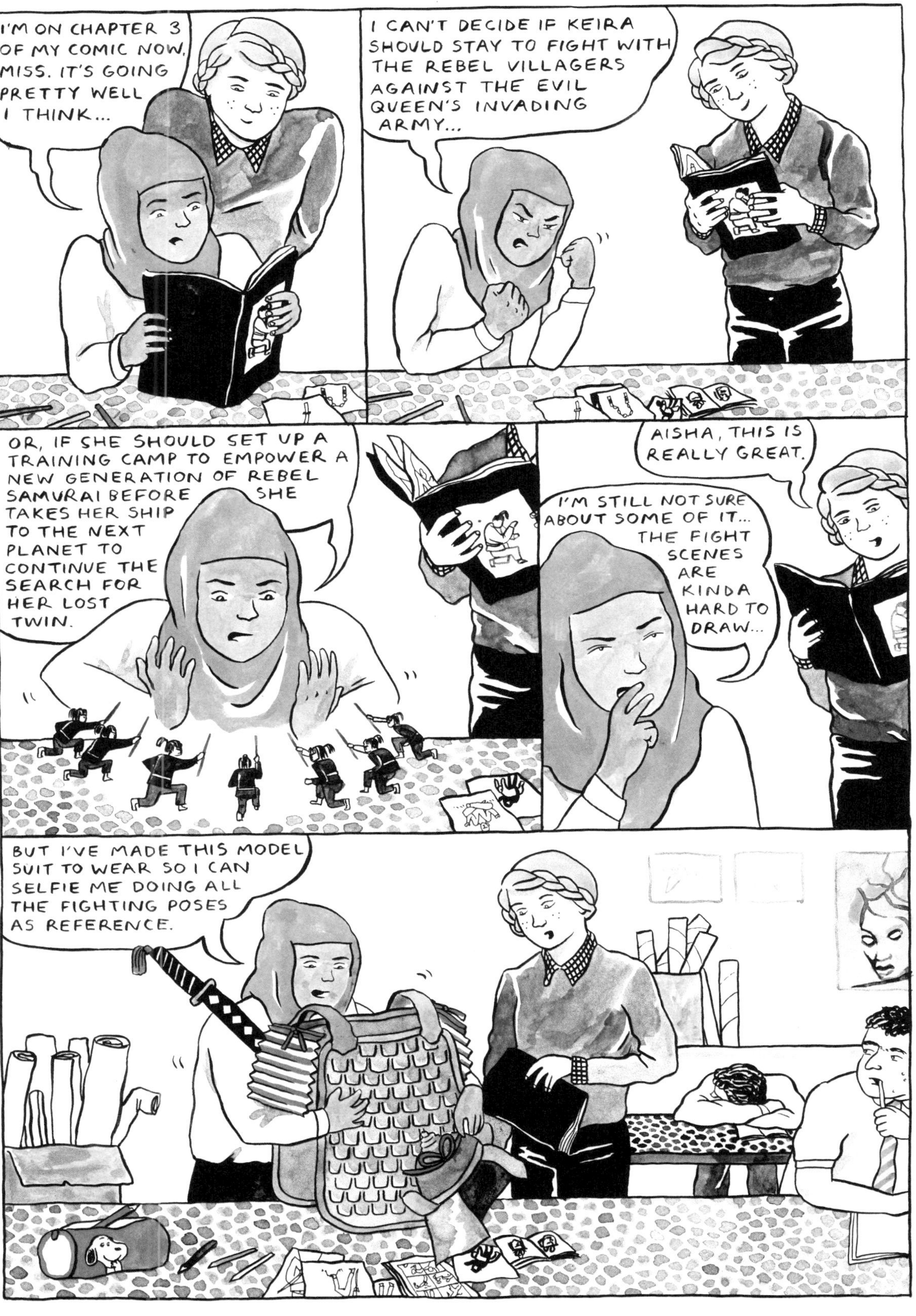
I'M ON CHAPTER 3 OF MY COMIC NOW, MISS. IT'S GOING PRETTY WELL I THINK...
I CAN'T DECIDE IF KEIRA SHOULD STAY TO FIGHT WITH THE REBEL VILLAGERS AGAINST THE EVIL QUEEN'S INVADING ARMY...
OR, IF SHE SHOULD SET UP A TRAINING CAMP TO EMPOWER A NEW GENERATION OF REBEL SAMURAI BEFORE SHE TAKES HER SHIP TO THE NEXT PLANET TO CONTINUE THE SEARCH FOR HER LOST TWIN.
AISHA, THIS IS REALLY GREAT.
I'M STILL NOT SURE ABOUT SOME OF IT... THE FIGHT SCENES ARE KINDA HARD TO DRAW...
BUT I'VE MADE THIS MODEL SUIT TO WEAR SO I CAN SELFIE ME DOING ALL THE FIGHTING POSES AS REFERENCE.

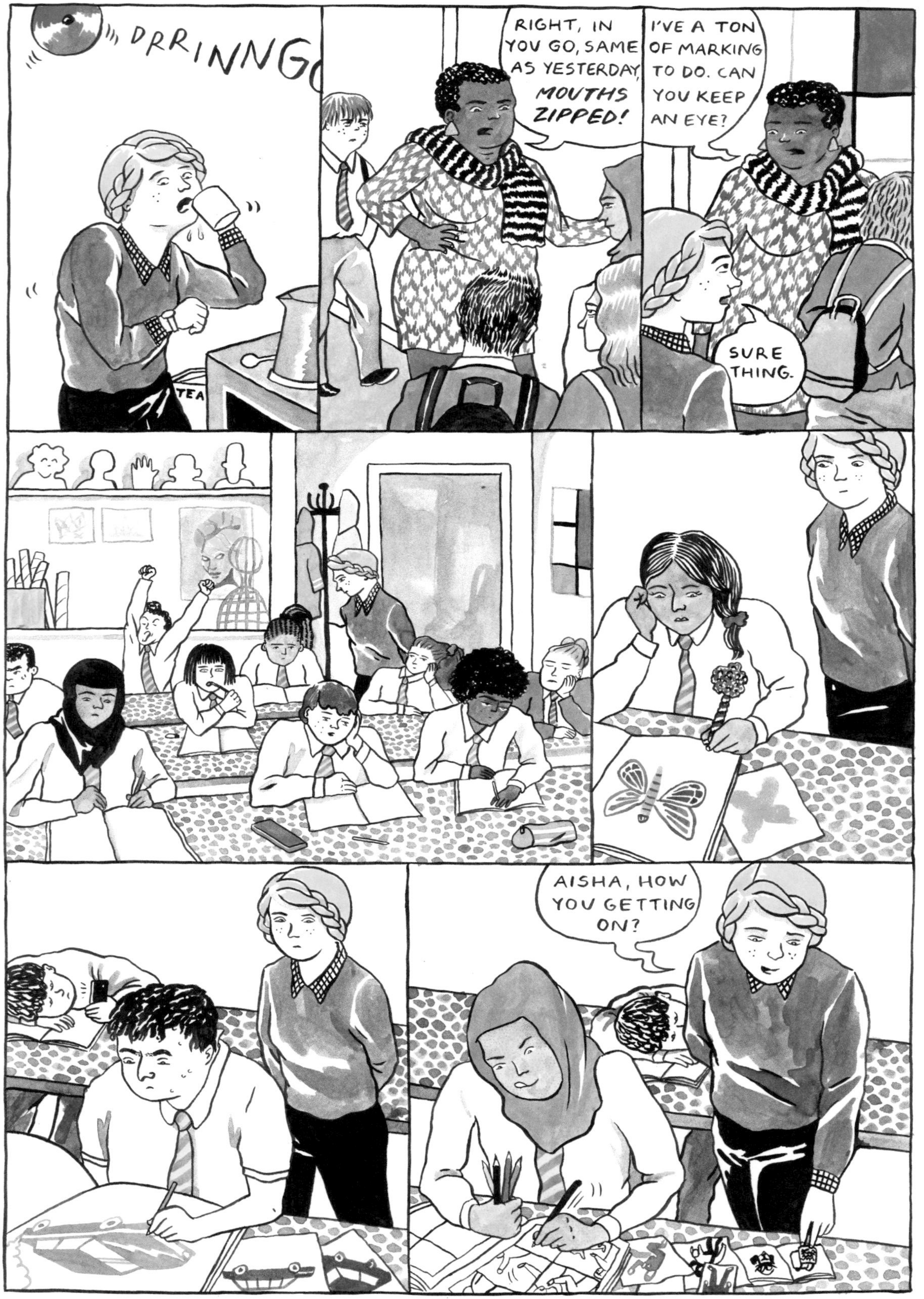
DRRINNG
RIGHT, IN YOU GO, SAME AS YESTERDAY, MOUTHS ZIPPED!
I'VE A TON OF MARKING TO DO. CAN YOU KEEP AN EYE?
SURE THING.
TEA
AISHA, HOW YOU GETTING ON?

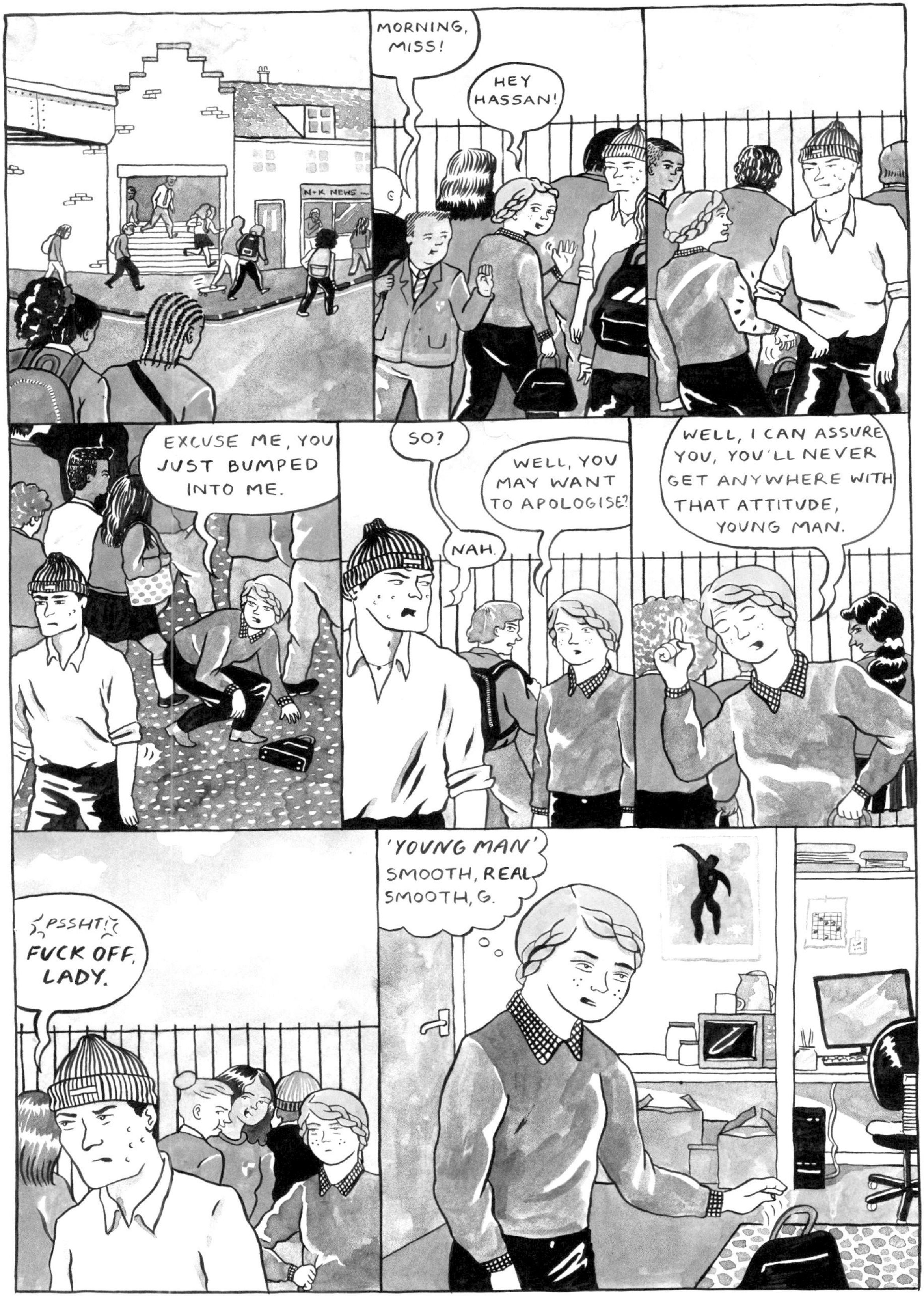
N+K NEWS
MORNING, MISS!
HEY HASSAN!
EXCUSE ME, YOU JUST BUMPED INTO ME.
SO?
WELL, YOU MAY WANT TO APOLOGISE?
NAH.
WELL, I CAN ASSURE YOU, YOU'LL NEVER GET ANYWHERE WITH THAT ATTITUDE, YOUNG MAN.
PSSHT!
FUCK OFF, LADY.
'YOUNG MAN' SMOOTH, REAL SMOOTH, G.

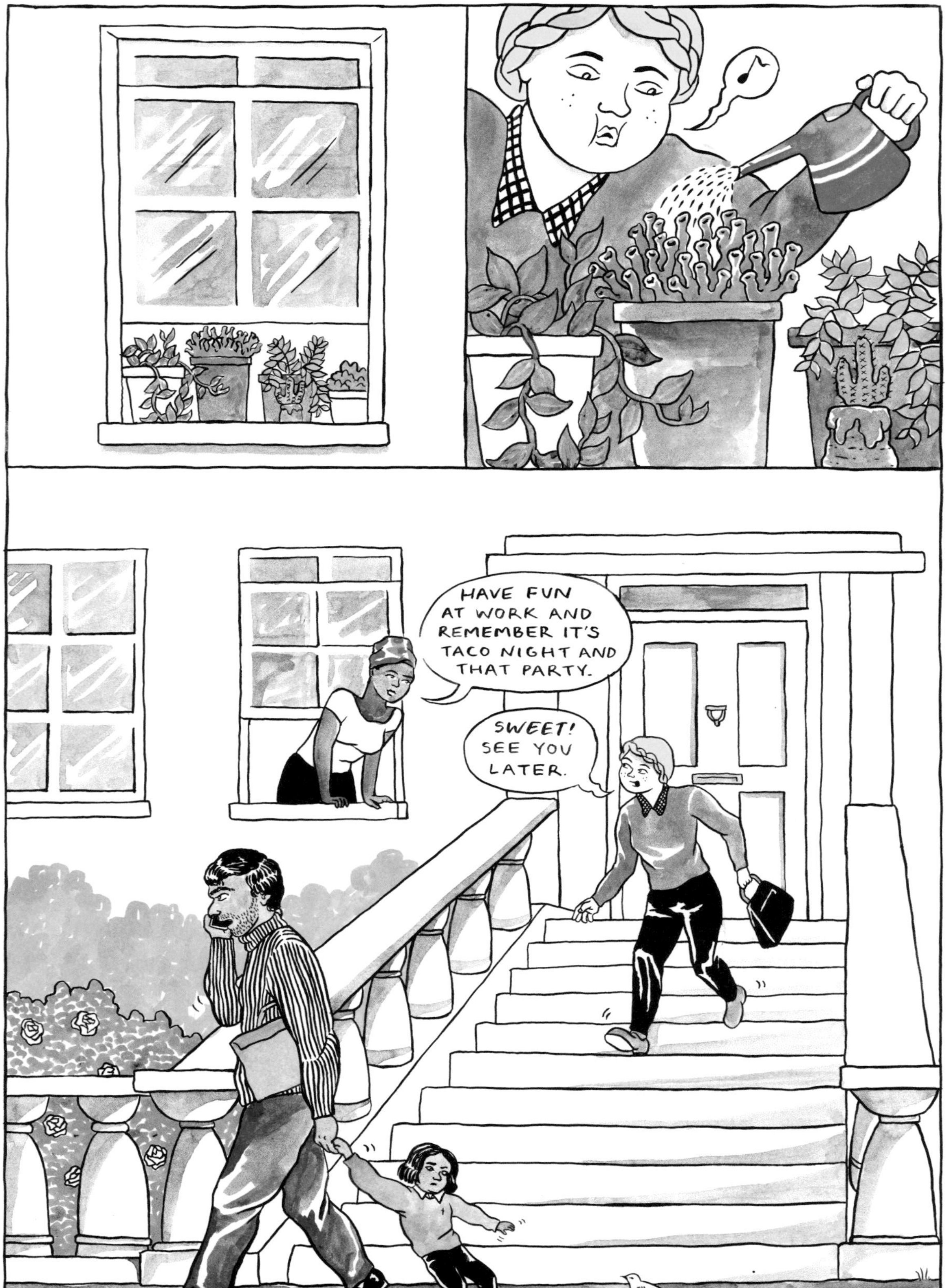
HAVE FUN AT WORK AND REMEMBER IT'S TACO NIGHT AND THAT PARTY.
SWEET! SEE YOU LATER.

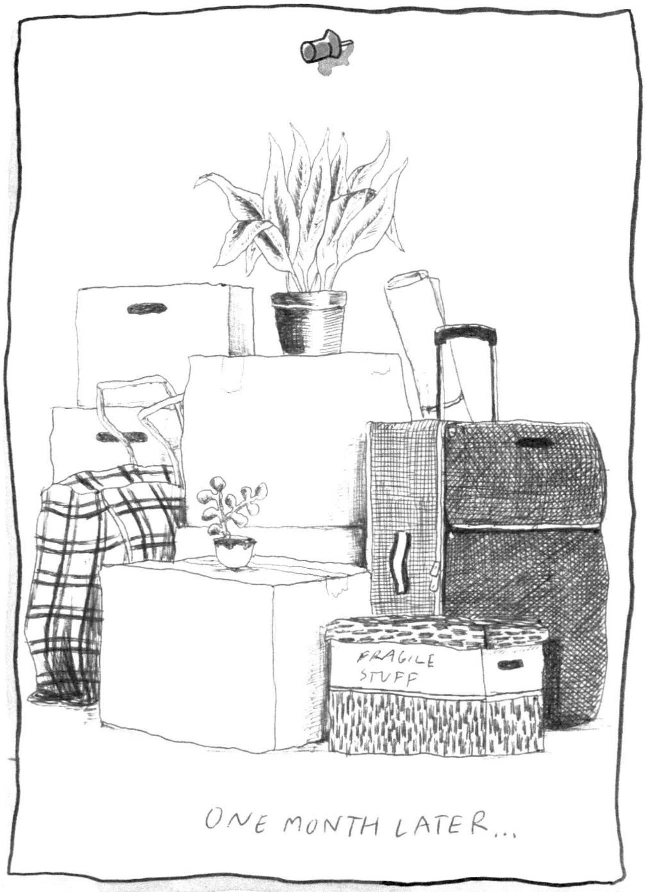
FRAGILE STUFF
ONE MONTH LATER...

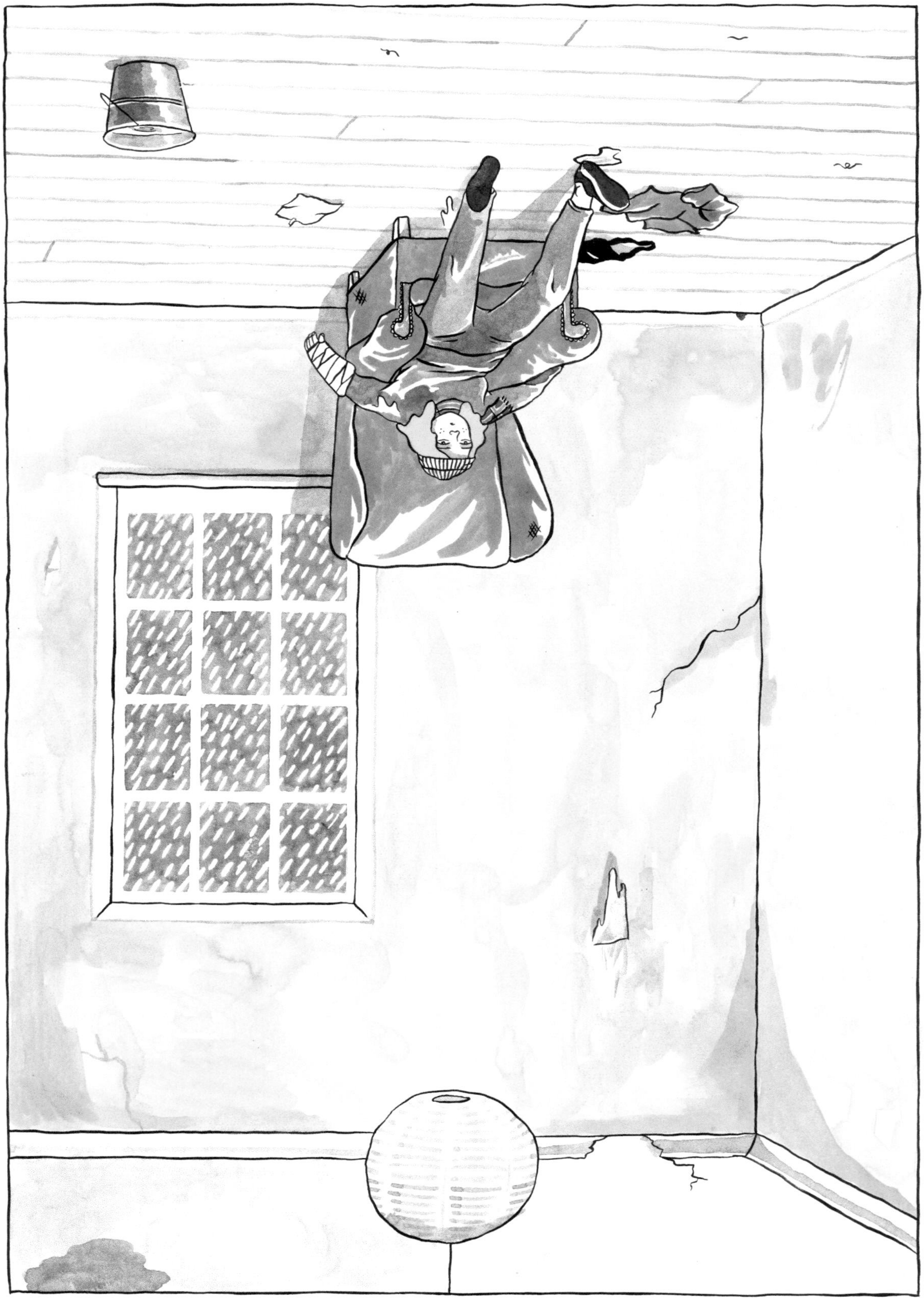

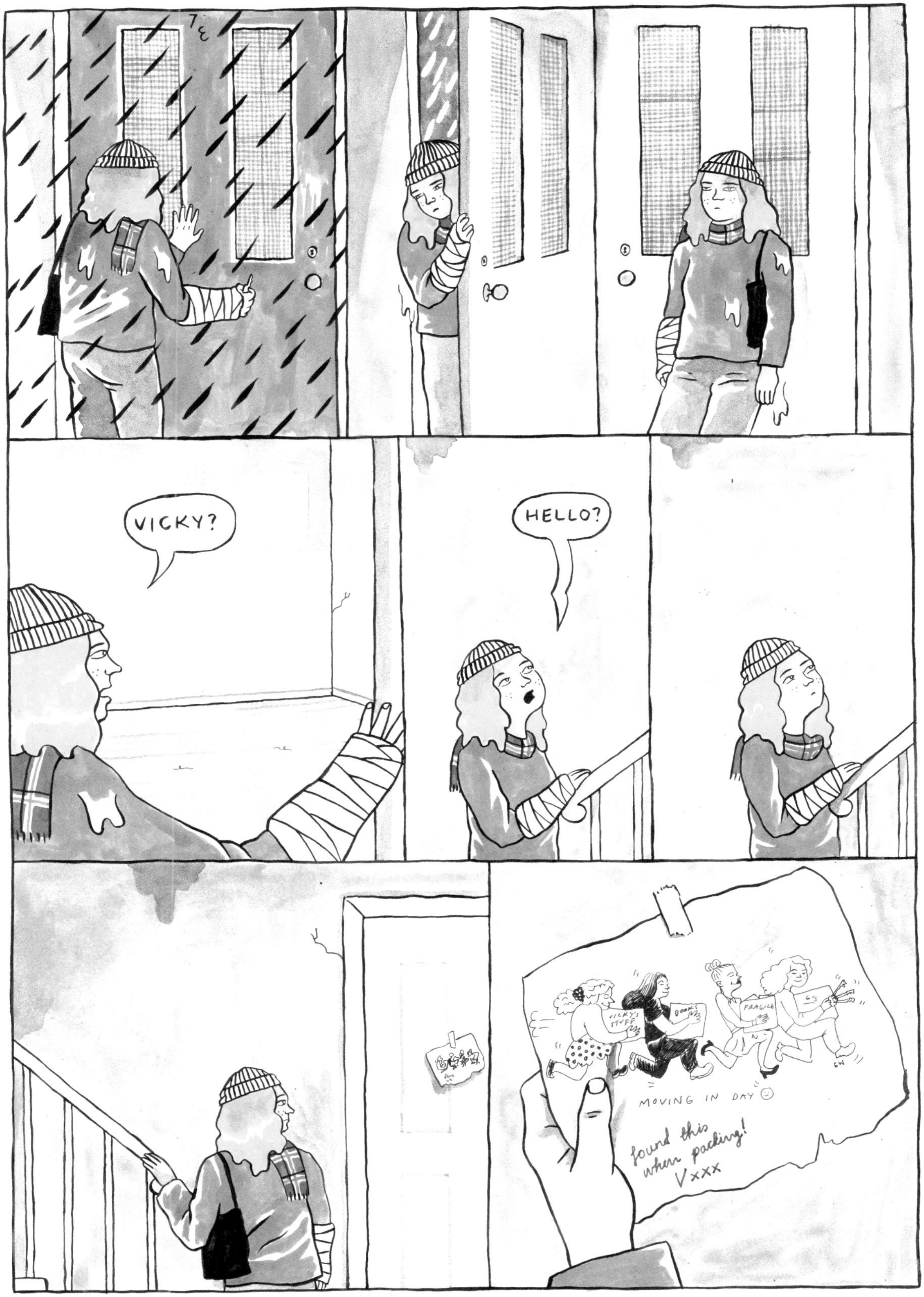
VICKY?
HELLO?
VICKY'S STUFF
BOOKS
FRAGILE
MOVING IN DAY
found this when packing!
Vxxx

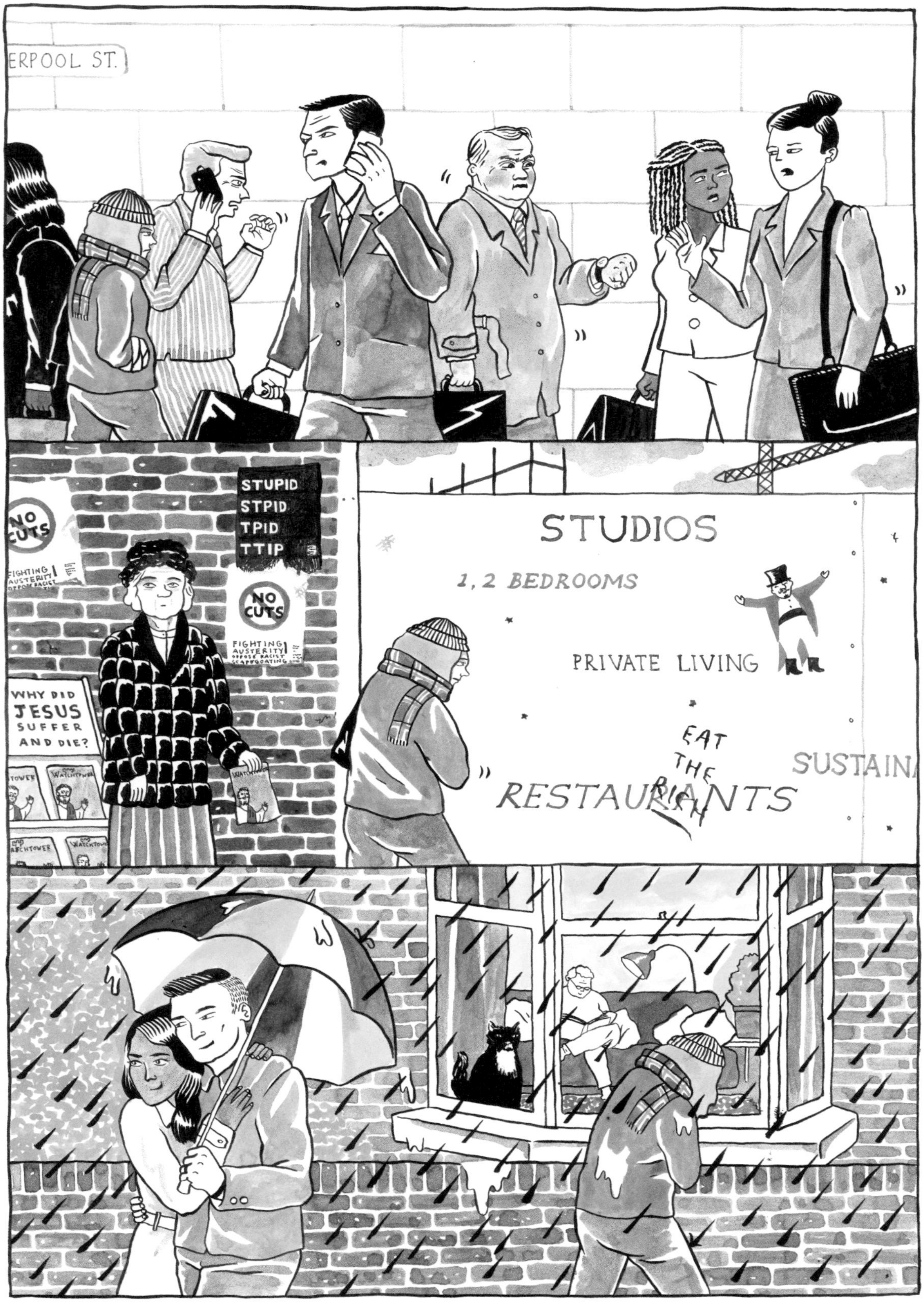

ERPOOL ST.
STUPID
STPID
TPID
TTIP
NO CUTS
FIGHTING AUSTERITY
NO CUTS
FIGHTING AUSTERITY OPPOSE RACIST SCAPEGOATING
WHY DID JESUS SUFFER AND DIE?
STUDIOS
1,2 BEDROOMS
PRIVATE LIVING
EAT THE RICH
RESTAURANTS
SUSTAIN

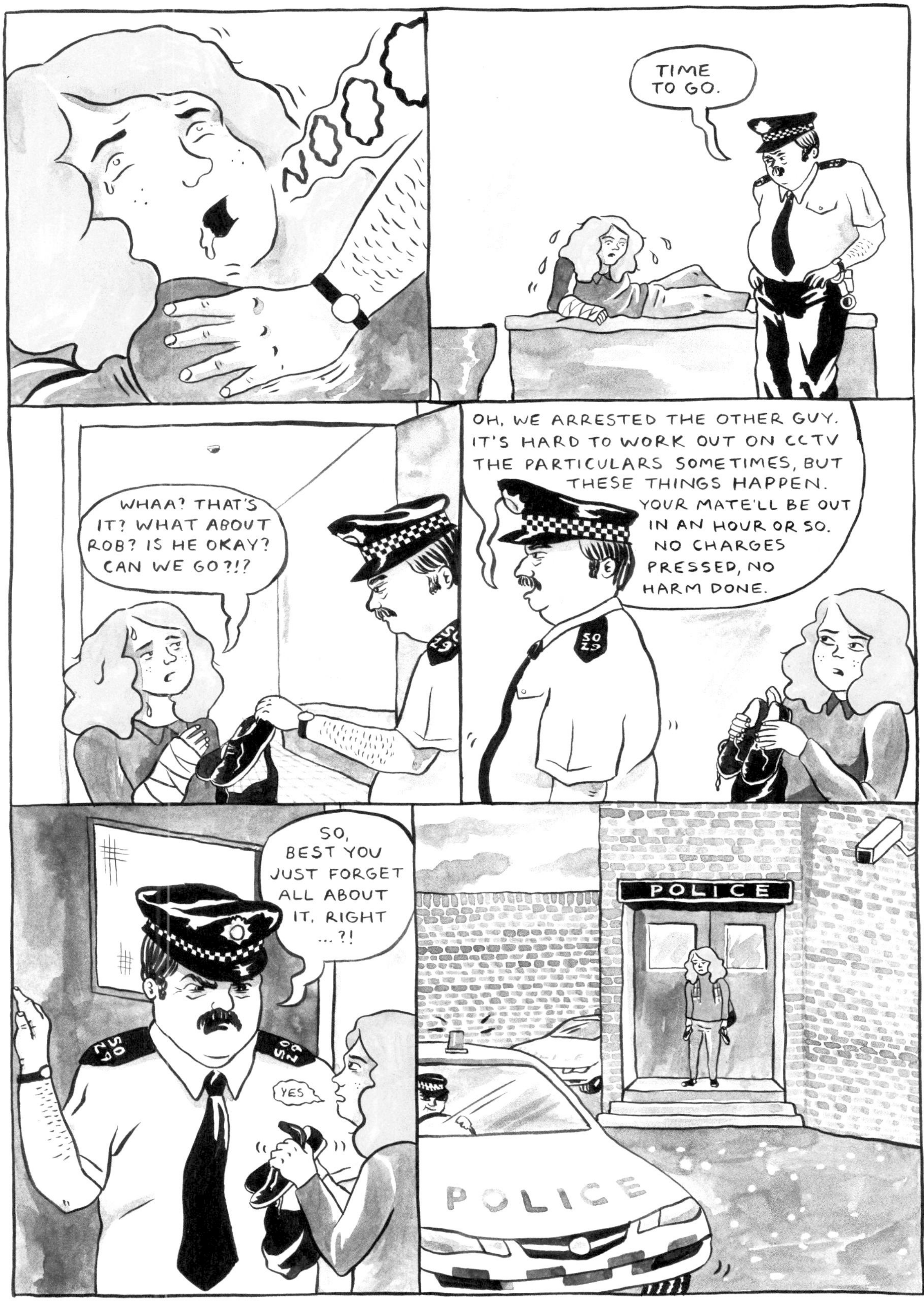
NOOO
TIME TO GO.
WHAA? THAT'S IT? WHAT ABOUT ROB? IS HE OKAY? CAN WE GO?!?
OH, WE ARRESTED THE OTHER GUY. IT'S HARD TO WORK OUT ON CCTV THE PARTICULARS SOMETIMES, BUT THESE THINGS HAPPEN. YOUR MATE'LL BE OUT IN AN HOUR OR SO. NO CHARGES PRESSED, NO HARM DONE.
SO, BEST YOU JUST FORGET ALL ABOUT IT, RIGHT ...?!
YES
POLICE
POLICE

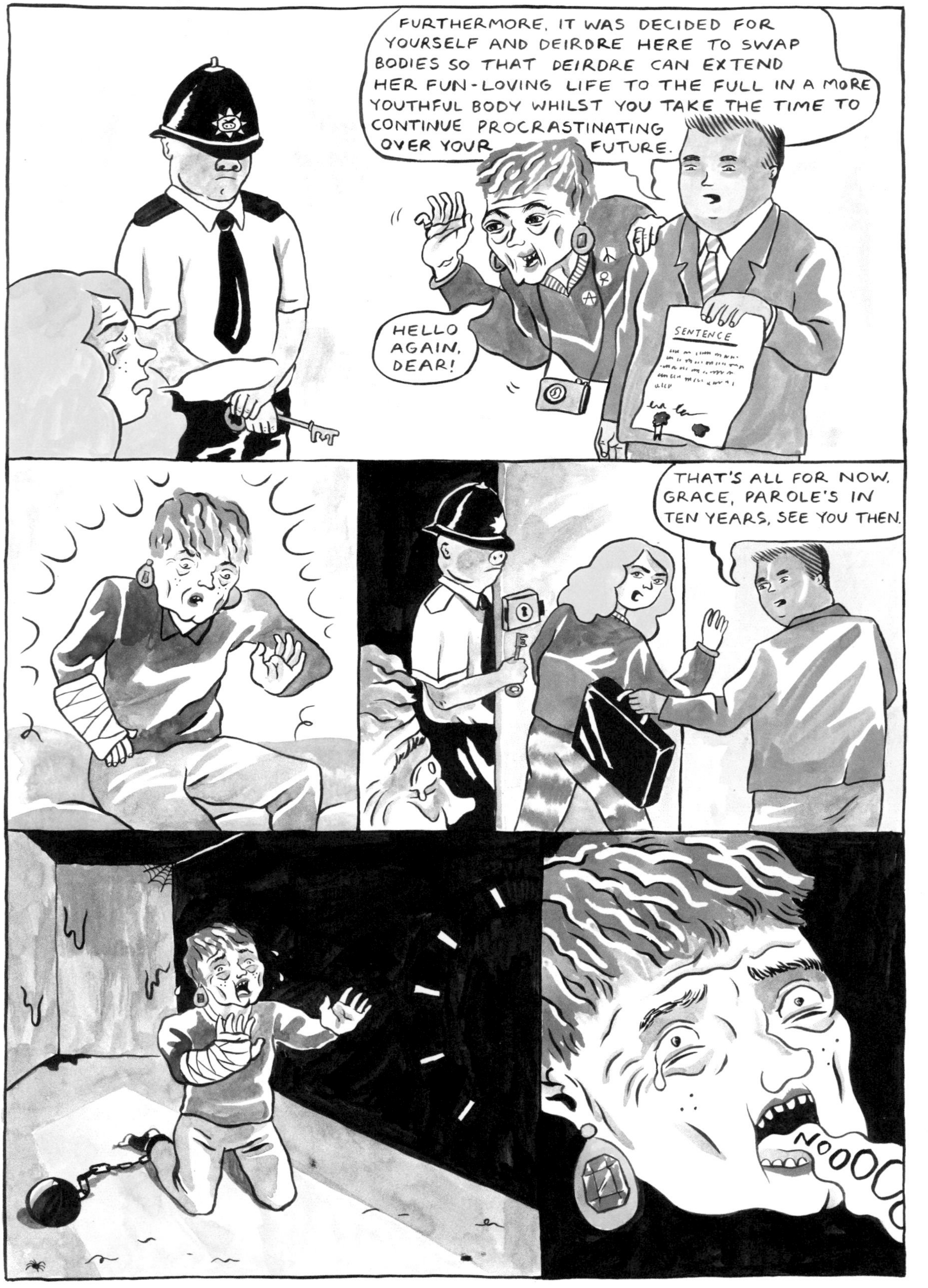
FURTHERMORE, IT WAS DECIDED FOR YOURSELF AND DEIRDRE HERE TO SWAP BODIES SO THAT DEIRDRE CAN EXTEND HER FUN-LOVING LIFE TO THE FULL IN A MORE YOUTHFUL BODY WHILST YOU TAKE THE TIME TO CONTINUE PROCRASTINATING OVER YOUR FUTURE.
HELLO AGAIN, DEAR!
SENTENCE
THAT'S ALL FOR NOW, GRACE, PAROLE'S IN TEN YEARS, SEE YOU THEN.
NOOOOO

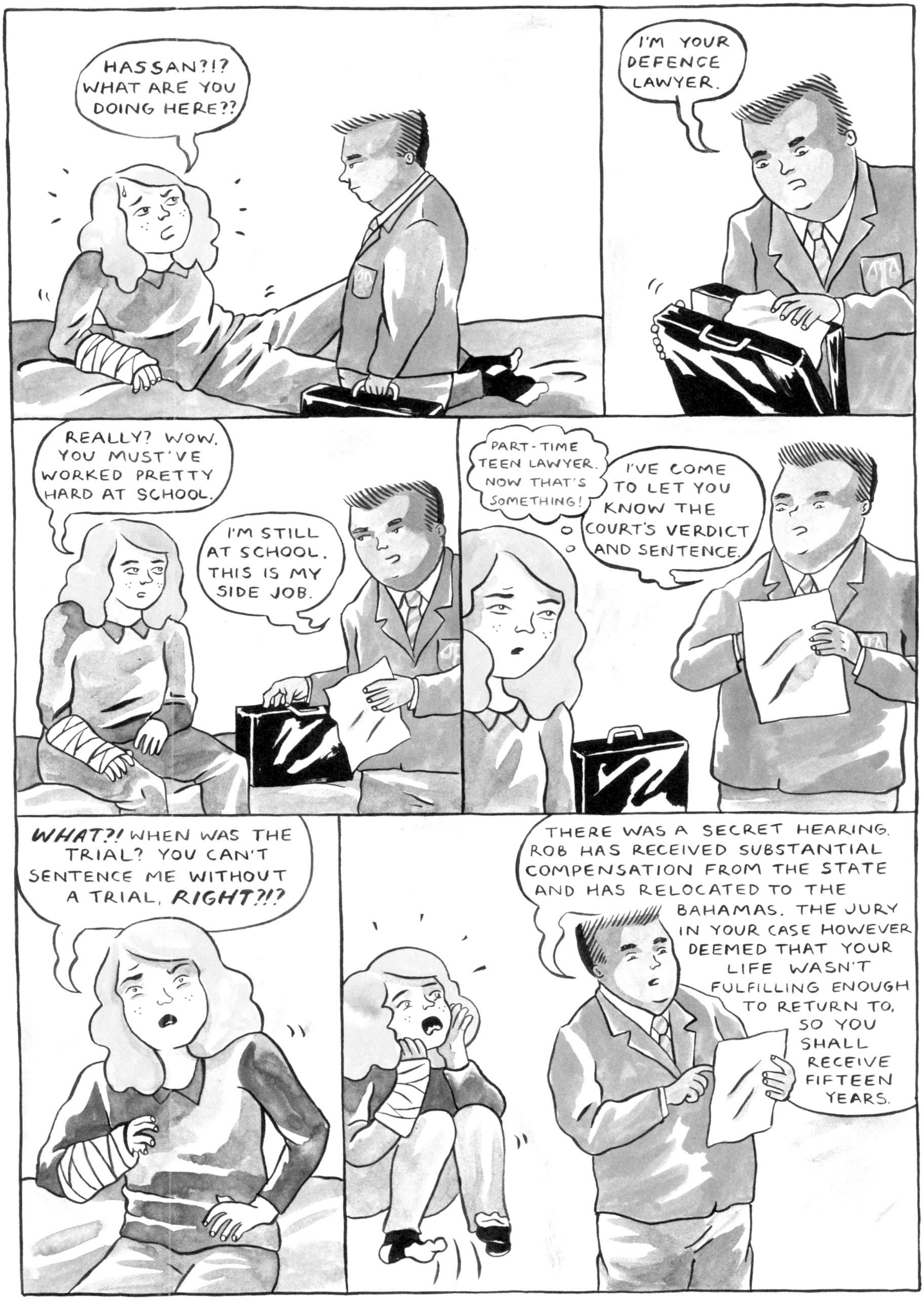
HASSAN?!? WHAT ARE YOU DOING HERE??
I'M YOUR DEFENCE LAWYER.
REALLY? WOW. YOU MUST'VE WORKED PRETTY HARD AT SCHOOL.
I'M STILL AT SCHOOL. THIS IS MY SIDE JOB.
PART-TIME TEEN LAWYER. NOW THAT'S SOMETHING!
I'VE COME TO LET YOU KNOW THE COURT'S VERDICT AND SENTENCE.
WHAT?! WHEN WAS THE TRIAL? YOU CAN'T SENTENCE ME WITHOUT A TRIAL, RIGHT?!?
THERE WAS A SECRET HEARING. ROB HAS RECEIVED SUBSTANTIAL COMPENSATION FROM THE STATE AND HAS RELOCATED TO THE BAHAMAS. THE JURY IN YOUR CASE HOWEVER DEEMED THAT YOUR LIFE WASN'T FULFILLING ENOUGH TO RETURN TO, SO YOU SHALL RECEIVE FIFTEEN YEARS.

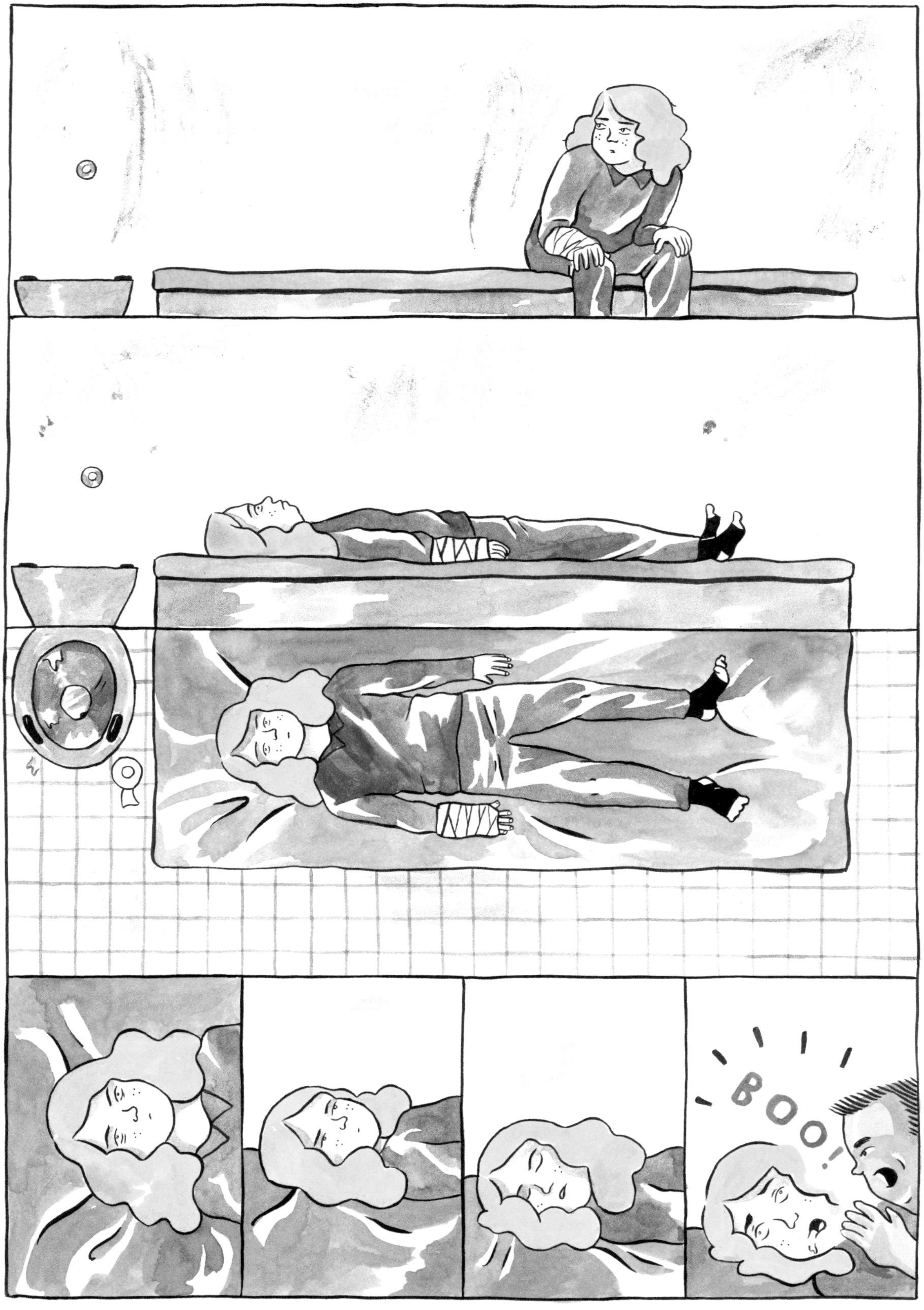
BOO!

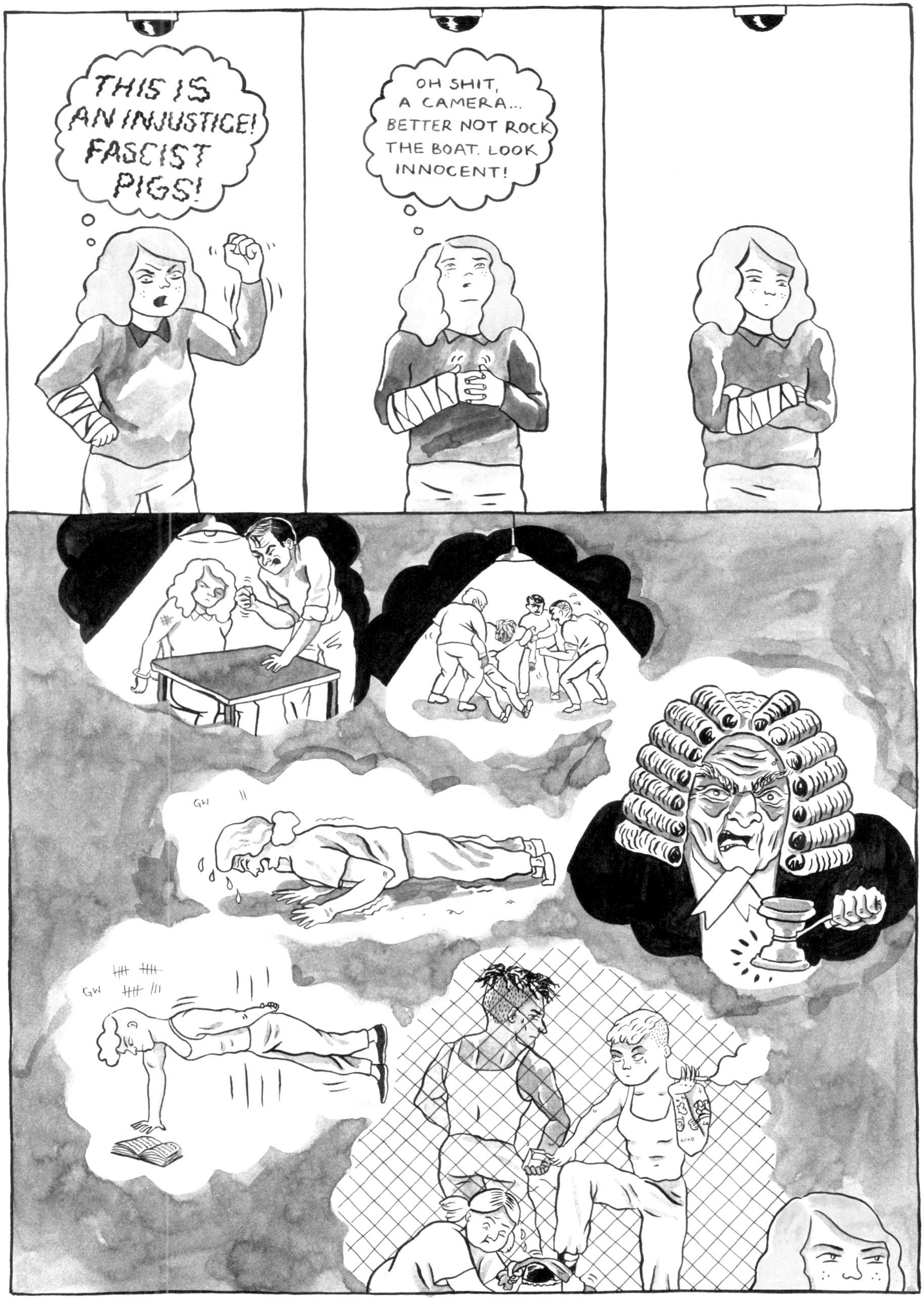
THIS IS AN INJUSTICE! FASCIST PIGS!
OH SHIT, A CAMERA... BETTER NOT ROCK THE BOAT. LOOK INNOCENT!

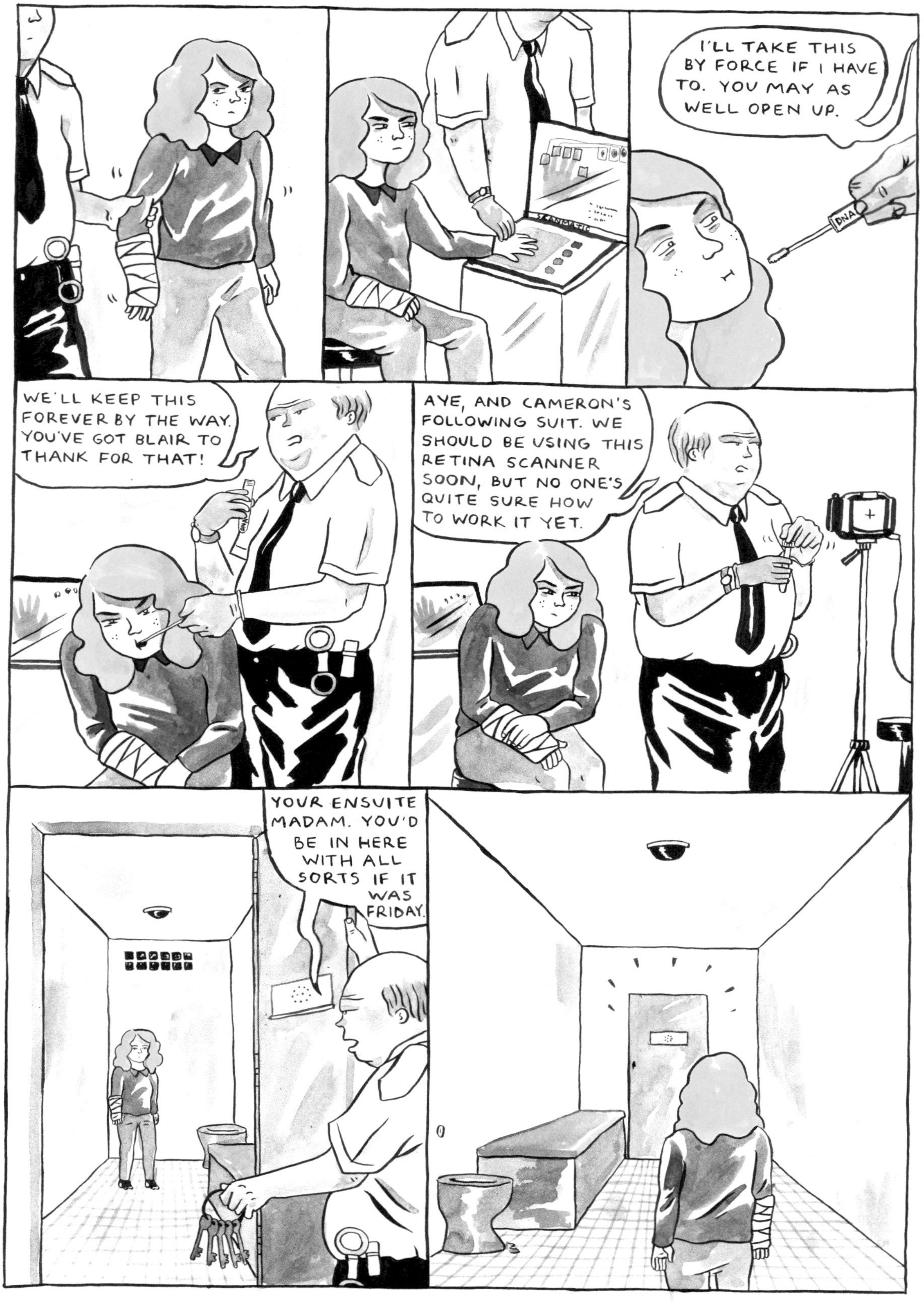
SCANMATIC
I'LL TAKE THIS BY FORCE IF I HAVE TO. YOU MAY AS WELL OPEN UP.
DNA
WE'LL KEEP THIS FOREVER BY THE WAY. YOU'VE GOT BLAIR TO THANK FOR THAT!
AYE, AND CAMERON'S FOLLOWING SUIT. WE SHOULD BE USING THIS RETINA SCANNER SOON, BUT NO ONE'S QUITE SURE HOW TO WORK IT YET.
YOUR ENSUITE MADAM. YOU'D BE IN HERE WITH ALL SORTS IF IT WAS FRIDAY.

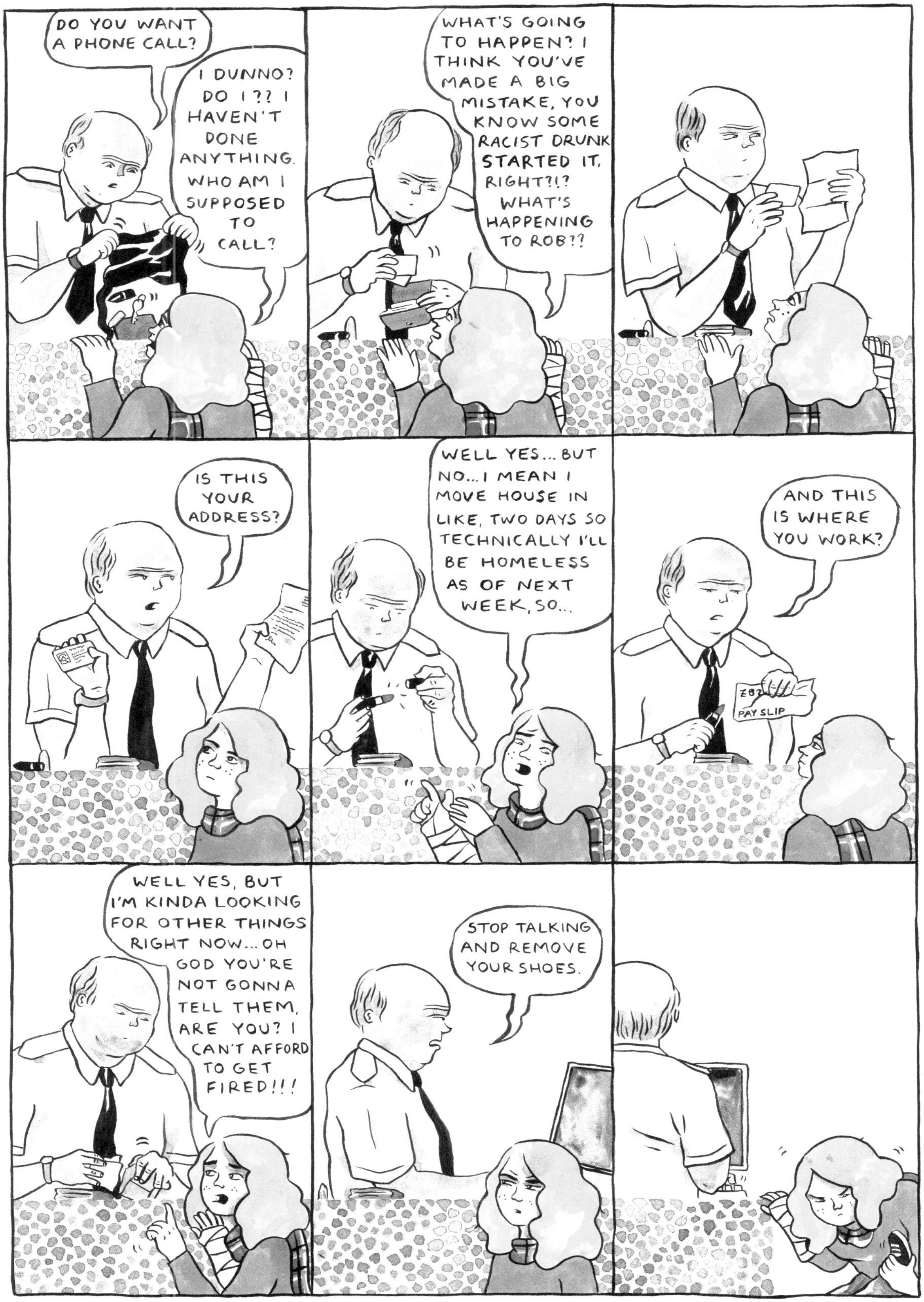
DO YOU WANT A PHONE CALL?
I DUNNO? DO I?? I HAVEN'T DONE ANYTHING. WHO AM I SUPPOSED TO CALL?
WHAT'S GOING TO HAPPEN? I THINK YOU'VE MADE A BIG MISTAKE, YOU KNOW SOME RACIST DRUNK STARTED IT, RIGHT?!? WHAT'S HAPPENING TO ROB??
IS THIS YOUR ADDRESS?
WELL YES... BUT NO... I MEAN I MOVE HOUSE IN LIKE, TWO DAYS SO TECHNICALLY I'LL BE HOMELESS AS OF NEXT WEEK, SO...
AND THIS IS WHERE YOU WORK?
PAY SLIP
WELL YES, BUT I'M KINDA LOOKING FOR OTHER THINGS RIGHT NOW... OH GOD YOU'RE NOT GONNA TELL THEM, ARE YOU? I CAN'T AFFORD TO GET FIRED!!!
STOP TALKING AND REMOVE YOUR SHOES.

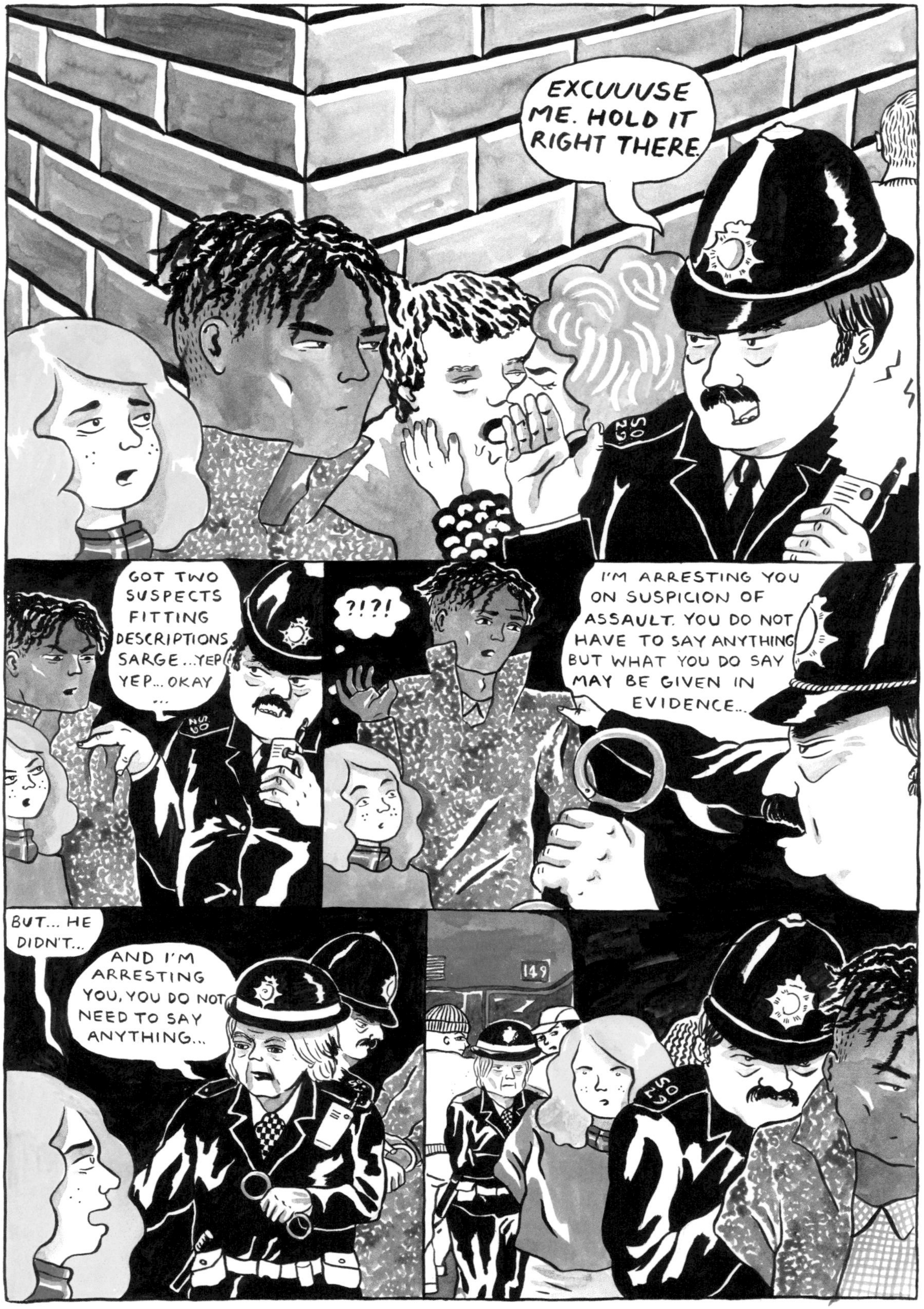
EXCUUUSE ME. HOLD IT RIGHT THERE.
GOT TWO SUSPECTS FITTING DESCRIPTIONS SARGE...YEP YEP...OKAY ...
?!?!
I'M ARRESTING YOU ON SUSPICION OF ASSAULT. YOU DO NOT HAVE TO SAY ANYTHING BUT WHAT YOU DO SAY MAY BE GIVEN IN EVIDENCE...
BUT... HE DIDN'T...
AND I'M ARRESTING YOU, YOU DO NOT NEED TO SAY ANYTHING...
149

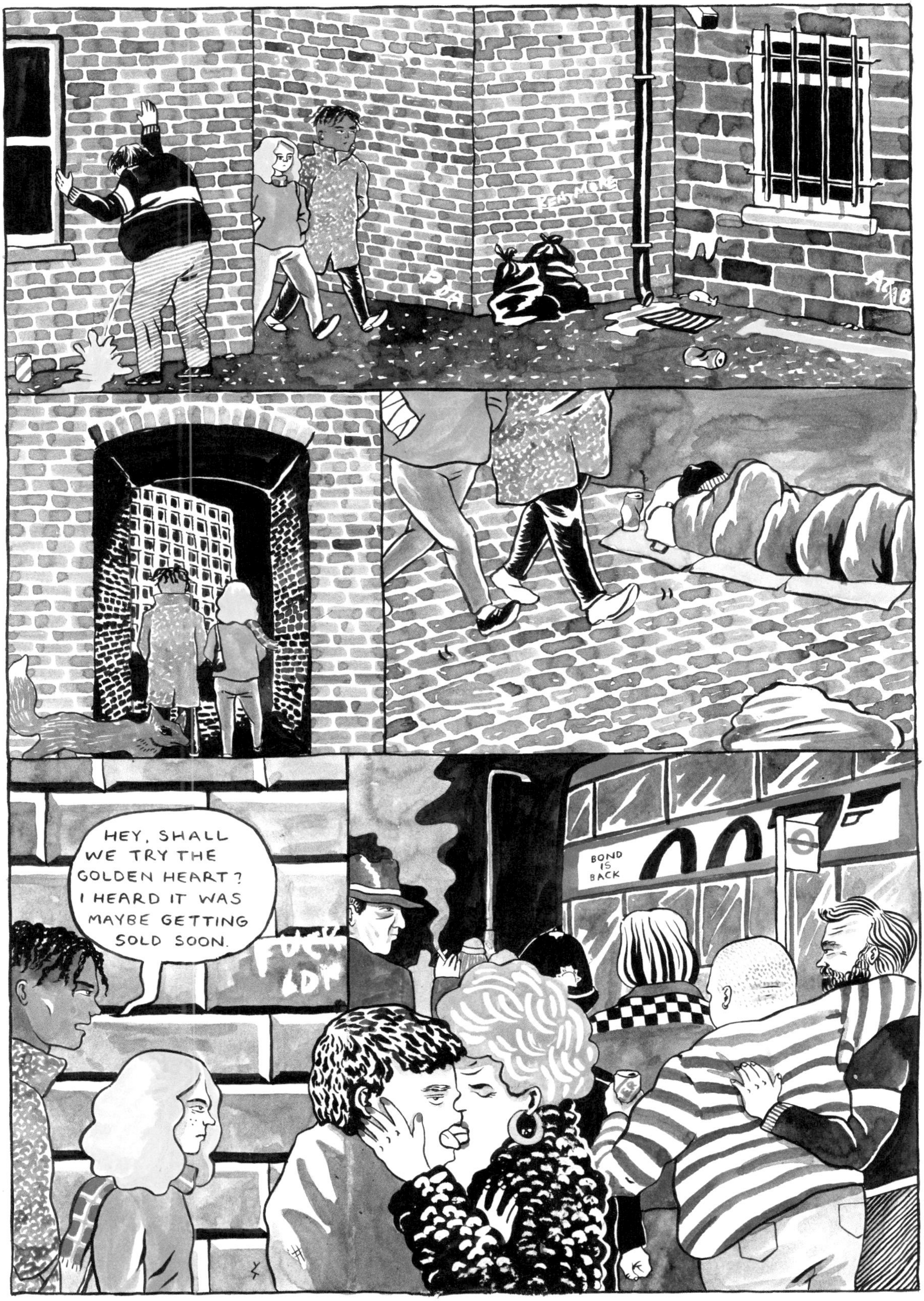
HEY, SHALL WE TRY THE GOLDEN HEART? I HEARD IT WAS MAYBE GETTING SOLD SOON.
BOND IS BACK

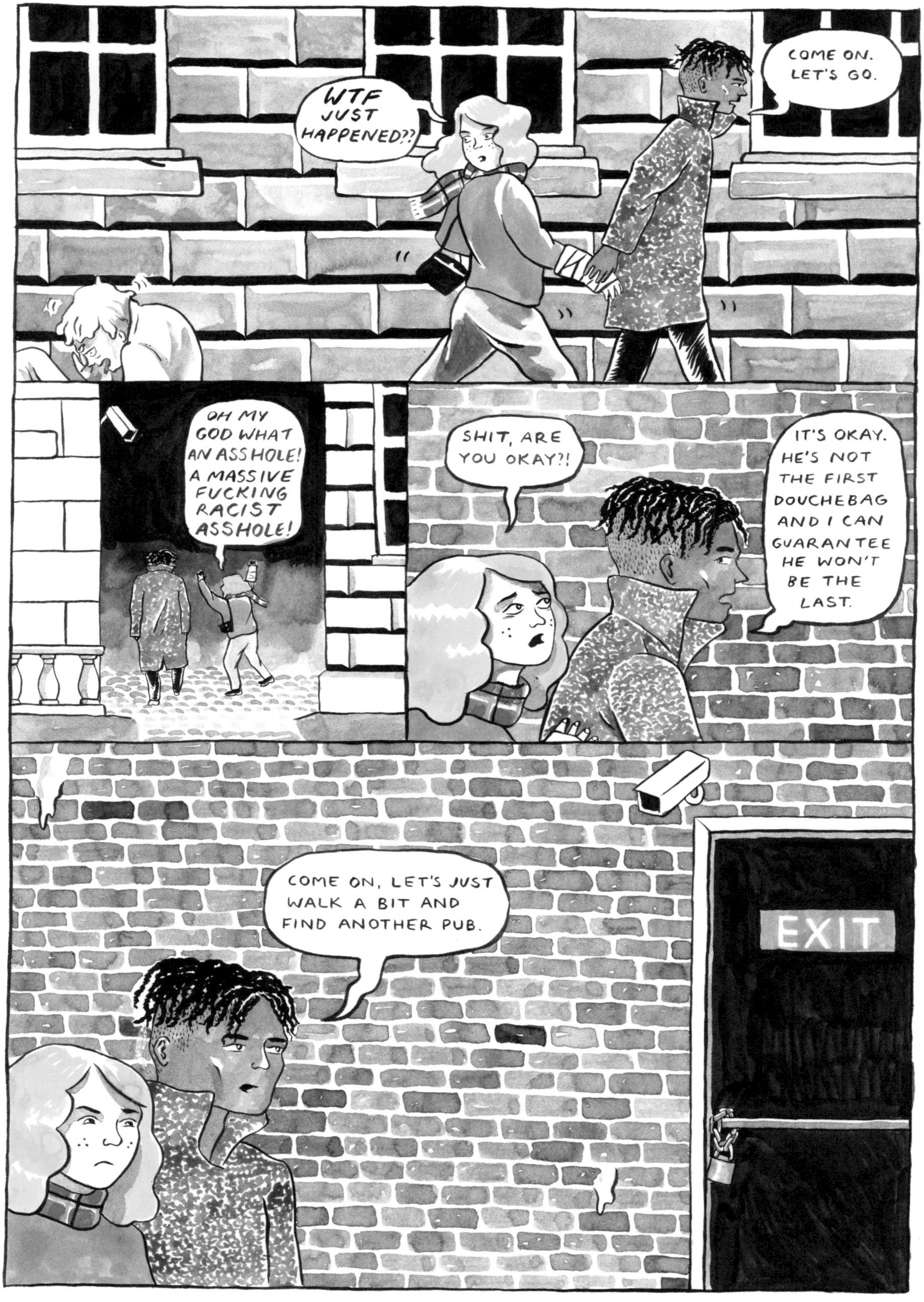
WTF JUST HAPPENED??
COME ON. LET'S GO.
OH MY GOD WHAT AN ASSHOLE! A MASSIVE FUCKING RACIST ASSHOLE!
SHIT, ARE YOU OKAY?!
IT'S OKAY. HE'S NOT THE FIRST DOUCHEBAG AND I CAN GUARANTEE HE WON'T BE THE LAST.
COME ON, LET'S JUST WALK A BIT AND FIND ANOTHER PUB.
EXIT

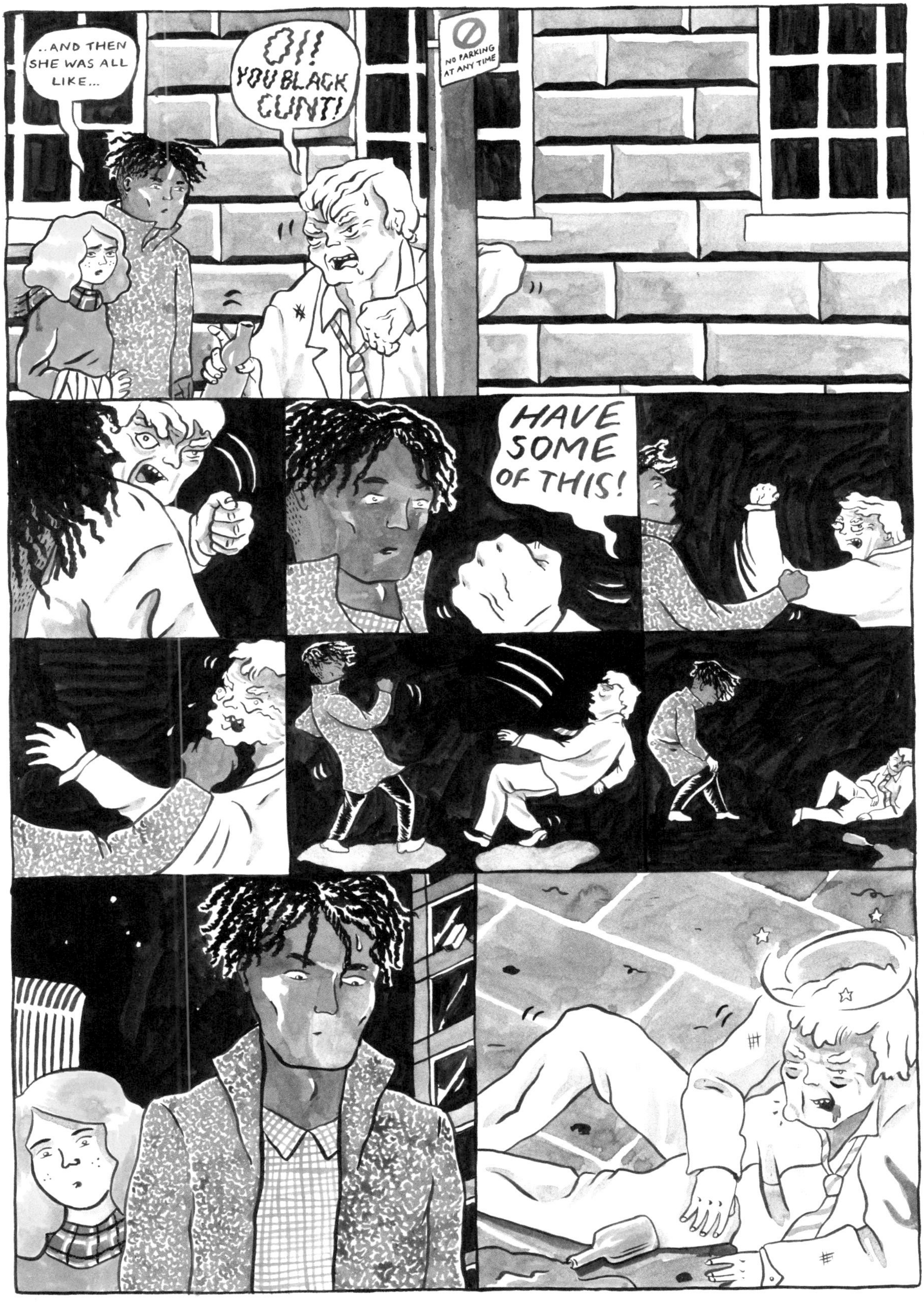
..AND THEN SHE WAS ALL LIKE...
OI! YOU BLACK CUNT!
NO PARKING AT ANY TIME
HAVE SOME OF THIS!

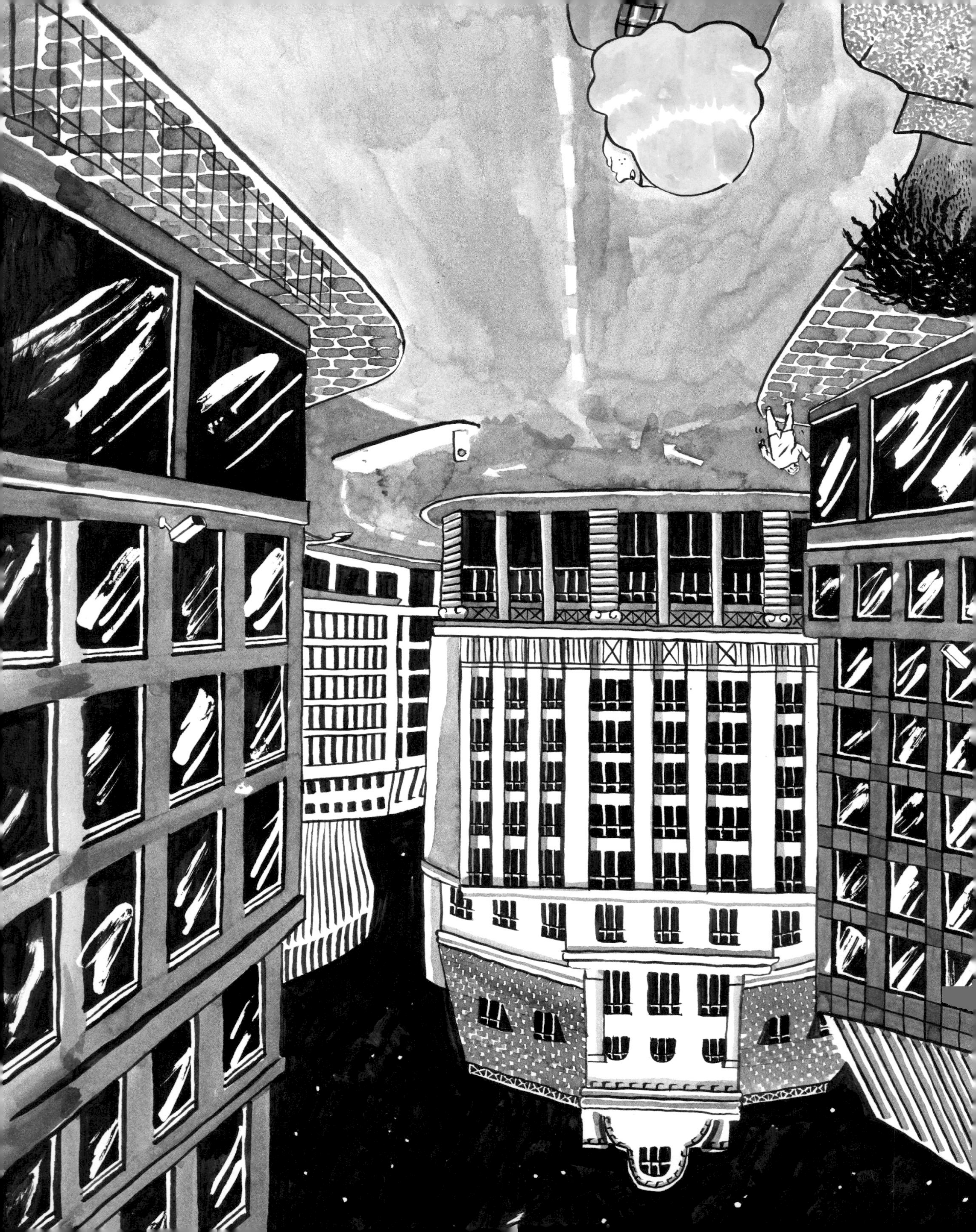